"Spanning the history of Christian guidance from the Desert Fathers and Mothers to contemporary expressions in literature and film, this groundbreaking book traces spiritual direction from its roots to its flourishing. Informed and inspired by this first-rate historical analysis, our own ministries as spiritual directors will become blessed by the saints who preceded us."

— Susan S. Phillips, author of *Candlelight: Illuminating the Art of Spiritual Direction*

"Written first as an important contribution to the Catholic tradition of spiritual direction, *A Science of the Saints* is also designed to be accessible to a more general audience. In this volume, a spiritual director will find many enriching reminders of what kind of person the director should be, the natural and unique unfolding of the spiritual life in each person, and the still-relevant wisdom of a 2000-year-old tradition of companionship designed to assist the human capacity to be enfolded in God."

— Norvene Vest, author of *Preferring Christ, a Devotional Commentary on the Rule of St. Benedict*

A Science of the Saints
Studies in Spiritual Direction

Edited by
Robert E. Alvis

LITURGICAL PRESS
Collegeville, Minnesota

www.litpress.org

1	2	3	4	5	6	7	8	9

Library of Congress Cataloging-in-Publication Data

Names: Alvis, Robert E., editor.
Title: A science of the saints : studies in spiritual direction / edited by Robert E. Alvis.
Description: Collegeville, Minnesota : Liturgical Press, 2020. | Summary: "Explores the dynamics of spiritual direction as revealed in the lives and writings of a wide array of disciples, from the Desert Fathers and Mothers to Thomas Merton, and from St. Teresa of Avila to St. Teresa Benedicta of the Cross (Edith Stein)"—Provided by publisher.
Identifiers: LCCN 2019040305 (print) | LCCN 2019040306 (ebook) | ISBN 9780814688045 (paperback) | ISBN 9780814688298 (epub) | ISBN 9780814688298 (mobi) | ISBN 9780814688298 (pdf)
Subjects: LCSH: Spiritual direction—Catholic Church. | Christian saints. | Desert Fathers. | Catholic authors.
Classification: LCC BX2350.7 .S37 2020 (print) | LCC BX2350.7 (ebook) | DDC 253.5/3—dc23
LC record available at https://lccn.loc.gov/2019040305
LC ebook record available at https://lccn.loc.gov/2019040306

To the students and alumni of
Saint Meinrad Seminary and School of Theology

Contents

viii A Science of the Saints

List of Contributors

Robert E. Alvis earned his PhD in church history from the University of Chicago. Currently, he serves as professor of church history and academic dean at Saint Meinrad Seminary and School of Theology. His publications include *Religion and the Rise of Nationalism: A Profile of an East-Central European City* (Syracuse University Press, 2005) and *White Eagle, Black Madonna: One Thousand Years of the Polish Catholic Tradition* (Fordham University Press, 2016). He coedited *Prisms of Faith: Perspectives on Religious Education and the Cultivation of Catholic Identity* (Pickwick Publications, 2016).

Fr. Guerric DeBona, OSB, is professor of homiletics at Saint Meinrad Seminary and School of Theology. He holds a PhD from Indiana University and is the author of numerous books and articles on film, preaching, and cultural history, including *Fulfilled in Our Hearing: The History of Christian Preaching* (Paulist, 2005), *Film Adaptation during the Hollywood Studio Period* (University of Illinois Press, 2010), and the three-volume *Between the Ambo and the Altar: Biblical Preaching and the Roman Missal* (Liturgical Press, 2013–15). He currently serves his community as novice/junior master.

Fr. Thomas Gricoski, OSB, holds a PhD in philosophy from the Catholic University of Leuven, Belgium, and is assistant professor of philosophy at Saint Meinrad Seminary and School of Theology, where he is also the director of pastoral formation. He is the series editor of the *Collected Works of Edith Stein* (ICS Publications). His first book is *Being Unfolded: Edith Stein on the Meaning of Being* (Catholic University of America Press, 2020).

Keith Lemna earned a PhD in systematic theology from The Catholic University of America. He is an associate professor of systematic theology at Saint Meinrad Seminary and School of Theology. He is the author of *The Apocalypse of Wisdom: Louis Bouyer's Theological Recovery of the Cosmos* (Angelico Press, 2019) and has published scholarly articles in numerous academic journals, including *Gregorianum*, *Communio*, *Irish Theological Quarterly*, and *Heythrop Journal*.

Fr. Mark O'Keefe, OSB, is professor of moral theology at Saint Meinrad Seminary and School of Theology. He holds a doctorate in sacred theology from The Catholic University of America. Among his most recent books are *Love Awakened by Love: The Liberating Ascent of Saint John of the Cross* (ICS Publications, 2014) and *The Way of Transformation: Saint Teresa of Avila on the Foundation and Fruit of Prayer* (ICS Publications, 2016). Forthcoming is *In Context: Teresa of Avila, John of the Cross, and Their World* (ICS Publications).

Fr. Christian Raab, OSB, earned his doctorate in sacred theology at The Catholic University of America. He is assistant professor of sacramental and systematic theology at Saint Meinrad Seminary and School of Theology. He is the author of *Understanding the Religious Priesthood: History, Controversy, Theology* (Catholic University of America Press, 2020) and the coeditor of *The Tradition of Catholic Prayer* (Liturgical Press, 2007).

Fr. Denis Robinson, OSB, a Benedictine monk of Saint Meinrad Archabbey, is president-rector of Saint Meinrad Seminary and School of Theology, where he also serves as associate professor of systematic theology. He earned doctorates in sacred theology and philosophy from the Catholic University of Louvain in 2007. He is the author of numerous articles and essays, and he edited *Sacerdos in Aeternum: Prayers and Blessings for Priests* (Abbey Press, 2010).

Kevin Schemenauer is associate professor of moral theology at Saint Meinrad Seminary and School of Theology. He earned a PhD in moral theology from The Catholic University of America in 2009.

He wrote his dissertation on Dietrich von Hildebrand's treatment of procreation, which was published as *Conjugal Love and Procreation: Dietrich von Hildebrand's Superabundant Integration* (Lexington Books, 2011). He is currently working on a book that analyses the relationship between family ethics and social ethics.

Sr. Jeana Visel, OSB, is a Benedictine sister of Monastery Immaculate Conception in Ferdinand, Indiana, and presently oversees the non-seminary programs at Saint Meinrad Seminary and School of Theology. She earned a DMin in spirituality from The Catholic University of America. She is the author of *Icons in the Western Church: Toward a More Sacramental Encounter* (Liturgical Press, 2016).

Introduction

Robert E. Alvis

Long before it was a term, spiritual direction was a practice. From the very beginnings of the faith, earnest followers of Christ recognized that the way of life they had embraced was more than just a set of tenets to believe, practices to perform, and virtues to embody. Regular guidance from a wise mentor could enable individuals to better recognize their own challenges and to move forward in the quest for holiness. In his letter to the Galatians, St. Paul encourages spiritually advanced members of the community to reach out to others who may be struggling: "Brothers, even if a person is caught in some transgression, you who are spiritual should correct that one in a gentle spirit" (Gal 6:1). In chapter 4 of the *Didache*, a Christian handbook written toward the end of the first century, the faithful are enjoined to meet regularly with individuals of spiritual distinction: "Frequent the company of the saints daily, so as to be edified by their conversation."[1]

As the Christian community has adapted to changing circumstances over time, the practice of spiritual direction has evolved in tandem while remaining enduringly relevant. Starting in the third century, growing numbers of spiritually ambitious Christians abandoned mainstream society in favor of an array of monastic

---

[1] Maxwell Staniforth, trans., "The *Didache*," in *Early Christian Writings* with rev. translation, introductions, and new editorial material by Andrew Louth (London: Penguin Books, 1987), 192.

movements. Fundamental to this way of life was the careful mentoring of disciples by experienced masters. The literary deposit of the Desert Fathers and Mothers offers the first detailed portrait of Christian spiritual direction in antiquity. By the fourth century, new generations of Christian leaders, formed in monastic contexts and called to serve in the upper echelons of the ecclesiastical hierarchy, were bringing monastic values to bear on the broader Church. These values included a high esteem for spiritual direction.[2] St. Gregory of Nazianzus, who grudgingly abandoned monastic life in favor of a clerical career, famously praised the practice of spiritual guidance as "the art of arts and the science of sciences."[3]

In the Middle Ages, monastic orders in both the East and the West continued to serve as vital centers of spiritual direction. A regimen of spiritual mentoring was integral to the monastic life, and many outsiders took advantage of the counsel of holy monks and nuns. In time, newer religious orders like the Dominicans and Franciscans brought fresh forms of pastoral outreach, including spiritual direction, to population centers across much of Europe. Meanwhile, laypeople embraced novel forms of intentional discipleship, such as third orders and the *Devotio Moderna*, in which spiritual direction was often an integral feature.

Amid the tumult of the early modern era, including the fracturing of the Western Church into rival confessions and the so-called wars of religion, the practice of spiritual direction reached new heights of popularity and sophistication. In his quest for sanctification, St. Ignatius of Loyola developed a program of "spiritual exercises" and a distinctive approach to spiritual direction that are practiced widely to this day. St. Francis de Sales, to whom the term *spiritual direction* is commonly attributed, offered another enduring model that has been preserved both in his published

---

[2] See George E. Demacopoulos, *Five Models of Spiritual Direction* (South Bend, IN: University of Notre Dame Press, 2006).

[3] Quoted in Christopher A. Beeley, *Gregory of Nazianzus on the Trinity and the Knowledge of God: In Your Light We Shall See Light* (Oxford: Oxford University Press, 2008), 242.

correspondence and *An Introduction to the Devout Life*, an immensely popular spiritual guidebook intended for a general audience. In the emerging Protestant confessions, prominent leaders such as Martin Luther, John Calvin, and John Knox engaged in direction, and Luther's writings on the topic have proven enduringly influential.

In the past two centuries, an expanding array of luminaries have provided novel iterations of spiritual direction through published works and public presentations and private counsel and correspondence. Their ranks include St. John Henry Newman, Evelyn Underhill, C. S. Lewis, and Fr. Thomas Merton, to name just a few. Their advice has resonated well beyond their original audiences, in part because they are carefully calibrated to the distinct challenges of modern life.

While spiritual direction has been a constant feature of the faith, interest in the practice has expanded markedly in the United States and other societies in recent decades. This interest is rooted in part in broader sociological developments. Growing numbers identify as "spiritual but not religious," a term that signals a hunger for cultivating a relationship with the transcendent alongside dissatisfaction with more institutional manifestations of religion. Spiritual direction, it seems, affords opportunities for personal, interior growth that are especially attractive to many in our day. The heightened demand for spiritual direction has given rise to a variety of initiatives focused on providing this ministry, as well as to a considerable body of literature on the topic.

Regarding the recent literature on spiritual direction, much of it is highly practical in nature. The authors typically are experienced spiritual directors who are writing in order to guide new generations of directors and directees. They base their guidance primarily on instructive encounters they have had in spiritual direction, and they often draw insights from related fields like psychology.

A Science of the Saints, the title of which is borrowed from an observation by the renowned spiritual director and cardinal Pierre de Bérulle, belongs to a modest subset of the literature that takes a more historical approach to the subject.⁴ Works of this type explore how spiritual direction has been practiced within distinct contexts across the Church's 2,000-year history. Such studies help illuminate an essential and often underappreciated dimension of the Christian experience. At the same time, they often yield timeless wisdom that can fruitfully inform the practice of spiritual direction in our own day.

The genesis of this project is closely linked to the mission of Saint Meinrad Seminary and School of Theology, where the authors of the following chapters teach. Spiritual direction is fundamental to the work of Saint Meinrad. Many on its faculty regularly receive spiritual direction, provide spiritual direction to others, and model the practice of direction to the future Catholic priests and lay ministers they are training. Many have also studied spiritual direction on a more theoretical level. This shared interest and expertise gave rise to the idea of an edited volume devoted to the topic. Each of the nine chapters is rooted in the individual author's larger area of expertise. In addition to contributing to the scholarly understanding of the Catholic tradition of spiritual direction, the chapters are designed to be accessible to a more general audience and useful to those engaged in offering or receiving spiritual direction.

The first two chapters of the volume focus on a pair of traditions of spiritual direction emerging in antiquity. In chapter 1, Sr. Jeana Visel, OSB, analyzes the legacy of the Desert Fathers and Mothers. Emerging in Egypt, Syria, Palestine, and Asia Minor around the fourth century, desert monasticism took various forms, from the hermit life, to small groups of disciples gathered around a spiritual father or mother, to large monasteries shaped by more communal elements. At the heart of desert spirituality was the wisdom gained by the *ammas* and *abbas*. Through personal experiences of wrestling

⁴ Bérulle once observed that spiritual direction "is part of the science of the saints, as Scripture speaks of it. It is a science which belongs to the saints, which the saints do and which directs saints in the ways of heaven." Quoted in *Writings on Spiritual Direction by Great Christian Masters*, edited by Jerome M. Neufelder and Mary C. Coelho (New York: Seabury Press, 1985), 89.

with sin, aiming for virtue, and ultimately coming to know God in love, these spiritual masters became equipped to help others along the spiritual journey. Visel extracts enduring lessons concerning spiritual direction from this legacy, including the personal integrity and commitment to growth required of spiritual directors, and the importance of customizing direction to address the distinctive trajectories of individual directees.

In chapter 2, Fr. Christian Raab, OSB, reflects on the underappreciated yet vital tradition of spiritual direction cultivated within Benedictine monastic circles. He begins by considering the wisdom of St. Gregory the Great in his *Pastoral Rule* concerning the qualities that a spiritual director should possess. He then examines the contributions of three modern Benedictine thinkers. Blessed Columba Marmion presents an example of spiritual direction in relation to the development of the directee's spiritual life. Fr. Thomas Merton offers advice concerning how to receive spiritual direction. Fr. André Louf crafts a synthetic vision of spiritual direction that incorporates the insights of monastic tradition, Ignatian spirituality, and contemporary psychology. Taken together, these four figures point to a distinctively Benedictine approach to spiritual direction that can serve as a worthy complement to the dominant Ignatian model.

The next two chapters discuss several figures of the early modern period who, each in their own way, significantly enriched the Catholic tradition of spiritual direction: St. Teresa of Avila, St. John of the Cross, and St. Francis de Sales. While previous scholars have examined the contributions of these three saints in considerable detail, the chapters in this part of the book offer fresh insights that enhance our understanding of their respective legacies.

In chapter 3, Fr. Mark O'Keefe, OSB, juxtaposes the insights of the Carmelite mystics John of the Cross and Teresa of Avila. Spiritual direction was a principal ministry of John of the Cross, and his prose writings have been described as written spiritual direction. His contemporary and collaborator Teresa of Avila had a great deal of experience with spiritual direction as her deep spiritual journey unfolded—some of it helpful, much of it not. Both

Carmelite authors offered valuable observations about spiritual direction and the qualifications of spiritual directors, emphasizing in particular the need to be learned in Scripture and theology, experienced in the journey toward holiness, and discerning of the movements of the Spirit in the soul. This chapter examines their counsel and suggests how it can serve spiritual directors today.

In chapter 4, Kevin Schemenauer discerns the distinctiveness of Francis de Sales's model of spiritual direction by viewing it through the lens of a saint's biography and piecing together the counsel he dispensed in his spiritual writings and letters. A portrait emerges of a saint focused on guiding people of all stations active in the world, emphasizing love of God and surrender to God's will. Schemenauer highlights three themes that echo throughout de Sales's corpus—total surrender to God, the need for gradual growth, and the cultivation of holy liberty—and considers the practical relevance of these themes for those engaged in the work of spiritual direction.

The volume's focus shifts next to several twentieth-century figures not commonly associated with the Catholic tradition of spiritual direction: St. Faustina Kowalska, St. Teresa Benedicta of the Cross (Edith Stein), and Fr. Louis Bouyer. The authors demonstrate how the diverse legacies of these figures have much to teach us about complicated work of spiritual direction.

In chapter 5, Robert E. Alvis considers the counsel that priestly confessors offered to St. Faustina Kowalska as she coped with a tumultuous interior life punctuated time and again by powerful mystical encounters. She was anguished by the skepticism of most of the priests in whom she confided, but not deterred from pursuing the work she believed God was calling her to undertake. The several priests who believed her claims provided emotional support and critical assistance. Her experience offers lessons to contemporary priests who offer spiritual direction to people claiming private revelations.

In chapter 6, Fr. Thomas Gricoski, OSB, gleans insights into spiritual direction from the life and extensive correspondence of St. Edith Stein. Roughly a third of Stein's correspondence shows her offering spiritual direction, vocational discernment, and personal encouragement for protégés and students. Gricoski's analysis illustrates how spiritual direction often occurs in unexpected times and places well beyond the boundaries of a formal relationship devoted to the same. He also underscores the role of personal holiness in the lives of would-be spiritual directors. The theme that resounds most prominently in Stein's guidance, though, is the summons to take up the crosses one encounters in life and to recognize them as invitations to participate more fully in the mystery of Christ's passion, death, and resurrection.

In chapter 7, Keith Lemna considers the model of spiritual direction developed by the French Oratorian priest Louis Bouyer, who was a decisive influence on some of the most important French Catholic ecclesial figures and intellectuals in the contemporary Catholic Church, including Jean-Luc Marion. This model is anchored in a deep appreciation and thorough familiarity with Scripture and the theological corpus of the church fathers and great mystics, and it invites earnest Christians to discover in these resources a higher order of knowledge around which to orient their lives, including the divine event of love and the trinitarian basis of creation and our human destiny. His model recovers the essential interdependence of spiritual theology and dogmatic theology, dimensions of the Christian experience which all too often have been considered in isolation from one another in recent centuries.

The final two chapters of this volume look to the arts to offer innovative insights regarding the practice of spiritual direction. Specifically, they offer nuanced analyses of a number of remarkable films and works of literature. While the characters in these films, short stories, and novels are fictional, they bear the imprint of their creators' profound wisdom regarding the human condition and thus deserve careful attention.

In chapter 8, Fr. Guerric DeBona, OSB, turns to cinema to illuminate some of the seminal lessons embedded in the Ignatian approach to discernment and spiritual direction. Drawing from his remarkable personal journey, St. Ignatius of Loyola developed an influential model for discerning the movements and stages of development within the soul, but how do his theories manifest in the messy lives of ordinary people? DeBona suggests that we can learn a lot in this regard from great films that depict the spiritual maturation of their central characters. To illustrate his point, he demonstrates how Elia Kazan's *On the Waterfront* and Robert Bresson's *The Diary of a Country Priest* offer particularly apt examples of the spiritual dynamics encompassed in the first and second of Ignatius's "rules" for the discernment of spirits.

In the ninth and final chapter, Fr. Denis Robinson, OSB, considers literature as a potential source of spiritual direction, and he unpacks some of the spiritual lessons embedded in the works of three modern Catholic authors. Flannery O'Connor's short stories employ the motif of the Southern Gothic to highlight the sometimes "violent" nature of spiritual discernment and how God's grace can be encountered in some of the most unsuspecting moments, places, and people. At the center of Muriel Spark's *The Prime of Miss Jean Brodie* is the fraught relationship between its two main characters, whose respective life choices shed light on the dynamics of spiritual seeking and the consequences of conversion. Finally, Robert Hugh Benson's dystopian *The Lord of the World* invites readers to contemplate the heavy cost of discipleship in the context of a triumphant and suffocating secularism. Robinson suggests that the distinctively compelling qualities of literature— its capacity to move us and delight us—make it a worthy complement to more traditional sources of spiritual direction.

Taken together, the nine studies in *A Science of the Saints* shed new light on the richness of the Catholic tradition of spiritual direction. It is the shared hope of the authors that their contributions advance the scholarly understanding of this tradition, stimulate further study of this important dimension of the Christian experience, and offer practical lessons for those engaged in the work of spiritual direction.

CHAPTER ONE

Spiritual Direction among the Desert Fathers and Mothers

Sr. Jeana Visel, OSB

Some of the earliest traditions of Christian spiritual direction have their roots in the practices of the Desert Fathers and Mothers, monastic men and women who lived either solitary or community-based lives outside of cities. The literature of these holy men and women appears around the fourth century, arising almost simultaneously in Egypt, Syria, Mesopotamia, Persia, and elsewhere.[1] As Jesus was led by the Spirit into the desert to be tempted by Satan, so these men and women also found the desert a place of spiritual struggle for holiness. Here they quickly discovered the importance of engaging the discerning guidance of others who

---

[1] André Louf, OCSO, "Spiritual Fatherhood in the Literature of the Desert," in *Abba: Guides to Wholeness and Holiness East and West*, ed. John R. Sommerfelt, Cistercian Studies Series #38 (Kalamazoo, MI: Cistercian Publications, 1982), 37; George E. Demacopoulos, *Five Models of Spiritual Direction in the Early Church* (Notre Dame, IN: University of Notre Dame Press, 2007), 1–9; Rosemary Rader, "Early Christian Forms of Communal Spirituality: Women's Communities," in *The Continuing Quest for God: Monastic Spirituality in Tradition and Transition*, ed. William Skudlarek (Collegeville, MN: Liturgical Press, 1982), 90; Gabriele Winkler, "The Origins and Idiosyncrasies of the Earliest Form of Asceticism," in *The Continuing Quest for God*, 11, 28, 29; Armand Veilleux, "The Origins of Egyptian Monasticism," in *The Continuing Quest for God*, 44ff.

likewise had been tested.[2] While most early Christians sought spiritual leadership from priests, bishops, family members, or other Christians, in the desert tradition God was understood to speak through elders.[3] Because of their ability to transmit spiritual life to others, these elders commonly have been called "mothers" and "fathers."[4] The true *amma* or *abba* was one who had been tried in virtue and found faithful, a wise and discerning guide for others, regardless of chronological age or educational background. What might the example of these spiritual leaders offer to spiritual directors today? In examining their style of direction, the subject matter they address, and the process by which Desert Fathers and Mothers became guides for others, we can find models of wisdom that may assist those called to direct souls today.

Sources

What we know of the Desert Fathers and Mothers comes to us via different forms of monastic literature. Most well-known are the *Sayings of the Desert Fathers*, or *Apophthegmata Patrum*, gathered and circulated among the monks and nuns themselves, and published in Greek in the latter fifth century by an unknown editor. The literature comprises a collection of about a thousand short vignettes and quotations from about 120 desert ascetics.[5] The sayings soon were followed by more formal biographies, or *vitae*, such as St. Athanasius's *Life of St. Antony the Great*. Other biographies followed in the fourth and fifth centuries, as travelers to

---

[2] Thomas Merton, *Spiritual Direction and Meditation* (Collegeville, MN: Liturgical Press, 1960), 3–4.

[3] Louf, "Spiritual Fatherhood," 42.

[4] Ibid., 37.

[5] The sayings are organized in two forms: either by the elder's name into the alphabetical collection or by topic in the systematic collection. See Benedicta Ward, *The Sayings of the Desert Fathers: The Alphabetical Collection* (Kalamazoo, MI: Cistercian Publications, 1975); Norman Russell, *The Lives of the Desert Fathers* (Kalamazoo, MI: Cistercian Publications, 1980), 3; Joseph Lienhard, SJ, "On 'Discernment of Spirits' in the Early Church," *Theological Studies* 41 (1980): 520; J. William Harmless, "Apophthegmata Patrum (Sayings of the Desert Fathers)," *The Oxford Dictionary of Late Antiquity*, ed. Oliver Nicholson (Oxford: Oxford University Press, 2018).

Egypt and Palestine met the monks and nuns firsthand and wrote of their experiences.[6] Palladius's *Lausiac History*, Rufinus's translation of the *Historia Monachorum in Aegypto*, and John Cassian's *Institutes* and *Conferences* were particularly influential in bringing some of these sayings and stories to Western monasticism.

Beyond the sayings and the lives, writings from the Desert Fathers and Mothers themselves also are a source of their wisdom. Early Coptic monks like Antony and then his follower Ammonas wrote letters; while Antony's letters tend to be somewhat abstract, the fourteen letters of Ammonas clearly address the changing circumstances of particular people.[7] Similarly, in the early sixth century, two desert monks named Barsanuphius and John lived near Gaza, counseling a number of different kinds of people via letters. Responding to the concerns of monastics, simple laypeople, church leaders, and political figures, these letters provide a beautiful example of how elders provided personalized spiritual guidance. While the sayings tend to be short, pithy responses to questions, and stories from the lives provide examples, the letters tend to provide more context, allowing us to see how the Desert Fathers and Mothers addressed the spiritual dynamics of actual people in sometimes ongoing situations.[8]

Many desert ascetics are described as being simple people of fairly humble background, but some more educated people of culture also spent time among their number. Some produced spiritual and theological writings. St. Basil the Great, for instance, was the son of a famous orator and was educated at some of the best schools, including the university at Athens. While he did not spend his whole life in the desert, in 356 Basil made visits to the monks and nuns of Syria, Mesopotamia, and Egypt. When he returned to solitary life in Cappadocia, he began to write the *Philokalia* and

---

[6] Russell, *Lives of the Desert Fathers*, 3–4.

[7] David Brakke, "The Making of Monastic Demonology: The Ascetic Teachers on Withdrawal and Resistance," *Church History* 70 (2001): 32; Derwas Chitty, trans., *The Letters of Saint Anthony the Great* (Oxford: SLG Press, 1979).

[8] John Chryssavgis, *Letters from the Desert: Barsanuphius and John* (Crestwood, NY: St. Vladimir's Seminary Press, 2003), 8–9, 19.

several monastic rules before going on to become a bishop.[9] Evagrius of Pontus, similarly, was a fourth-century intellectual of Constantinople, ordained lector by Basil and deacon by St. Gregory Nazianzen, who became his lifelong friend. He enjoyed great worldly success before fleeing to Jerusalem and then, at the direction of St. Melania, to the Egyptian monastic life at Nitria and the Cells.[10] While living in great austerity, he gave spiritual direction and wrote about the spiritual and psychological dynamics of dealing with one's thoughts and temptations. He was known for great discretion.[11] While his more speculative *Kephalaia Gnostika* was condemned, his *Praktikos, Gnostikos, Chapters on Prayer, Antirrhetikos, Sentences for Monks,* and other works influenced generations of spiritual teachers.

The Style of Spiritual Direction among the Desert Fathers and Mothers

The various sources of desert wisdom indicate that the *abbas* and *ammas* used different styles of spiritual direction. While some practices might apply only to monastic usage, or might reflect culturally conditioned values that have shifted with time, some of these styles of direction still are worth imitating today. It is important to note that to some extent, both the nature of the relationship between an elder and a follower, and their style of spiritual direction, were determined primarily by the elder's way of life, and secondarily, by the form of life of the follower. Regardless, those seeking direction usually had to take the initiative to build the relationship.[12] In the desert tradition, some men and women

---

[9] Olivier Clément, *The Roots of Christian Mysticism: Texts from the Patristic Era with Commentary* (Hyde Park, NY: New City Press, 1993), 315–16.

[10] John Eudes Bamberger, introduction to Evagrius Ponticus, *The Praktikos & Chapters on Prayer*, trans. John Eudes Bamberger (Kalamazoo, MI: Cistercian Publications, 1981), xxxvi–xlii.

[11] Ibid., xliii–xliv.

[12] Claudia Rapp, " 'For Next to God, You Are My Salvation': Reflections on the Rise of the Holy Man in Late Antiquity," in *The Cult of the Saints in Late Antiquity and the Early Middle Ages: Essays on the Contribution of Peter Brown*, ed. James Howard-Johnston and Paul Antony Hayward (New York: Oxford University Press, 1999), 78.

pursued a solitary life, perhaps with a loose affiliation with other hermits. Those of great holiness inevitably attracted regular visitors seeking spiritual advice. Callers might come from near or far to confess their sins and to receive encouragement, reprimand, or teaching from the *abba* or *amma*.[13] Among those who came, some disciples might stay on and attach themselves to the spiritual master, either for a period of time or for life. Sometimes these disciples would live nearby, or even in the same cell as the *abba* or *amma*. Thus closely connected to their elders, these disciples learned humility and virtue through daily rather than occasional invitations to obedience, and by imitation of the life they saw. Regarding the desert hermits and their followers, the words of Dorotheos of Gaza are apropos: "The fathers say that staying in a cell is half [of monastic observance], and to see the elders the other half."[14] Both solitary reflection and staying close to those of good example and wisdom promote growth.

In contrast with the eremitic or semi-eremitic tradition, more community-minded monastics, or cenobites, gathered in a group around a particular spiritual father or mother. Imitating the early Christian community described in the Acts of the Apostles, cenobites sought to practice charity, holding everything in common and serving their neighbors. While individuals might have a personal spiritual relationship with the leader, in the cenobitic life, spiritual wisdom was learned in part via the style of life itself, often codified into a written rule.[15] As in the eremitic tradition, however, obedience was still a core spiritual value, and giving up one's own

[13] Demacopoulos, *Five Models of Spiritual Direction*, 9.

[14] Quoted in Louf, "Spiritual Fatherhood," 42.

[15] Armand Veilleux has argued in *La liturgie dans le cénobitisme* that in Pachomian monasteries, the abbot was more the organizer of the common life than a spiritual father to each monk. He says that Cassian's mis-transmission of the northern Egyptian tradition of cenobitic life caused these roles to be fused in Western monasticism. Claude Peifer, on the other hand, argues that plenty of literature describes Pachomius as a spiritual father to the monks of his monasteries; he does not believe that a stress on community negates the role of the spiritual father. See also Claude Peifer, "Appendix 2: The Abbot," in Timothy Fry et al., eds., *RB 1980: The Rule of St. Benedict in Latin and English with Notes* (Collegeville, MN: Liturgical Press, 1981), 337–40; Thomas Keating, "The Two Streams of Cenobitic Tradition in the Rule of Saint Benedict," *Cistercian Studies* 11, no. 4 (1976): 257–68.

will in humility was considered a trustworthy path to holiness. While a rule of life and communal expectations provided a level of basic spiritual guidance, the superior was considered to hold the place of Christ and could be expected to teach and advise the members. In large communities, a leader might delegate authority to others. Both Basil and Pachomius led large communities where spiritual direction was divided among the elders and supervised by the abbot.[16]

In terms of the master-disciple relationship, then, among the solitaries, a disciple might ask for onetime advice or meet with a teacher regularly. This could happen in person or via letters. A long-term follower might live with or near an elder and receive direction in a way similar to that of the cenobites, where spiritual direction might come via a personal meeting, or from general preaching to the community, or through an elder's own example or response to situations arising in the regular ebb and flow of life. Today, we see a similar range of ways for spiritual direction to happen, from a single encounter after Mass or during a retreat, to regular meetings, phone calls, or electronic communications, to full entry into a form of religious life that allows one to follow more sustained spiritual guidance.

Spiritual direction in the desert often began with a person approaching an elder asking, "Give me a word," or "How can I be saved?"[17] The word of the *abba* or *amma* was seen as a movement of the Holy Spirit in the soul of the hearer. Indeed, in the desert tradition, spiritual direction was a process of guiding a disciple such that the individual might respond to his or her own calling with the graces of the Holy Spirit.[18] The director offered a level of clarity for the directee. We are told that a disciple of Antony's

[16] Demacopoulos, *Five Models of Spiritual Direction*, 9; Peifer, "Appendix 2: The Abbot," 341; "Bohairic Life of Pachomius," 26, in *Pachomian Koinonia, Volume 1*, trans. Armand Veilleux (Kalamazoo, MI: Cistercian Publications, 1980).

[17] Louf, "Spiritual Fatherhood," 38; cf. "On Abba Helle," 12: "One of the brethren, desiring to be saved, asked him if he might live with him in the desert" (Russell, *Lives of the Desert Fathers*, 91); "The Monks of Nitria," 10: "If there were many who came to him wishing to be saved, he called together the whole community." (Russell, 106).

[18] Merton, *Spiritual Direction and Meditation*, 5.

named Paul came to him immediately after discovering his wife committing adultery and, wishing "to be saved," asked to live with him. "Antony said to him, 'You can be saved if you have obedience; whatever I tell you, that is what you will do.' Paul replied, 'I shall do everything you command.'" Paul indeed went on to be astoundingly obedient and ultimately became a revered spiritual father in his own right.[19] Amma Syncletica also taught about the importance of discerning one's call and living it authentically. She said that many living in monastic communities "act like those living in cities and are lost while many of those living in cities do the works of the desert and are saved. Indeed, it is possible to live with a multitude and still be solitary in spirit just as it is possible to live as a solitary while one's thoughts are with the crowd."[20] One call might be different from another, but the wise elder could help a seeker discern the appropriate path of holiness in his or her own life. This was done in part by assisting in evaluating a disciple's strengths and limitations. When a brother went to Abba Matoës, asking what to do about his inability to control his speaking ill of others, "[t]he old man replied, 'If you cannot contain yourself, flee into solitude. For this is a sickness. The person who dwells with brothers must not be square, but round, so as to turn himself towards all.' He went on, 'It is not through virtue that I live in solitude, but through weakness; those who live in the midst of people are the strong ones.'"[21] The Holy Spirit guides each to a way that will lead to healing and wholeness; the elder helps discern the way.

Beyond the guiding word itself, an elder's example, prayer, and sanctity could themselves be a sacramental expression of God's will, guiding those they led to holiness.[22] Actions speak. It was said that "even when silent, Pachomius made his actions a discourse."[23] When Abba Sisoes became impatient with having to

---

[19] "On Paul," 1, in Russell, *Lives of the Desert Fathers*, 114.

[20] Tim Vivian, ed., *Becoming Fire: Through the Year with the Desert Fathers and Mothers*, Cistercian Studies Series, no. 225 (Collegeville, MN: Liturgical Press, 2008), 36.

[21] Ibid., 406.

[22] Merton, *Spiritual Direction and Meditation*, 9.

[23] "Psenthaisios," 1, quoted in Louf, "Spiritual Fatherhood," 51.

give spoken direction, he asked: "Why do you insist on my speaking idly? Do what you see."[24] And to other elders who would direct disciples, Abba Poemen famously advised, "Be their model, not their lawgiver."[25] Dorotheos of Gaza, similarly, wrote, "Teach by deeds and by words what must be practiced, but most of all by your deeds, for examples are much more efficacious."[26] In many cases, actively living the Christian life is the best way of showing others what is to be done and how. Example proves that virtue is possible. Imitating an elder, disciples could discover on their own how such action reorients the rest of life in a more coherent way. For the elder, teaching by example also protected against the hypocrisy of not practicing what one preaches.[27] These are timeless virtues still worth practicing today.

Among the Desert Fathers and Mothers, elders often taught by means of symbolic actions, a practice used by Old Testament prophets.[28] Among the most well-known is the story of Abba Moses, a former brigand who became a holy man:

> A brother at Scetis committed a fault. A council was called to which Abba Moses was invited but he refused to go to it. Then the priest sent someone to say to him, "Come, for everyone is waiting for you." So he got up and went. He took a leaking jug, filled it with water and carried it with him. The others came out to meet him and said to him, "What is this, father?" The old man said to them, "My sins run out behind me and I do not see them, and today I am coming to judge the errors of another." When they heard that they said no more to the brother but forgave him.[29]

---

[24] "Sisoes," 45, quoted in Louf, "Spiritual Fatherhood," 51; Ward, *Sayings of the Desert Fathers*, 185.

[25] "Abba Poemen," 174, quoted in Peifer, "Appendix 2: The Abbot," 337; Ward, *Sayings of the Desert Fathers*, 160–61.

[26] Dorotheos of Gaza, *Letter* 2, 184, quoted in Louf, "Spiritual Fatherhood," 52.

[27] Peifer, "Appendix 2: The Abbot," 336.

[28] See also "Zacharias," 3, "Pior," 3, and "Ammonas," 8 and 9; Peifer, "Appendix 2: The Abbot," 336.

[29] "Moses," 2, Ward, *Sayings of the Desert Fathers*, 117.

The symbolic action in this case provides an image of a spiritual reality to be addressed. The truly humble Christian is self-aware enough not to condemn another person for his or her sins, but in mercy entrusts them to God. In another case, the elder symbolically acts out the image of the monk who embodies the crucified Christ:

> A brother asked an old man, "How can I be saved?" The latter took off his habit, girded his loins and raised his hands to heaven, saying, "So should the monk be: denuded of all things in this world, and crucified. In the contest the athlete fights with his fists; in his thoughts the monk stands, his arms outstretched in the form of a cross to heaven, calling on God. The athlete stands naked when fighting in a contest; the monk stands naked and stripped of all things, anointed with oil and taught by his master how to fight. So God leads us to the victory."[30]

Such symbolic actions would be memorable. They point to important core values not to be forgotten. Here, the brother is given a striking image of how depending on God makes a monk like Christ, both vulnerable and strong.

Beyond providing one's own living example, when helping their disciples, elders also would share stories of other holy people. In some cases, this could be a quiet act of deference and humility, passing on good advice without pointing to oneself in the process.[31] John Cassian's stories of idealized heroes of the desert teaching wisdom exemplify this model, with the conferences he wrote being credited to various fathers, while also advancing Cassian's own goals of reforming monasticism in Gaul.[32] In his *Epistle 12*, the elder Ammonas presents the examples of Elijah and John the Baptist. He notes that after seeking God in solitude in

---

[30] *Wisdom of the Desert Fathers*, §11, p. 3, as quoted in Russell, *Lives of the Desert Fathers*, 34.

[31] Aelred Gidden, foreword to *Becoming Fire*, ed. Vivian, 17.

[32] See John Cassian, *The Conferences*, trans. Boniface Ramsey (New York and Mahwah, NJ: Newman Press, 1997; Demacopoulos, *Five Models of Spiritual Direction*, 114.

the desert, they then were sent to serve God by tending the souls of people.[33] While this may be a good pattern for other elders to consider imitating, it may also express quietly Ammonas's sense of his own experience and call to serve. Among the *Sayings*, an anonymous "abba of Rome," who may be Arsenius, "recalled that there was an elder who had a good disciple. Because of some narrowness of mind, he chased him out. The brother remained seated outside, and when the elder opened the door and found him still seated, he bowed to him saying, 'O father, the humility of your patience has won over my narrowness of mind. Come in; from now on you are the elder and father and I shall be the younger and disciple.' "[34] Both the teacher and the exemplars of the story remain unnamed, yet the humility and obedience to be imitated shine through clearly.

Across all of these forms of desert teaching, we see a style of spiritual direction marked by knowledge, care, and prayer for directees. Knowledge allows for personalized, appropriate direction. In one letter, Barsanuphius instructs a certain Paul to avoid discussions of the faith (which trouble him) because the spiritual father judges him "not capable of studying the mysteries." Instead, Paul is instructed to contemplate his own sins.[35] Elsewhere, Barsanuphius directs a sick monk named Andrew to be joyful and give thanks in the midst of it, enduring suffering with patience.[36] Knowledge of his disciple allows Barsanuphius to challenge wisely. A disciple must be able to trust in the loving concern of the elder if he or she is to be completely open and honest about matters of the soul.[37] Amma Talis was said to be so trusted and

[33] Ammonas, *Epistle 12*, in *The Letters of Ammonas, Successor of Saint Antony*, trans. Derwas Chitty and Sebastian Brock (Oxford: SLG Press, 1979), as quoted in Demacopoulos, *Five Models of Spiritual Direction*, 8.

[34] "An Abba of Rome," 2, Ward, *Sayings of the Desert Fathers*, 175–76. Note that Arsenius was known to give examples as though referring to others, when they actually referred to himself. See Arsenius 33, Ward, *Sayings of the Desert Fathers*, 13.

[35] *Epistle 57–58*, as referenced in Adalbert de Vogüé, "The Letters of Barsanuphius and John of Gaza to Some Hermits," trans. Terrence G. Kardong in *American Benedictine Review* 69:2 (June 2018): 151.

[36] *Epistle 76.9–10*, as referenced in de Vogüé, "Letters of Barsanuphius," 153.

[37] Louf, "Spiritual Fatherhood," 55.

beloved by her young sisters that their community had no need of a key to lock them in the monastic enclosure; it was considered remarkable that they freely chose to stay close to her.[38] Love and care also mean that the wise elder does not act shocked when a directee reveals thoughts or behaviors reflecting humanity's fallen nature. The true *amma* or *abba* knows human weakness, but also can see the image of God in each person.[39] Among the desert monastics, struggles with bodily asceticism, especially, called for a level of both compassion and discipline. To a brother dealing with gluttony and "other movements of the flesh," Abba John gives encouragement, saying that God is more powerful than the monk's spiritual enemies. He also suggests that when lustful thoughts occur at night, the brother should perform forty-nine genuflections, saying, "I have sinned, Lord, pardon me because of your name." At the same time, Abba John consoles him and encourages him to go to community prayer and to partake in the sacraments, knowing that they are not for condemnation, but for purification of body, soul, and spirit.[40] Many desert elders who counsel others regarding challenges with sexuality confide that they, too, have dealt with these same struggles.

The intercessory prayer of an *abba* or *amma* also was a common part of early spiritual direction. Letters to Abba Paphnutius ask for his prayers, and sometimes express prayer for his health and longevity. A certain Justinius writes to him, "for we believe that your citizenship is in heaven, and therefore we regard you as our master and common patron." A woman named Valeria refers to herself as his daughter and calls him "bearer of Christ," saying, "I trust by your prayers to obtain healing, for by ascetics and devotees revelations are manifested."[41] When a monk asked Abba Apollo to pray that he might be granted a particular grace, "the

---

[38] *Lausiac History* 138, cited in Louf, "Spiritual Fatherhood," 56.

[39] Peifer, "Appendix 2: The Abbot," 335.

[40] Abba John, *Epistles* 168.15–21, 170.9–13, cited in Vogüé, "Letters of Barsanuphius," 159–60.

[41] From H. I. Bell, *Jews and Christians in Egypt* (London, 1924), nos. 1923–29, 100–20, as cited in Rapp, " 'For Next to God, You Are My Salvation,' " 69.

grace of humility and gentleness was granted to him, so that all were amazed at him and the extraordinary degree of gentleness which he had attained."[42] The prayer of one's spiritual father or mother was seen to be powerful, a part of God's will being expressed through the guidance of the elder. Such prayer also is an expression of the elder's spiritual assistance when conversion or clarity is needed. St. Antony the Great writes to "all the dear brethren who are at Arsinoe and in its neighborhood" and expresses grief over their confusion but encourages them, promising his unceasing prayer, that God might give them "a heart of knowledge and a spirit of discernment, that you may be able to offer your hearts as a pure sacrifice before the Father, in great holiness, without blemish."[43] Interceding for one another is a basic act of Christian charity.

Some elders were charismatically gifted with the ability to see into the hearts and minds of those they directed. Without wasting time, these directors could go right to the point needing attention. Abba Apollo, for instance, was known to notice if people were gloomy or downcast, and to ask them about it; he then told them the secrets of their own hearts and urged them to rejoice.[44] Abba Helle, likewise, was said to be able to read hearts, and after teaching the monks for a few days, he declared that "one was troubled by fornication, another by vanity, another by self-indulgence, and another by anger. He declared that this man was meek and that one was a peacemaker, bringing under his scrutiny the vices of some, the virtues of others. On hearing these things they were amazed and said, 'Yes, it is just as you say.' "[45] Then, as now, such charismatic gifts were given not for the fame or personal benefit of the elder, but for the spiritual building up of those they served.

[42] "On Apollo," 42–43, Russell, *Lives of the Desert Fathers*, 76.

[43] Antony the Great, *Epistle 6*, in *The Letters of Saint Antony the Great*, trans. Chitty, 17–18.

[44] Peifer, "Appendix 2: The Abbot," 336; "On Apollo," 52–53, Russell, *Lives of the Desert Fathers*, 78.

[45] "On Abba Helle," Russell, *Lives of the Desert Fathers*, 91.

Discernment (in Greek, *dia krisis*, or in Latin, *discretio*) was perhaps the key element of spiritual guidance offered by Desert Fathers and Mothers, the mark of spiritual authority.[46] Elders prayed for their followers to gain discernment, but their own ability to help directees sort through their thoughts and experiences was at the heart of the relationship. Discernment meant analyzing thoughts, temptations, and other spiritual experiences and being able to clarify what was of God, what was from oneself, and what was from a demon. In both the *Sayings* and the *Lives*, Abba Pityrion was said to be an authority on discernment of spirits: "He said that there were certain demons which followed the passions and often made us disposed to do evil. 'Therefore, my children,' he said to us, 'whoever wishes to drive out the demons must first master the passions.' For whichever passion one overcomes, one also drives out its corresponding demon."[47] According to Ammonas, discernment was an uncommon gift said to come with "ascetic progress, trial, and prayer."[48] Such asceticism and trial often was experienced through obedience. Obedience to an elder allowed practice of giving up one's own will, so as to become more readily obedient to God. Then, after long experience of giving up one's own will, one could gain the ability to "make the choice of what is good or useful" more easily.[49] When one was inwardly purified enough to be obedient to God, then one might be ready to assist others.[50] Fundamentally, discernment was about knowing God's will; the practice of asceticism, particularly of obedience, was training to gain clarity and strength to follow it.

Besides the techniques of desert spiritual direction mentioned above, Cassian gives examples of a couple others. First is the process

---

[46] Demacopoulos, *Five Models of Spiritual Direction*, 8.

[47] "On Pityrion," 2, Russell, *Lives of the Desert Fathers*, 99; "Pityrion," Ward, *Sayings of the Desert Fathers*, 168.

[48] See Ammonas, *Epistle* 4.10, as quoted in Demacopoulos, *Five Models of Spiritual Direction*, 9.

[49] Basil, *Longer Rules*, 41, as quoted in Demacopoulos, *Five Models of Spiritual Direction*, 10–11. See also Louf, "Spiritual Fatherhood," 47–49.

[50] See Ammonas, *Epistle* 6, as quoted in Demacopoulos, *Five Models of Spiritual Direction*, 8.

of gradual correction. Depending on the age, health, or spiritual status of the person to be directed, the strategy used by the elder might be more or less strict. Those just joining monastic life might need more experience of humility and obedience, while those long-practiced at such virtues might need less.[51] Cassian notes that different monks struggle with different vices, and argues that those wrestling with physical passions, such as gluttony or lust, need physical remedies, such as fasting and vigils, while those struggling with spiritual passions, such as vainglory and pride, need more spiritual medicines, such as the practice of love and humility.[52] An elder might begin by focusing on where physical strategies are useful, then move on to the more spiritual. In this vein, Cassian notes that elders may also make use of the method of *condescensio*, temporarily relaxing a prior directive in order to deal with a more serious vice needing attention in the moment.[53] Finally, desert spiritual direction could attend to both action and contemplation. While contemplation was the preferred spiritual state promoted by early Christian authorities, practice of charity and communal discipline also could be important.[54]

In terms of the styles and techniques of spiritual direction among the Desert Fathers and Mothers, then, we see a few common themes. It was common for elders to offer disciples "a word," either in the form of a wise maxim or perhaps a saying or example from another wise elder. Often the elder gave a performative example of what was to be done. Often the elder gave explicit directives that required obedience and humility. Some elders had the charismatic gift of seeing into souls and giving appropriate direction; others heard more about the situation and then offered their discerned advice. Elders often were intercessors for their follow-

---

[51] Demacopoulos, *Five Models of Spiritual Direction*, 114–16; see John Cassian, *The Institutes*, trans. Boniface Ramsey (New York: Newman Press, 2000), IV (pp. 75ff).
[52] Demacopoulos, *Five Models of Spiritual Direction*, 115–16; John Cassian, *The Conferences*, trans. Boniface Ramsey (New York: Paulist Press, 1997), V.13ff (pp. 194ff).
[53] Demacopoulos, *Five Models of Spiritual Direction*, 116.
[54] Ibid., 120–22; Columba Stewart, *Cassian the Monk* (New York: Oxford University Press, 1998), 50. Cassian, *The Conferences*, XXIV.8.3; XVII.19; Cassian, *The Institutes* IV.19.

ers. Their deep care and prayer for their spiritual sons and daughters pervaded whatever direction they might give, even if some of their directives might have seemed harsh. While today we tend to be less comfortable with an expectation of such complete obedience among spiritual directors and directees, many of these other styles continue to be useful.

Subject Matter for Spiritual Direction

The topics brought to spiritual direction with the Desert Fathers and Mothers in some ways are similar to matters discussed today. In the literature we see examples of direction dealing with everyday issues such as illness, legal or economic matters, marriage, death, property, charity, right relationships, and dealing with temptations. People sought direction regarding how to discern the best way of life and how to balance action and contemplation appropriately. Less similar to today are issues such as treatment of slaves, how to deal with non-Christians, asceticism in city life, and determining the importance of dreams and visions.[55] While dealing with temptations is a timeless spiritual struggle, the way in which it was addressed in early Christianity was marked by a particular character that, if found today, probably is present more among monastic audiences than the general Christian public. Likewise, concern about how monastic men and women relate with the laity was and continues to be a topic for spiritual direction, at least among religious; the subject was approached differently in the early centuries of Christianity, however. Today, we share a greater appreciation for the *universal* call to holiness, and so we are quicker to point out the presence of grace in secular lay life. Finally, at the heart of spiritual direction is the ageless matter of how to grow in prayer and the love of God.[56]

---

[55] Chryssavgis, *Letters from the Desert*, 20; Demacopoulos, *Five Models of Spiritual Direction*, 121–22.

[56] Vogüé, "Letters of Barsanuphius," 171.

The matter of temptations is significant. As people seek virtue, temptations test resolve.[57] In the desert approach to addressing temptations, key to dealing with this subject matter was the practice of exposing one's thoughts for scrutiny and analysis. This practice of observing one's thoughts was particularly promoted by Evagrius, who built on the work of Origen. Evagrius's system of eight thoughts, or *logismoi*, was a precursor to what has come to be known as the seven deadly sins.[58] In this system, the vices begin as evil thoughts proposed by demons, which one can either entertain or ignore. Given full attention, the thought becomes a temptation, which one might actively resist or perhaps eventually decide to accept. The temptation then becomes a passion, which if not resisted leads to sinful behavior. Each demon specializes in its own kind of evil thought, and these tend to be linked: Gluttony leads to lust, which leads to the other sins, all the way to vainglory and pride.[59] According to Evagrius, by analyzing thoughts, one can see and combat them before they became pure temptation or sin: "We must take care to recognize the different types of demons and note the special times of their activity . . . so that when these various evil thoughts set their own proper forces to work we are in a position to address effective words against them, that is to say, those words which correctly characterize the one present. . . . In this manner we shall . . . pack them off, chafing with chagrin, marveling at our perspicacity."[60] Evagrius's approach, then, illustrates the widely held understanding of the early Church that seeking God through ascetic life will mean battling demons.[61] While today we tend to be less ready to name demonic forces as such, the same dynamics apply to the spiritual life, and Evagrius's system bears renewed attention.

[57] Brakke, "Making of Monastic Demonology," 33.

[58] Cassian linked Evagrius's eight thoughts with the medieval idea of seven or eight deadly sins (gluttony, lust, greed, anger, despair, laziness, vainglory, and pride); Gregory the Great reduced the vices from eight to seven. See Demacopoulos, *Five Models of Spiritual Direction*, 117–20.

[59] Evagrius, *Praktikos*, pars. 7–8.

[60] Ibid., par. 43.

[61] Bamberger, introduction to *Praktikos*, 5; Demacopoulos, *Five Models of Spiritual Direction*, 12.

As the Desert Mothers and Fathers expounded on the subtleties of vice and virtue, they sometimes counseled with the teachings of Evagrius. For example, against anger, he recommends the singing of Psalms, patience, and almsgiving. Against lust, he recommends "hunger, toil and solitude."[62] While not often specifically named, the thought of Evagrius echoes through direction given by other Desert Fathers and Mothers. Amma Theodora says, "You should realize that as soon as you intend to live in peace, at once evil comes and weighs down your soul through *accidie*, faintheartedness, and evil thoughts. . . . But if we are vigilant, all these temptations fall away."[63] Similarly, when Abba Poemen asked Abba Joseph of Panephysis about what to do when attacked by the passions, Abba Joseph responded that he ought to fight them.[64] Amma Syncletica echoes Evagrius on the linkages between vices and virtues: "Just as dreadful qualities are attached to one another (for example, envy follows upon avarice, as do treachery, perjury, anger, and remembrance of wrongs), so the opposite qualities of these vices are dependent upon love; I mean, of course, gentleness and patience, as well as endurance, and the ultimate good—holy poverty."[65] In every age, the role of the spiritual father or mother includes seeing how vice corrupts the journey to God, and proposing appropriate strategies to address it.[66] To observe and control one's thoughts is one way to bring them into greater alignment with the things of God.

A common theme for spiritual direction among the Desert Fathers and Mothers was how to find the right balance between action and contemplation. How much silence and solitude were possible? If contemplation was the desired state among early Christian authorities, it usually was preceded by a life of charitable action and practical service.[67] Among the *Sayings* and the *Lives*,

---

[62] Evagrius, *Praktikos*, par. 15.

[63] "Theodora," 3, in Ward, *Sayings of the Desert Fathers*, 71.

[64] "Joseph of Panephysis," 3, in Ward, *Sayings of the Desert Fathers*, 87.

[65] Pseudo-Athanasius, *The Life and Regimen of the Blessed and Holy Syncletica*, trans. Elizabeth Bryson Bongie (Eugene, OR: Wipf & Stock, 2003), no. 72, p. 45.

[66] Demacopoulos, *Five Models of Spiritual Direction*, 119.

[67] Ibid., 121.

we are given many examples of how holy elders would step away from their personal prayer or ease their fasting in order to accommodate visitors with hospitality.[68] Moreover, the value of work to support oneself or one's community was not denied. The Desert Fathers and Mothers knew themselves to be both body and spirit, and so labor to support one's physical life had its own dignity.[69]

For those seeking the pure contemplation of God, though, the desert elder provided guidance on what to expect at each stage of spiritual growth. After expounding on the prerequisite examples of obedience, humility, patience, and charity, elders could share stories of ecstatic prayer to give a sense of the goal—union with God. A well-known saying concerns how Abba Lot consulted with Abba Joseph on what to do beyond the habits he already kept: saying his office, fasting, praying, meditating, being at peace with others, and purifying his thoughts as best he could. "Then the old man stood up and stretched his hands towards heaven. His fingers became like ten lamps of fire and he said to him, 'If you will, you can become all flame.'"[70] A story about Abba Silvanus similarly relates how his disciple Zacharias "entered and found him in ecstasy with his hands stretched towards heaven." Going away and returning several times over the next few hours, Zacharias again found Silvanus in this state, until at the tenth hour, he found him at peace. He asked, "What has happened today, father?" and Silvanus claimed he had been sick. "But the disciple seized his feet and said to him, 'I will not let you go until you have told me what you have seen.' The old man said, 'I was taken up to heaven and I saw the glory of God and I stayed there till now and now I have been sent away.'"[71] These stories demonstrate that after spiritual purification, deep contemplative prayer can lead to union

---

[68] See also Barsanuphius and John, Letters 304–26, dealing with hesychasm and the practice of silent prayer when visitors come; Louf, "Spiritual Fatherhood," 171.

[69] See "Silvanus," 5, in Ward, *Sayings of the Desert Fathers*, 187; Barsanuphius, Letters 327–30 and John, Letters 286–303, dealing with an infirmarian; Louf, "Spiritual Fatherhood," 170, 173–74.

[70] "Joseph of Pnephysis," 7, in Ward, *Sayings of the Desert Fathers*, 88.

[71] "Silvanus," 3, in Ward, *Sayings of the Desert Fathers*, 186–87.

with God that transcends earthly experience for the joy of heaven. The journey of ascetic practice and spiritual growth is worth it.

Becoming an *Abba* or *Amma*

If those called to the ministry of spiritual direction today sometimes balk at the prospect, they are in good company with the Desert Fathers and Mothers. In the desert tradition, the genuine elder does not usually seek to become a spiritual father or mother. Rather, humility and perhaps terror at the offer are more typical.[72] Usually the elder is one who has lived the life for a long time, who has gained the wisdom of experience with which to advise others.[73] Abba Horsiesus, a follower of Pachomius, says that those who govern souls should be "perfect men" and shares a parable: "If an unbaked brick is set in a foundation near a river, it does not last for a single day; but if it is baked, it endures like stone."[74] According to Cassian, spiritual authority is granted to those who have achieved perfect love, with humility, obedience, and discernment.[75] The spiritual mother or father is one who has been tried and found true.

At the same time, sometimes God chooses younger people to be spiritual fathers and mothers. These men and women tend to be discovered by an act of the Holy Spirit, their words, or perhaps a miracle.[76] Abba Zacharias, the son of Abba Carion, apparently became a humble, holy man at a young age. According to the *Sayings*, Abba Moses saw the Holy Spirit descend on him, and so he felt compelled to consult the young Zacharias on what he ought to do. At this Zacharias "threw himself on the ground at the old

---

[72] Louf, "Spiritual Fatherhood," 45; Peifer, "Appendix 2: The Abbot," 333; see *The First Greek Life of Pachomius* 126, in *Pachomian Koinonia Volume 1, The Life of St. Pachomius and His Disciples*, trans. Armand Veilleux, Cistercian Studies Series, no. 45 (Kalamazoo, MI: Cistercian Publications, 1980), 386.

[73] Peifer, "Appendix 2: The Abbot," 332.

[74] Ibid., 341; *The First Greek Life of Pachomius,* 126, in *Pachomian Koinonia Volume 1*, 386.

[75] Demacopoulos, *Five Models of Spiritual Direction*, 111.

[76] Louf, "Spiritual Fatherhood," 44, 60.

man's feet and said, 'Are you asking me, Father?' " Told that Abba
Moses had seen the Holy Spirit descending on him and that he
now was "constrained to ask," Zacharias then "drew his hood off
his head and put it under his feet and trampled on it, saying, 'The
man who does not let himself be treated thus, cannot be a monk.' "
Abba Macarius, likewise, felt called by God to consult Zacharias
and received a similarly incredulous response. On hearing that
God had urged it, though, Abba Zacharias again gave counsel.[77]
In another example, we are told that Abba Poemen called Agathon
an *abba* and was questioned about why he would call him that,
given that Agathon was so young. Abba Poemen then responded,
"Because his speech makes him worthy to be called 'abba.' "[78] In
these stories we see that wisdom will reveal itself, whether it is
made manifest in the young or the old.

All this said, while most spiritual elders are advanced in years,
it is good to remember that age does not automatically confer
wisdom. According to Cassian, Abba Moses said that one should
follow an elder not because of his gray hair, but "on the basis of
his commitment to the traditions of the fathers—a sign that he
possesses not only integrity but discernment."[79] Besides a whole-
some sense of the Christian tradition, the genuine elder also possesses other gifts, sometimes charismatic gifts. Most important,
however, are the gifts of discernment, discretion, and purity of
heart; these help people to know both their true selves and God.[80]
Moreover, the person called to be an elder must be able to set a
good example for those entrusted to his or her care, particularly
by following biblical models. To resemble Christ and the apostles
in one's actions is to express the reality of the Holy Spirit dwelling
within oneself and to invite others to participate in the same life.[81]
In the Pachomian community, a young monk was entrusted to an

[77] "Zacharias," in Ward, *Sayings of the Desert Fathers*, 58.
[78] "Poemen," 61, in Ward, *Sayings of the Desert Fathers*, 147.
[79] Cassian, *Conferences*, II.13.1–3.
[80] Peifer, "Appendix 2: The Abbot," 333–36; Demacopoulos, *Five Models of Spiritual Direction*, 118.
[81] See "Sahidic Life of St. Pachomius," 3, in *Pachomian Koinonia, Volume 1*, 426–27; Peifer, "Appendix 2: The Abbot," 336.

elder with these words: "Here is your father after God: everything that you see him do, you shall do. If he fasts, you will fast with him, and you will act just as he does; if he sits at table to eat, you will sit beside him and eat; when he gets up, you will get up with him; you will do nothing without him, and go nowhere without his permission."[82] The example of the *abba* or *amma* should be a trustworthy guide for others. In the desert tradition, the true spiritual father or mother was one who communicated the life of the Holy Spirit to others and begat in them the work of God, by both their words and actions.[83] Such presence of the Holy Spirit comes with a lifetime practice of asceticism and prayer.

The Desert Fathers and Mothers as Models for Spiritual Directors Today

In summary, if we were to ask what those called to the ministry of spiritual direction today can take from the example of the Desert Fathers and Mothers, a few themes emerge. First, if one is to be a spiritual leader for others, one's own human maturity and spiritual discipline must be in order. We cannot be good guides for others if we are not ourselves self-aware, converted, and well on the way toward God. Integrity matters. Good example matters. We need to have wrestled with our own demons before we know how the demons are likely to tempt someone else, and we need to know a pathway of prayer and virtue that has been proven true. If at some point we discover ourselves not as far along the way as we had thought we were, humility is the proper response. God will reveal the moment when we are ready to be called into service.

Second, we see in the Desert Fathers and Mothers that it is possible to assist others spiritually in different ways. Even today, some people are more hidden from the world and write letters, or spiritual reflections, or books. These men and women offer their spiritual

---

[82] "Sahidic Life of St. Pachomius," 93, quoted in Peifer, "Appendix 2: The Abbot," 340.

[83] See "Sahidic Life of St. Pachomius," 3, in *Pachomian Koinonia, Volume 1*, 426–27; Peifer, "Appendix 2: The Abbot," 333.

wisdom and help numerous people without necessarily knowing them. It is humbling not to see the fruits of one's own labor, but God can work through such people nonetheless. Others meet with people one-on-one and accompany individual souls on their journeys. These people are called to know and love those entrusted to their care. Such faithful love may be expressed in the language of support and encouragement, or perhaps the tough love of challenge and invitation to something new. Others may be called to lead whole groups or congregations in a more public way, leading by example, preaching, and teaching, as well as by offering individual guidance. As in early Christianity, we need many kinds of spiritual leaders. The skill sets and personalities appropriate to each may differ.

We see in the Desert Fathers and Mothers that keen awareness of human nature is important for those who would direct others. We have both the capacity for crushing weakness and for great integrity in the face of temptation and challenge. The discerning director knows when and how to encourage with mercy and confidence in God, and when to put vainglory or pride in its place. Spiritual growth may take a long time, and progress may come in fits and starts. Those called to direct others should be patient with this process, knowing how to focus energies strategically. They are attentive to the ways we can be deceived and recognize the signs of genuine movements of the Holy Spirit. They draw from a treasury of knowledge of Scripture and tradition, and they can use the examples and wise sayings of others to help their directees.

Finally, those who provide spiritual direction must continue to be faithful to their own spiritual journey into the life of God. As the Desert Fathers and Mothers themselves consulted with other elders, so spiritual directors today need to be in direction themselves. Engaging another in reflective supervision of their ministry is a responsible way of keeping one's own unconverted mess from interfering with ministry to the other. Moreover, a deep life of prayer and charity expressed through the works of mercy keeps one rooted in the heart of the Christian tradition, and it guards against hypocrisy. Humility is a protective virtue bearing continual cultivation. While few of us today likely pursue the desert asceticism of all-night vigils or extreme fasts as a regular matter of course, the example of the *abbas* and *ammas* shows us that a level of bodily discipline also affects our spiritual discipline. What are the practices that keep us faithful and ready to serve? Like the Desert Fathers and Mothers, those called to be spiritual directors know and follow spiritual practices that ground their own lives, and they provide tools for guiding others.

CHAPTER TWO

Gregory, Marmion, Merton, and Louf: Insights from the Benedictine Religious Family for the Practice of Spiritual Direction

Fr. Christian Raab, OSB

In this chapter, I do not intend to identify or profile a Benedictine approach to spiritual direction that is distinct from or in any way in competition with other approaches. Instead, I wish to highlight some wisdom about giving and receiving spiritual direction that comes from monastic sources for the benefit of all. This task is important because monastic sources have been underappreciated in recent years. In contemporary literature, Ignatian approaches to spiritual direction are the most prominent and influential, and rightfully so. Ignatius presented a user-friendly method for growing in relationship with Christ and a comprehensive set of principles for discernment that will likely remain unsurpassed. By investigating some monastic sources, monastic spiritual directors can become better aware that this ministry is something they can claim as part of their own patrimony. Non-monastic spiritual directors can have their own approaches further supplemented and enriched by wisdom from the Benedictine tradition.

The chapter begins by examining the major insights of St. Gregory the Great in his *Pastoral Rule*. It then shows how the Benedictine tradition of spiritual direction has continued to be developed closer to our own time by Columba Marmion, Thomas Merton, and André Louf. Although these four sources are only a limited sample, they are thematically diverse enough that, when taken together, they provide a rather thorough portrait of the practice of spiritual direction in the Benedictine tradition. Each one highlights a different aspect of spiritual direction. Gregory's *Pastoral Rule* focuses especially on what kind of person the director should be. Marmion's *Union with God: Letters of Spiritual Direction* portrays a Benedictine vision of the spiritual life into which a director initiates and mentors his directees. Merton's *Spiritual Direction and Meditation* describes how to receive spiritual direction. Finally, Louf's *Grace Can Do More: Spiritual Accompaniment and Spiritual Growth* models an approach to spiritual direction that integrates the best insights from Ignatian spirituality and contemporary psychology into an otherwise Benedictine framework.

The *Pastoral Rule* of Gregory the Great

Two Objections

Before probing deeply into Gregory's *Pastoral Rule*, it is necessary to confront two objections that may be made to the inclusion of this famous text in a chapter on Benedictine spiritual direction. The first objection is that the sense in which Benedictines can claim Gregory as one of their own is not clear. The second objection is that the text itself may not really be about spiritual direction.

Let us first say something about Gregory's connection to the Benedictine world. Before ascending to the papacy in 590, Gregory was a monk. After his conversion (around 573), he used his sizable inheritance to establish a number of monasteries and went to live in one of them, St. Andrew's on Caelian Hill.[1] We do not know, however, which rule the monks of St. Andrew's followed, and it would be anachronistic to call Gregory a Benedictine the way we

---

[1] Jean LeClercq, "Monasticism and Asceticism: II. Western Christianity," in *Christian Spirituality: Origins to the Twelfth Century*, ed. Bernard McGinn, John Meyendorff, and Jean LeClercq (New York: Crossroad, 1985), 113–31, esp. 116–19.

mean it today. In the sixth century, there were no religious orders. There were only monasteries. A given monastery might author its own rule, borrow an extant rule from another monastery, or collate a piecemeal governing document assembled from various rules.

Gregory's inclusion in this chapter is based on the following set of mostly uncontroversial truths. Gregory and St. Benedict came from the same milieu.[2] They were both monks on the Italian peninsula during the sixth century. Gregory was familiar enough with Benedict to devote a book of his *Dialogues* to telling the story of the saint's life. In that text, Gregory reports meeting monks who knew Benedict. He also claims familiarity with the rule in the context of that work.[3] The *Dialogues* is probably the second most important document for informing the Benedictine charism from the Middle Ages to today, and so a case can be made that Gregory is, after Benedict, the second most important historical figure for determining Benedictine identity.

Furthermore, Benedictines have always included monastic sources beyond just Benedict in their formation. Indeed, Benedict instructs them to do precisely this at the end of his Rule when he encourages the monks to read the lives of the Desert Fathers, the *Conferences* and *Institutes* of John Cassian, and the *Rule of Saint Basil*.[4] Gregory is an ideal candidate to be a supplementary source for Benedictine formation not only for the reasons already named but also because he incorporates the best of monastic tradition into his teaching: Augustine, Cassian, and Benedict himself, as well as Eastern fathers such as Evagrius, Athanasius, and Gregory Nazianzen.[5]

---

[2] See ibid., 116–19.

[3] Gregory writes: "[Benedict] wrote a rule for monks that was outstanding for its discretion and limpid in its diction." Terrence Kardong, *The Life of St. Benedict by Gregory the Great* (Collegeville, MN: Liturgical Press, 2009), 139.

[4] Timothy Fry et al., eds., *RB 1980: The Rule of St. Benedict in English* (Collegeville, MN: Liturgical Press, 1981), 73.

[5] George E. Demacopoulos, introduction to St. Gregory the Great, *The Book of Pastoral Rule*, trans. George E. Demacopoulos (Crestwood, NY: St. Vladimir's Seminary Press, 2007), 10–11. For more on Benedict's influence on Gregory, see George E. Demacopoulos, *Five Models of Spiritual Direction in the Early Church* (Notre Dame, IN: University of Notre Dame Press, 2007), 127–64.

A second objection is that it is not clear that Gregory's *Pastoral Rule* is in fact written for spiritual directors. Scholars debate who Gregory's intended audience was. Marc Reydellet has argued that Gregory wrote his rule for the widest of possible audiences, having both church and political rulers in mind. Bruno Judic and Wilhelm Gessel claim, to the contrary, that Gregory's true audience was bishops. George Demacopoulos, meanwhile, has argued that Gregory's audience was all spiritual leaders. Brendan Lupton, who has summarized these arguments, contends quite convincingly that Gregory's primary audience was bishops but not in an exclusive way.[6] Lupton shows that Gregory was aware that his advice to bishops translated well for other leaders and was not averse to his work being given to them as a guide. In fact, as Lupton notes, Gregory instructed a bishop to deliver copies of the rule to priests working in his diocese.[7]

Many people in the English-speaking world reading Gregory's *Pastoral Rule* today rely on the 2007 translation by George Demacopoulos. Demacopoulos makes a somewhat unusual choice of translating the terms *sacerdos, rector, praedicator,* and *pastor* all as "spiritual director."[8] In light of Lupton's analysis, this translation

[6] Brendan Lupton, "Reexamining Gregory the Great's Audience for the *Pastoral Rule*," *Downside Abbey Review* 133.468 (April 2015): 178–204, at 180–84. See also Marc Reydellet, *La royauté dans la littérature latine, de Sidoine Apollinaire à Isidore de Seville* (Rome: École française de Rome, 1981), 463; Bruno Judic, introduction to Gregory the Great, *Régle pastorale*, vol. 1, 2 vols., SC 381 (Paris: Editions du Cerf, 1992), 76; Wilhelm Gessel, "Reform am Haupt: Die Pastoralregel Gregors des Grossen und die Besetzung von Bischofsstühlen," in *Papsttum und Kirchenreform: Historische Beiträge. Festschrift für Georg Schwaiger zum 65. Geburtstag,* ed. Manfred Weitlauff and Karl Hausberger (St. Ottilien: EOS Verlag, 1990), 17–36.

[7] Lupton, "Reexamining Gregory the Great's Audience," 193.

[8] Demacopoulos, introduction, 23–24. The choice serves Demacopoulos's agenda of demonstrating that Gregory, who is writing a manual for clergy, wanted these figures to cultivate the characteristics of the Desert Fathers and Mothers—who were, in fact, charismatic wisdom figures practicing a more one-on-one spiritual mentorship. It was part of Gregory's reform that the qualities developed in the ascetic-monastic milieu, to which he belonged, be adopted and developed among secular clergy. Viewed from this angle, Gregory is distilling and systematizing centuries of the desert tradition of spiritual direction as it was practiced by *abbas* and *ammas* and presenting it to the secular clergy and encouraging them to adopt it. Insofar as that is the case, the *Pastoral Rule* remains for us today a window into the earliest tradition of spiritual direction and thus an invaluable resource of timeless wisdom.

choice is disadvantageous insofar as it obscures the original autho-
rial intent of writing to clergy, especially bishops. On the other
hand, it advantageously highlights that the wisdom found herein
is analogously applicable to a wider scope of spiritual leadership,
including spiritual directors. The translation choice is disadvantageous in a second way if it misleads the reader into thinking the
text is primarily about the ministry of one-on-one guidance in a
conversational setting. To the contrary, Gregory's *Pastoral Rule*
concerns the whole range of ministerial activity, with particular
emphasis on the preaching ministry. However, the translation
choice is thereby advantageous if it helps us to realize that we
need not limit our understanding of spiritual direction to what
happens in the parlor or the confessional. The whole range of
ministerial activity has spiritual directive potential. As Thomas
Merton puts it, spiritual direction is "guiding Christians to their
proper interior and exterior perfection according to their particular
vocation as manifested by their gifts, capabilities, ideals, duties
of state and above all, by their place in God's plan for His Church.
This means first of all helping them to recognize their personal
vocation and encouraging them, by means of instructions and
guidance, to correspond with God's will in their regard by the
best means at their disposal according to their state of life."[9] Demacopoulos's translation choice helps us realize that this task is accomplished through preaching and teaching and administrating
as much as through what we have come to recognize as formal
spiritual direction.

The Qualities of the Director

At the beginning of the *Pastoral Rule*, Gregory states: "Necessity
demands that one should carefully examine who it is that comes
to the position of spiritual authority; and coming solemnly to this
point, how he should live; and living well, how he should teach;
and teaching rightly, with what kind of self-examination he should

---

[9] Thomas Merton, *Spiritual Direction and Meditation* (Collegeville, MN: Liturgical
Press, 1960), 6.

learn of his own weakness."[10] In these words one can see that Gregory is utterly concerned with the personal qualities of spiritual directors. Indeed, he prioritizes these personal qualities and will only proceed to discuss ministerial method after laying the foundation for ministry in the character of the minister. While Gregory mentions many qualities, virtues, and charismatic gifts of would-be spiritual directors, the most important ones fall under the following three headings: humility; contemplative experience and moral rectitude; and the gift of discernment.

Let us begin then with humility. Gregory was heir to a monastic tradition that was often skeptical toward those who sought positions of spiritual authority.[11] The mantle of leadership could be a temptation to pride and seeking it out could be a result of pride. Accordingly, Gregory opines that it is only the "weak man" who "yearns to assume the weight of honor."[12] But such office seekers are not rare. Gregory humorously observes that while no one without appropriate credentials would ever dare to practice medicine, for some reason many unqualified people present themselves as "physicians of the heart."[13] By way of contrast he warns: "No one who is imperfect should dare to seize a position of spiritual leadership."[14] Gregory thus chides ill-equipped, would-be spiritual leaders who out of pride presume readiness for the mantle of spiritual leadership.

Gregory's intention, however, is not to steer everyone away from becoming spiritual leaders. Michael Casey interprets Benedict's chapter on humility as a "guide to living in the truth."[15]

---

[10] Gregory the Great, "Gregory, to the Most Reverend and Holy Brother John, a Fellow Bishop," introductory note to *The Book of Pastoral Rule*, trans. George E. Demacopoulos (Crestwood, NY: St. Vladimir's Seminary Press, 2007), 27–28, at 27. Henceforth, I will cite from the *Pastoral Rule* by providing chapter and section enumeration, e.g., *PR* 1.1, but this opening note has no such numbering.

[11] See Brian E. Daley, "The Ministry of Disciples: Historical Reflections on the Role of Religious Priests," *Theological Studies* 48.4 (December 1987): 605–29.

[12] *PR* 1.7.

[13] Ibid., 1.1.

[14] Ibid., 1.4.

[15] Michael Casey, *A Guide to Living in the Truth: Saint Benedict's Teaching on Humility* (Liguori, MO: Liguori/Triumph, 2001).

Humility is a God-given ability that enables one to see oneself accurately. The other side of "living in the truth" is recognizing when one has the capacity to serve in some way and generously offering one's potential for the aid of others. Gregory very much wanted to draw suitable candidates to ministry. Accordingly, he writes: "Whoever does not care to serve others out of the gifts he has received is found guilty before the holy church."[16] Potential spiritual directors need to ask themselves if they have the right qualities for the ministry and if they are holding back in any way out of a lack of generosity. If he is unsure of himself, "it is best for him to decline,"[17] but if he continues to be called, he should accept as an expression of obedience to God. According to Gregory, humility can be as manifest in the one who says yes to ministering as it is in the one who refuses it. He writes: "No one is truly humble if he understands by the judgment of the supreme Will that he ought to . . . but then refuses."[18]

The second set of qualifications for spiritual directors includes ascetic/contemplative experience and moral rectitude. These traits can be seen in two of the summaries Gregory provides on the necessary character of the spiritual director. He writes:

> He must be devoted entirely to the example of good living. He must be dead to the passions of the flesh and live a spiritual life. He must have no regard for worldly prosperity and never cower in the face of adversity. He must desire the internal life only. His intentions should not be thwarted by the frailty of the body, nor repelled by the abuse of the spirit. He should not lust for the possessions of others, but give freely of his own. He should be quick to forgive through compassion, but never so far removed from righteousness as to forgive indiscriminately. He must perform no evil acts but instead deplore the evil perpetrated by others as though it was his own. In his own heart, he must suffer the afflictions of others and likewise rejoice at the fortune of his neighbor,

---

[16] *PR* 1.4.
[17] Ibid., 1.7.
[18] Ibid., 1.6.

as though the good thing was happening to him. He must set such a positive example for others that he has nothing for which he should ever be ashamed. He should be such a student of how to live that he is able to water the arid hearts of his neighbors with the streams of doctrinal teaching. He should have already learned by the practice and experience of prayer that he can obtain from the Lord whatever he requests.[19]

It is necessary, therefore, that he should be pure in thought, exemplary in conduct, discerning in silence, profitable in speech, a compassionate neighbor to everyone, superior to all in contemplation, a humble companion to the good and firm in the zeal of righteousness against the vices of sinners. He must not relax his care for the internal life while he is occupied by external concerns, nor should he relinquish what is prudent of external matters so as to focus on things internal.[20]

Monastic readers will recognize that these passages have deep resonances with Benedict's descriptions of the ideal abbot and the cellarer.[21] That is no coincidence. Though Gregory was writing a manual primarily for secular clergy, he nonetheless wanted these figures to cultivate the characteristics for which monastic leaders were celebrated—namely, ascetic/contemplative experience and moral rectitude.[22] Directors are further described as generous, compassionate, forgiving, long-suffering, and as persons of integrity whose lives are consistent with their teachings.

While this portrait is lofty to the point of being intimidating, there are reasons for Gregory's high expectations. First, in Gregory's understanding, directors can only lead along paths that they themselves have traveled and continue to travel. Teaching happens more from example than from words and so a person who does not practice the spiritual and moral life cannot model it.[23] The

[19] Ibid., 1.10.
[20] Ibid., 2.1.
[21] Ibid., chaps. 2, 31, and 64.
[22] Demacopoulos, *Five Models of Spiritual Direction*, 130.
[23] Ibid., 134.

people will follow their directors' examples, and it will be a case of the blind leading the blind.[24] Directors who do not have their own experiences of God cannot introduce others to God, and directors who have not cultivated their own virtues will not be able to aid others in becoming more virtuous. He is accordingly skeptical toward the leadership of those who have learned only through study and not by their own experience in the spiritual life.[25]

Second, Gregory is convinced that a central task of spiritual directors is to pray for their people. To be successful in this task, they need a well-established relationship with God. Gregory writes: "If, for example, someone came asking us to intercede for them before some powerful man who was angry with him but did not know us, we would immediately respond that we were unable to intercede on his behalf because we do not have a relationship with the man in question. . . . How could anyone reasonably assume the role of intercessor before God on behalf of others [then] if he does not know himself to be in the intimacy of his grace by the merits of his life?"[26] In this light, Gregory's exhortations toward contemplation and righteous living take on the added meaning of being necessary for one's intercessory role and not simply so that one can teach from experience and by example.

A third necessary qualification of directors, according to Gregory, is the gift of discernment. The concept of *discretio* has deep roots in monastic tradition. The Rule of Benedict, following John Cassian, calls it the "mother of all virtues" (RB 64), and it is a major theme linking the Rule with Gregory, who uses the term over 140 times in his corpus.[27] Its Latin meaning is "practical understanding or wisdom."[28] In ascetical practice, it connoted "the ability to judge where the middle is to be found" between

---

[24] *PR* 1.1.

[25] Ibid., 1.1 and 1.2.

[26] Ibid., 1.10.

[27] Harry Hagan, "Benedictine Orthodoxy and the Relationship between the Rule of the Master and the Rule of Benedict," *American Benedictine Review* 66.2 (June 2015): 124–43, at 130.

[28] Harry Hagan, "The Mother of Virtues and the Rule of St. Benedict," *American Benedictine Review* 60.4 (December 2009): 371–97, at 383.

extremes of rigor and laxity, and thus was a "presupposition for the virtue of temperance or self-control."[29] Beyond being practical wisdom for monks seeking to avoid extremes in their own spirituality, *discretio* was a pastoral virtue of perceiving correctly what would be helpful rather than harmful to say to the other whom one was spiritually guiding, and this is the sense we most often find of *discretio* in the *Pastoral Rule*. Gregory writes: "The spiritual director should be discerning in his silence and profitable in his speech, otherwise he might say something that should have been suppressed or suppress something that should have been said. For just as reckless speaking leads someone into error, so indiscreet silence leaves in error those who may have been instructed."[30]

More than any other virtue, *discretio* takes us right to the heart of the practice of spiritual direction. It undergirds the entirety of the third and longest section of the *Pastoral Rule* where Gregory discusses "How the Spiritual Director Should Teach." He begins this section by stating: "Long before us, Gregory Nazianzus of blessed memory taught that one and the same exhortation is not suited for everyone because not everyone shares the same quality of character. For example, what often helps some people will cause harm in others. . . . Therefore the discourse of the teacher should be adapted to the character of his audience so that it can address the specific needs of each individual."[31] Gregory proceeds from here to identify seventy-two possible traits of directees paired into thirty-six oppositional sets, such as "the meek and the easily provoked"[32] and "those who do not speak enough and those who speak too much."[33] For each, he provides a "pastoral regimen."[34] For example, he says that impatient people "should be told that when they fail to curb their spirit they are carried into many types of iniquity that they do not [truly] desire," whereas patient people "should be advised that they not pity themselves on the inside for

---

[29] Ibid., 383.
[30] *PR* 2.4.
[31] Ibid., 3. prologue.
[32] Ibid., 3.16.
[33] Ibid., 3.14.
[34] Demacopoulos, *Five Models of Spiritual Direction*, 130.

what they appear to tolerate on the outside."[35] Gregory's ideal director is someone who can see clearly what needs to be said, how it needs to be said ("a wound is made worse by unskilled mending"), and when it needs to be said ("wounds are made worse by untimely surgery").[36]

Discretio does not stand alone, however. Its application requires the development of other related capacities. A gift for discerning the right message for a particular soul must be accompanied by the courage to say what needs to be said, particularly if the message is admonishing.[37] If compassion is needed, directors must also have cultivated their own wells of empathy.[38] *Discretio* requires that one know when and how to apply the "loving kindness" of a mother and the "discipline" of a father.[39]

To conclude this section, Gregory has given us a great insight into the necessary qualities of spiritual directors. Directors must be humble and not presume to this role unless they are qualified. They should be contemplative and virtuous people. Finally, directors should have *discretio*, practical wisdom that allows them to determine the kind of advice their directees need. At times, Gregory's idealized portrait can feel intimidating and we might wonder who could ever live up to it. Perhaps Gregory's litany of qualifications is best viewed simply as a healthy reminder that unless directors are taking their own prayer life and moral life seriously, they should not be offering direction to others.

Columba Marmion

Our second source is *Union with God: Letters of Spiritual Direction by Blessed Columba Marmion*. Marmion (1858–1923) was an Irish priest who became a monk of the Belgian Abbey of Maredsous. In 1899, he was named the prior of Mt. César, Maredsous's foun-

---

[35] *PR* 3.9.
[36] Ibid., 2.6 and 2.10.
[37] Ibid., 2.10 and 2.4.
[38] Ibid., 2.5.
[39] Ibid., 2.6.

dation at Louvain. In 1909, he was elected abbot of Maredsous where he served until his death in 1923.[40] He authored three important works of spiritual theology: *Christ the Life of the Soul*, *Christ in His Mysteries*, and *Christ the Ideal of the Monk*.[41] A fourth book, *Christ the Ideal of the Priest*, was compiled from various retreat conferences he had given and was published posthumously.[42] Marmion's writings, which emphasize participation in Christ through the liturgy and sacraments of the Church, were influential for many major Catholic figures of the twentieth century.[43] He was beatified in the year 2000 by Pope John Paul II.

As Lambert Beaudoin puts it, Marmion "was a theologian from tip to toe,"[44] but his scholarly passion in no way diminished his also being a pastoral figure, a revered abbot and spiritual guide. His broad correspondence with many souls made possible the text of *Union with God*, a collection of excerpts from Marmion's letters in which he provides spiritual advice to a wide range of persons. Dom Raymond Thibault, Marmion's confrère at Maredsous and principal biographer, assembled and edited the collection.[45]

Marmion possessed those qualities that Gregory says the spiritual director must have. He was a man of contemplative experience. Alban Goodier notes: "He wrote always from the experience of his own soul. He described God to others as he knew Him within himself; when he spoke of union with God, its elements and its conditions, all unconsciously, because so spontaneously, he revealed the course, and the development, and the perfection

---

[40] For more on the life of Marmion, see Mark Tierney, *Blessed Columba Marmion: A Spiritual Biography* (Collegeville, MN: Liturgical Press, 2000).

[41] Columba Marmion, *Christ the Life of the Soul* (Bethesda, MD: Zaccheus, 2005); *Christ in His Mysteries* (Brooklyn, NY: Angelico, 2013); *Christ the Ideal of the Monk* (Orleans, MA: Paraclete, 2014).

[42] Columba Marmion, *Christ the Ideal of the Priest* (San Francisco: Ignatius, 2005).

[43] Alduin Deck and Mark Tierney, "The Legacy of Dom Columba Marmion," *The Priest* 54 (January 1998): 37–38.

[44] Lambert Beauduin, "From Other Lands: Abbot Marmion and the Liturgy," *Orate Fratres* 22.7 (May 1948): 303–14, at 310.

[45] Columba Marmion, *Union with God: Letters of Spiritual Direction by Blessed Columba Marmion*, trans. Mart St. Thomas (Bethesda, MD: Zaccheus, 2006).

of his own spiritual life."[46] He was also a man of great discernment. Thibault observes that Marmion exchanged letters of spiritual direction with people of various walks of life, and he always tailored his advice to their station and needs of the moment, and that he used language that each could understand.[47]

As a compilation of Marmion's letters providing spiritual guidance, *Union with God* is a very different book from the *Pastoral Rule*, which was written as a manual for ministers. Where the *Pastoral Rule* was most helpful for investigating the qualities a spiritual director should possess, *Union with God* affords us the opportunity to explore the content of the spiritual life as described by a master spiritual director to his directees.

Admittedly, as a model of spiritual direction, the book is limited. Direction is a two-way conversation between director and directee. For the director, it involves at least as much listening as it does speaking. As a collection of letters addressed by Marmion to others, *Union with God* is unable to capture the very important aspect of listening that is involved in spiritual direction. It shows only what Marmion's advice looked like, not what the whole process of direction looked like. Since advice really ought to be conditioned by the particular needs of the directee, the fact that *Union with God* only provides half of the conversation limits the text's instructional value for spiritual directors. Nonetheless, if we read *Union with God* with an eye out for the perennial themes in a true spiritual master's teaching, themes that all spiritual directors ought to consider appropriating and communicating in their own direction, we will not be disappointed. Happily, Thibault has arranged the book precisely in this thematic way.

The first two chapters are devoted to the theme "Union with God." Goodier—recognizing that most spiritual treatises of the neo-scholastic era followed the classic scheme of the purgative way, followed by the illuminative way, followed by the unitive way—explains the appropriateness of Thibault's arrangement of Marmion's writings. He states: "Other, more systematic writers,

[46] Alban Goodier, introduction to *Union with God*, by Columba Marmion, xiv.
[47] Raymond Thibault, preface to *Union with God*, by Columba Marmion, xix.

give Union with God as the climax of the spiritual life; it is usually given, and quite rightly, as the last chapter of spiritual books. Still, in describing the spirituality of Dom Columba, you have felt that you must place it, not last, but first; and not only first, but dominating all the rest."[48] For Marmion, union with God is the goal, but God is the way to reach the goal, and God's grace starts us on the journey to begin with. Reflecting on divine initiative, Marmion writes: "God who is 'the beginning' wills to take the initiative in the direction of your life."[49] Through baptism, God first adopts the Christian and makes a dwelling in the soul. God continues to accompany the soul throughout the entirety of the spiritual journey until it reaches its destiny of complete union. Marmion writes: "Little by little this Divine Spirit will become your guide and bear you with Him into God's bosom."[50]

Unsurprisingly then, a key feature of Marmion's direction is encouragement of the *practice of awareness* of God's presence, assistance, and the goal of final union. To various persons Marmion gives similar advice: "Keep your eyes fixed on God. 'Consider the end'—that will keep you in the truth"; "If you keep the eye of your soul fixed on God alone, you will receive many graces"; "Consider the end, namely God alone."[51] This awareness should be accompanied by loving devotion so that the heart is oriented to God and not just the mind.[52] He writes: "Try to do all for the love of Jesus"; "Try to love Our dear Savior with all your heart"; "Give him your whole heart and your whole love"; "Offer each action to Jesus out of love."[53] Marmion encourages the frequent return of the mind and heart to awareness of the presence of God and Christ in activities both mundane and important.[54]

---

[48] Goodier, introduction to *Union with God*, xv.

[49] Marmion, *Union with God*, 11.

[50] Ibid., 6.

[51] Ibid., 9–11.

[52] Interestingly, as Marmion's advice becomes more affective it also becomes more christological.

[53] Marmion, *Union with God*, 13–15.

[54] Ibid., 18.

As a model for spiritual direction, Marmion's emphasis on awareness of God and devotion to God is helpful because it is theocentric. He is encouraging the soul to be God-centered rather than self-centered. "Look at God," he writes, "much more than at yourself."[55] Accordingly, his direction helps the soul avoid the psychologism and navel-gazing that sometimes happens when one envisions the spiritual life as solely a quest for greater self-knowledge and self-awareness. It also helps to avoid the plague of Pelagianism that occurs when one undertakes a series of spiritual practices but ignores the presence of aiding grace. This theocentrism is one way in which Marmion's guidance bears a strong Benedictine stamp. Some commentators see the seventh chapter of Benedict's Rule as a key to Benedictine spirituality. This chapter describes the spiritual life as a progression along a "ladder of humility." Significantly, the very first step on this ladder exhorts the monk to cultivate awareness that God is always present. While subjective union with God is certainly deepened as a monk progresses, awareness of God must be there at the beginning in order to orient the journey rightly at all. As Robert Barron puts it, conversion is essentially a shift from living an "ego-drama" to living a "theo-drama."[56] Recognition of the divine presence initiates and sustains the spiritual life while it anticipates the final goal.

The next several chapters of *Union with God* describe "Conditions for Progress" in the spiritual life, "Growth through the Virtues," and "The Life of Prayer." These chapters portray the manifold ways in which a soul should respond to the divine presence and initiative. Marmion describes only two "conditions for progress." These are "desire for perfection" and the "spirit of detachment."[57] "Perfection" should probably be understood here as meaning "totality" or "completion" in spiritual self-gift rather than in a moralistic sense of rule following or flawlessness in personal virtue. The desire for totality in self-gift to God is ex-

[55] Ibid., 42.

[56] Robert Barron, *To Light a Fire on the Earth: Proclaiming the Gospel in a Secular Age* (New York: Image, 2017), 163.

[57] Marmion, *Union with God*, 46–52 and 53–80.

pressed through submission and obedience to God. Marmion writes: "The virtue which will lead you to the acquisition of all the others is the spirit of submission. Often unite yourself to the sentiments of obedience that the Heart of Jesus had towards His Father, above all in prayer and Holy Communion. Submit yourself not only to God's commands but to His every good pleasure, to the events which He permits, to all that he arranges for you. This virtue of submission will lead you to true abandon."[58] The language of obedience, submission, and abandon can sound intimidating at times. It is helpful to not lose sight of the fact that it is deeply connected to Marmion's understanding of spiritual childhood, which he shared with Thérèse of Lisieux (whose cause for canonization Marmion had a role in advancing).[59] It is not so much a violent conquering of the self as it is a humble recognition of one's littleness before God and a decision to show complete trust and dependence to God. This decision is similarly linked to the other "condition for progress" Marmion acknowledges: the "spirit of detachment." The choice to trust and depend on God is simultaneously a purgative renunciation of false gods.

Union with God is not only at the beginning and end of the spiritual journey; it is possible along the way. This is the great theme of the book's longest chapter, "Growth through the Virtues." The soul *in via* remains close to God through sacramental participation, especially the Eucharist. Through the Eucharist, Jesus "works in the spiritual part of the soul, far from the senses, and he produces grace and virtue of which we are unaware."[60] Christ's goal is to include us in his life, to make our lives conform

[58] Ibid., 112. He also states: "It is this spiritual childhood that is wanting to you. The more of a child you are, the more light and joy you will have" (28); "One is happy and becomes an instrument for God's glory according to the degree of his absolute abandon to the will from on high" (174); "Place yourself at His entire disposal, He will do the rest" (37); and "Abandon yourself absolutely into God's Hands" (61).

[59] See *Union with God*, 20. For deeper analysis of Marmion's understanding of filiation, see David Fagerberg, "*Theosis* in a Roman Key?: The Conferences of Columba Marmion," *Antiphon* 7.1 (2002): 30–39; Justin Rigali, "Blessed Columba Marmion: Doctor of Divine Adoption," *Josephinum Journal of Theology* 13.2 (Summer–Fall 2006): 132–42.

[60] Marmion, *Union with God*, 84–85, at 85.

to the pattern of his life, and to make us to share in his mysteries.[61]
The virtues (especially faith, hope, and love) are not simply imita-
tions of Christ. They flow from the sacraments and are participa-
tions in the life of Christ. The theological virtues are central to
how Marmion thinks we should engage the problem of suffering,
which is at the heart of many concerns in spiritual direction.
Marmion knows that "as long as we live we shall have our little
miseries."[62] He does not romanticize suffering or promote an
unhealthy seeking out of it. But Marmion's favorite line to quote
from the Rule of Benedict reads: "We shall through patience share
in the sufferings of Christ" (RB Prol. 50). The line is telling because
it reminds us that suffering is related to the cross and through the
cross Christ has transformed suffering, making it redemptive, a
place of encounter with him, and a place to be united with him.
Since the Christian knows that, he can navigate suffering in a new
way by liturgical participation in Christ's passion. He can have
patience and endure suffering with faith and hope. Insofar as he
exercises these virtues in suffering, he will find in suffering an
opportunity for deepened union with Christ.

Marmion's discussion of charity closes the chapter on the virtues. He answers the question of how to love God, the final goal
of spiritual life. It is not, in fact, obvious how one loves one who
cannot be seen or how one gives to one who has no needs. As
already noted, according to Marmion, love of God is expressed
by obedience. It is right and just for the creature to submit freely
to the rule of the Creator, which one does, for example, by living
a moral life and accepting the movements of Providence. But love
of God is also expressed by gratitude. God has no needs, and so
there is nothing we can give him, but we can offer thanks. Finally,
we can love God by loving and taking care of our neighbors.[63]

A striking feature of the guidance Marmion gives is that it is
heavily attitudinal: focused, that is, on the attitudes, dispositions,

[61] See William M. Fitzgerald, "Marmion's Appreciation for the Place of the Sacred
Liturgy in the Spiritual Life," *Josephinum Journal of Theology* 13.2 (Summer/Fall 2006):
143–48.

[62] Marmion, *Union with God*, 97.

[63] Ibid., 111–31.

and virtues he wishes his directees to cultivate rather than on specific ascetical or prayer practices he wishes them to undertake. His prioritization of the interior continues in his chapter on "The Life of Prayer." Though Marmion occasionally prescribes practices such as ejaculatory prayers, spiritual reading, and of course sacramental participation, his main focus is on encouraging consistent loving attention to God.[64]

The heart of Marmion's message is that the soul has been adopted by God in baptism and has received a new identity as a child of God. The essence of the spiritual life is to live out this relationship by trusting God and being docile to his initiative, participating in the sacraments, practicing the theological virtues, maintaining a spirit of gratitude to God, and loving God and all his creatures. Marmion's guidance is helpful for contemporary spiritual directors to contemplate. Avoiding Pelagianism and psychologism, he continually centers his advice on God, Christ, and the sacraments. He encourages the development of attitudes, dispositions, and virtues more than the adoption of a litany of spiritual practices. He teaches the love of God that begins in knowing God's presence and love.

Thomas Merton

Our third book for review is Thomas Merton's *Spiritual Direction and Meditation*. Merton (1915–1968), a monk of Gethsemane Abbey in Bardstown, Kentucky, was the most famous monk of the twentieth century and needs little introduction.[65] The book first appeared in 1960 and it seems to have been developed from formation conferences Merton first gave to young monks while he was serving as novice master.[66] This would help to explain the book's major

[64] Ibid., 132–57.

[65] Thomas Merton, like André Louf, who will be discussed in the next section, belonged to the Order of Cistercians of the Strict Observance, also known as the Trappists. The Cistercians are a reform within the Benedictine monastic tradition.

[66] This popular book is very similar—in places identical—to Merton's conference for novices, "Spiritual Direction in the Monastic Setting," in *Monastic Observances*, vol. 5 of *Initiation into the Monastic Tradition*, ed. Patrick F. O'Connell (Collegeville, MN: Cistercian, 2009), 251–78.

contribution. Most texts on the subject of spiritual direction focus on how to give it to others. This book does that to some extent, but it focuses more on how to *receive* spiritual direction. Men entering monastic life would have needed an orientation to a practice that would be central to their ongoing conversion, and it was Merton's duty as novice master to give it to them. Thankfully, through this book, Merton made his insights on the matter available to the wider public.

After describing the aim of spiritual direction as aid in discernment, facilitation of the awareness of grace, and encouragement toward a life of Christian freedom in the true self,[67] Merton describes who he thinks should receive spiritual direction. A formal spiritual direction relationship is most important at the time of discerning one's primary vocational commitment. Ongoing spiritual direction is a great help to those in religious life, ministry, and other professions where one has to regularly make decisions affecting many lives.[68] Merton makes the point that formal spiritual direction is not necessary for everyone. According to Merton, most ordinary Christians can receive all the support they need from regular confession.[69] Given the poor quality of some confessors, we might wonder whether or not that is the case. However, it does seem that many Christians who seek out formal spiritual direction do not always realize the support they might receive through other channels, not only sacramental confession, but also through faith-sharing groups and deep Christian friendships. Since it can sometimes be difficult to find good spiritual directors, these other channels really ought to be more widely encouraged.

Merton next offers much-needed reflection on how to receive spiritual direction. He begins by highlighting at least three key attitudes a directee should have. The first is *gratitude* that one has the opportunity to receive this ministry. Gratitude keeps one focused on the goals of spiritual direction and keeps one attentive to the graces and blessings God provides through the process. It

---

[67] Merton, *Spiritual Direction and Meditation*, 13–17.
[68] Ibid., 20–22.
[69] Ibid., 21.

sometimes happens that one speaks for an hour with a director and comes away from the conversation with only one small helpful insight. Gratitude for that nugget is a strong support for perseverance in the ongoing, never quick, process. It thus also helps to stave off disappointment stemming from unrealistic expectations about the wonders a director can perform. This brings us to the second attitude, which is *realism*. Many directees have inflated expectations that a director can or will solve all of their problems. A directee must be realistic enough to know that there is no perfect spiritual director and that the fruits that the process will bear will take time. The third attitude Merton highlights is *humility*. He notes that some directees are looking for flattery and approval. Honestly engaged spiritual direction involves stripping away the pretenses of the false self. Only those with the virtue of humility are able to truly participate.[70]

Merton's comments on the importance of humility are a good bridge to a more complete description of the actual process of spiritual direction, where, to the best of their abilities, directees need to make themselves transparent before their directors. Merton puts it like this:

> What we need to do is bring the director into contact with our real self, as best we can, and not fear to let him see what is false in our false self. Now this right away implies a relaxed, humble attitude in which we *let go* of ourselves and renounce our unconscious efforts to maintain a façade. We must let the director know that we really think, what we really feel, and what we really desire, even when these things are not altogether honorable. We must be quite frank about our motives insofar as we can be so. The mere effort to admit that we are not as unselfish or as zealous as we pretend to be is a great source of grace.[71]

Merton recognizes that sometimes it is our better qualities that are even harder to manifest, but these must be made transparent

---

[70] Ibid., 28–30.
[71] Ibid., 33.

as well. We must manifest our desires whether they be for things we think are good or for bad. Only then can the director really be of help.[72] Sometimes, what we think are our good desires reveal themselves as having dark motivations. Sometimes what we think are wicked desires are actually noble impulses that are just misdirected. And sometimes the purest and best parts of ourselves are hard to express because our desire to live as saints scares us. Indeed, the key contribution of the directee to spiritual direction is courageous transparency. Merton writes: "We must learn to speak according to our own inner truth, as far as we can perceive it. We must learn to say what we really mean in the depth of our souls, not what we think we are expected to say, not what somebody else has just said."[73]

Merton is not silent about the qualities directors should have. They should have a true love of souls. They should be able to establish a comfortable nonjudgmental conversation environment. They should be patient and sympathetic and attentive to the presence of Christ in the other. These qualities help them earn the trust of directees that is so necessary for the transparent disclosure which is at the heart of spiritual direction. They should have some theological sophistication, but that is secondary to love of souls and humility. Lovers of souls want to know the true self of their directees, and nothing will aggrieve them so much as entrenched phoniness.[74] Truly humble directors realize they are only there to help directees follow the ultimate spiritual director, the Holy Spirit. They emphasize the awareness of God as the object of prayer more than any particular prayer methods.[75]

The above description of the qualities of a director is helpful not only for those who exercise this ministry but also for those

---

[72] Ibid., 35.

[73] Ibid., 37.

[74] On this note, one of Merton's own directees had this to say about the experience of having Merton himself as a director: "He was conscious of that true self present in each person and he was attentive to help the person become more familiar with that and to strive to live more fully from that level. He saw falsity not just as a defense mechanism but as a lack of living from that level and that reality which the Lord sees and loves." James Conner, "Thomas Merton as Spiritual Director," *Cistercian Studies Quarterly* 19.4 (1994): 471–84.

[75] Merton, *Spiritual Direction and Meditation*, 33–43.

who receive it (Merton's primary audience). It informs the latter about what they should be looking for in a director and helps them to discern whether to remain with their director. Along these lines, Merton considers the question of when it is acceptable to change directors. He seems to think directees are often too quick to seek a change. So long as a director is not wicked or incompetent, God can work through the spiritual director. Yes, there are sometimes reasons for a switch, but one should test the situation before seeking a change. One should ask if, in fact, the director has not provided some helpful perspectives. So long as the relationship is bearing some fruit, one should hesitate to abandon the director and the process.[76]

Merton concludes by answering some other practical questions. He cautions against long-distance spiritual direction that might take place by mail (or today by email or Skype). While long-distance communication may be an acceptable stopgap measure, it should not be the norm of one's spiritual direction relationship where nonverbal communication can be as important as what is spoken or written. In response to the question of whether one should always obey a spiritual director, he answers that the key virtue is docility rather than humility. The director is not a superior but a teacher and a counselor. The directee should be receptive to the director's influence and advice, but choosing to follow or not to follow the director's lead is a matter of prudence rather than justice. It is not owed to the director. If a director is insisting on obedience, there is likely a problem of role clarification. Similarly, both director and directee should be clear that the relationship is not psychotherapy. The director should have some awareness of and respect for modern psychology, but in the final analysis the spiritual direction relationship has different aims.[77]

Merton's little book on spiritual direction is helpful especially for directees. It clarifies the goals of spiritual direction, the dispositions a good directee and director should cultivate, and what their conversation ought to look like. It also offers practical guidance for questions that often emerge from directees such as: What

[76] Ibid., 46–47.
[77] Ibid., 48–50.

should one look for in a spiritual director and when should one make a change? Should one engage in long-distance spiritual direction? Must one obey a spiritual director? And, how is spiritual direction different from psychotherapy? To the last question, Merton's response is rather brief. As psychology becomes more prominent in the culture, it is an increasingly important question. André Louf engages the question much more thoroughly.

André Louf

André Louf (1929–2010), a monk of Mont-des-Cats, in France, was born in Leuven, Belgium, entered his monastery in 1947, and was elected abbot there in 1963. After serving thirty-four years as abbot, he lived as a hermit and served as a chaplain to a community of nuns in southern France. He was a prolific spiritual author.[78] If I could recommend just one book from the Benedictine religious family on spiritual direction, it would be his *Grace Can Do More*. What makes the book special is Louf's synthetic approach. He interweaves insights from contemporary depth psychology, the monastic tradition, and the Ignatian tradition to show how these can be integrated in a contemporary approach to spiritual direction.

Louf begins by introducing discernment as a vital component of any authentically Christian life. Christian life involves conversion and repentance, turning away from the world and toward God. Discernment is recognizing which of those roads is which. The centrality of discernment to Christian life was historically forgotten, Louf argues, when morality became overly rationalistic in the early modern period, which led to a rules-centered vision of Christian morality. The advent of clinical psychology was actually an aid in turning us back to consideration of the subject.

[78] For more on Louf's biography, see Charles Wright, *Le Chemin du Coeur: L'expérience spiritualle d'André Louf (1929–2010)* (Salvator: Paris, 2017). Better known in the French world than the English, Louf is also the subject of Allessando Saraco's 2016 book *Discernement et accompagnement dans les écrits spirituelle d'André Louf* (Nouan-le-Fuzelier: Béatitudes, 2016).

In the ancient monastic tradition, discernment was facilitated by the two practices of *lectio divina* and spiritual direction. Through a committed practice of *lectio divina*, the soul is sensitized to the sound of the Lord's voice. As one becomes familiar with the voice of the Lord through *lectio*, the soul is better positioned to hear and obey the voice of the Lord in the context of daily life.[79] In addition to the practice of *lectio*, one is helped in discernment by a spiritual "accompanist."[80] Louf prefers this title to that of spiritual director. One reason for this preference is Louf's recognition that the Holy Spirit is the true director. "Grace can do more" and will do more than either the director or directee in this process.[81] The goal or object of spiritual direction is the birth of the true self marked by freedom and vitality; it is the new self in Christ, whose seed is already there from baptism but which we are in labor pains to manifest. Since the Holy Spirit is the true generator of this process, the director's role is really a kind of midwifery.[82]

Spiritual direction is different from therapy. No one today can do spiritual direction ignorant of psychology,[83] but the two processes have different goals. While both may foster self-awareness, psychotherapy aims to heal, or at least to help one cope with life, on a natural level. Spiritual direction aims at fostering an encounter with and surrender to God in the midst of one's suffering

---

[79] André Louf, *Grace Can Do More: Spiritual Accompaniment and Spiritual Growth*, trans. Susan Van Winkle (Collegeville, MN: Liturgical Press, 2002), 13–17.

[80] Ibid., 45. Though Louf uses the word *accompanist*, for the purpose of this essay's consistency I have chosen to maintain the term *director* as the name for the spiritual mentor's role.

[81] Louf writes: "We can contribute very little, perhaps some extremely simple disciplines which favor asceticism and create within us the space through which we may more easily slip over into our interiority at the appropriate time. It is not so much progress to be made or a distance to be covered as suffering, undergoing, letting happen, letting things come to the surface. We must instead learn to let go of a number of things, to stop many movements, to relax, abandon ourselves and even to lose our footing, to let ourselves sink into this deep reality in our heart, where Christ and the Spirit come to meet us. It is not that we go to meet them; they set out a long time ago to meet us. The important thing is not to miss their arrival, to be waiting at exactly the right place, the only place where the meeting can happen." Ibid., 38.

[82] Ibid., 39 and 59.

[83] Ibid., 63 and 161.

whether or not one's condition improves (though that certainly can be a fruit of the process).[84]

Provided we have the true nature of spiritual direction properly in view, we can utilize insights from the human sciences like psychology as a means of facilitating the spiritual life.[85] Louf shows how a number of concepts from modern psychology are useful tools in spiritual direction. The first is *transference*. Transference occurs in the direction relationship when directees seek, often unconsciously, to recapitulate the historical roles they are most comfortable playing by inviting their directors to play alternate roles that correspond to their needs. For example, one may try to be the good child to the director's approving parent. Countertransference involves the same dynamic in the opposite direction. Transference (and countertransference) always occur to some degree. The key is to be aware of it and to some extent make use of it.

Two typically Benedictine values are helpful for dealing properly with transference: humility and hospitality. From directees, what is required most is humility. From directors, what is required most is hospitality. These virtues work in tandem. Directees bravely and humbly make themselves more and more transparent through manifesting their thoughts, desires, and actions, some of which may be taboo. Directors are to listen in love without judging, in such a way that directees feel true acceptance and safety. Such acceptance breeds trust, which allows directees to deepen their self-revelation and to widen their self-concept as they discover they no longer need to hide parts of their selves. This overcoming of the hiding of parts of the self is the defeat of transference. Countertransference is similarly mitigated by the hospitality of directors. Instead of acting on the desire to have directees play particular roles (e.g., the victim the director gets to rescue), hospitable directors focus on meeting the true needs of directees, which, in the context of spiritual direction, fosters the birth and flourishment of the true self. In this context, Louf makes the wonderful point that direction

[84] Ibid., 65.
[85] Ibid., 44.

becomes an opportunity for spiritual growth for directees and directors alike. He writes: "Managed correctly, [the direction relationship] can finally force [the director] positively to renounce his desires, teach him to want something without being granted it, by obliging him to step aside constantly before the other person's growing freedom and autonomy. In short: it is an uncommon chance to learn to love truly. It is well-known that in spiritual accompaniment, both partners benefit equally."[86]

The second concept from psychology employed by Louf is the *super-ego*, which he calls "the policeman."[87] Louf rightly notes that a healthy psyche must have a super-ego and an ego and that these should not be treated like dragons to slay or diseases to be gotten rid of. The policeman, the super-ego, is a part of the self which protects the self by steering one away from thoughts, desires, and behaviors that were long ago internalized as taboos according to parental (especially paternal) reactions in the family of origin. The policeman was formed in early childhood and played an essential role in keeping the directee safe. Unfortunately, the policeman is often attached to a view of growth as perfectibility through rule adherence, a view which is contrary to the Gospel. Furthermore, a mistake most of us make is to identify the policeman with the authentic conscience. Directors encourage their directees to listen to the voice of the Holy Spirit in the conscience rather than to the condemning voice of the policeman.

As a matter of transference, the policeman of the directee will often make appeals to the director to ally with him as an authority in shaming the other parts of the self. Directors who make a habit of excusing or condemning their directees have, perhaps unwittingly, accepted the invitation and can feed the pattern of the policeman's dominance or position themselves as externalized policemen. Good directors resist this alliance and remain hospitable to the other parts of their directees' selves, not allowing them to become exiled in the direction process. Instead they use silence, understanding, and very prudent words.

[86] Ibid., 72.
[87] Ibid., 97–125.

The third psychological concept employed by Louf is the *ego*, which he calls "the mirror."[88] It is one's idealized sense of self. The mirror has satisfied enough of the policeman's expectations that he or she believes in one's personal value and worthiness to receive love. The problem is that the mirror part of the self has accepted the policeman's false belief that self-worth depends on rule adherence in the first place. Sooner or later one discovers that he or she does not in fact match the idealized self and the mirror inevitably cracks. This is scary, but it also liberating. The imperfect self behind the mirror is feared more than he or she should be. This is the part of the self that is most receptive to the Holy Spirit. Wise directors neither break the mirror nor put it back again. Instead, they encourage directees to go deeper into befriending the self behind the mirror so as to live with greater authenticity.

Shifting the spotlight from the internal dynamics of directees to those of directors, and building on a theme we already saw in Gregory, Louf describes how directors need to be in touch with their internal "father" and internal "mother."[89] In accord with Jungian typologies, but supporting himself with Scripture, Louf presents the mother as representing acceptance, affirmation, and gentleness to the psyche and the father as representing strength and challenge. The childhood experience with one's own mother and father and other parental figures is crucial for determining how one relates in adult life to these complementary aspects of love. Directors who are properly stewarding their own growth are integrating both sets of qualities so that they can draw on what they learned from both parents as resources for ministry according to the needs of directees. Since we live in a broken world, there are always gaps in what directors ought to have internalized from their relationships with parents. Directors are thus called to grow in awareness of their own limitations, but also to work toward their own healing by reconciling with their own pasts.

---

[88] Ibid., 127–41.
[89] Ibid., 141–61.

Louf concludes his book by bringing much of what he has said into direct conversation with the Christian spiritual tradition. He describes the goal of Christian life as conversion from living out of the superficial self to living out of the deep self. While this language sounds heavily psychological, it can be understood through a traditional Christian lens. Through baptismal grace, God resides in the deep self and authors and nurtures our best desires. Dying to the superficial self and living out the deep self is precisely what the monastic tradition means when it speaks of overcoming self-will through obedience. In its best sense, overcoming self-will is not a denial of the self, but a letting go of sin and superficiality which keep us residing on the surface. Obedience, in its best sense, is listening to the Spirit dwelling within and honoring holy desire, and thus growing in integrity. Stated otherwise, it is not the will of the deep self that must be overcome but the will of our superficial parts that have yet to be properly integrated. The birth of the true self is a birth into love and freedom. Monastic practices such as external obedience are simply a means toward this end.

In this same final discussion, Louf demonstrates the convergence of monastic wisdom with that of the Ignatian tradition. The key to Ignatian-style discernment is to work toward "indifference" by practicing detachment from possible choices until the will of God becomes manifest through deep desire accompanied by consolation and joy. Louf draws from monastic sources predating Ignatius that share the same insight. Accordingly, the Ignatian approach is not alien to the monastic tradition. Monastic spiritual directors can therefore learn from those trained in the Ignatian method and vice versa.[90] Louf's great contribution, then, is to show how a contemporary monastic approach to spiritual direction can draw from its own sources as well as those of contemporary psychology and the wider Christian spiritual tradition in order to be as rich as possible.

---

[90] Ibid., 166–72.

Conclusion

In this chapter, we have explored the insights of Gregory the Great, Columba Marmion, Thomas Merton, and André Louf. They are representatives of the Benedictine religious family who provide considerable wisdom on the qualities a spiritual director should have, the content of the spiritual life a director should communicate, practical tips for the reception of spiritual direction, and how the monastic tradition of spiritual direction can incorporate insights from both modern psychology and the Ignatian approach. Taken together, they illustrate the richness of the long Benedictine legacy of spiritual direction, which can serve as a valuable resource for directors and directees in our own day.

CHAPTER THREE

Learned, Experienced, and Discerning: St. Teresa of Avila and St. John of the Cross on Spiritual Direction

Fr. Mark O'Keefe, OSB

St. Teresa of Avila (1515–1582) and St. John of the Cross (1542–1591), mystics and doctors of the church, are rightly acknowledged as two of the central teachers of the entire Christian spiritual and mystical tradition. Their written works are true classics of Christian spirituality, and their descriptions, definitions, and analyses of the movements and experiences of the Christian journey and of prayer are often the reference points for subsequent reflections throughout the intervening centuries. Among Teresa's works are *The Book of Her Life*, *The Way of Perfection*, and her mature masterpiece, *The Interior Castle*.[1] Among John's are *The Ascent of Mount*

---

[1] Teresa of Avila's collected works are available in translations into English of contemporary critical Spanish editions, in three volumes (plus two volumes of letters) from the Institute of Carmelite Studies (ICS): Kieran Kavanaugh, OCD, and Otilio Rodriguez, OCD, trans./eds., *The Collected Works of St. Teresa of Avila*, 3 vols. (Washington, DC: ICS Publications, 1976/1987 [rev.], 1980, 1985). Her letters appear in two volumes: Kieran Kavanaugh, OCD, *The Collected Letters of St. Teresa of Avila*, 2 vols. (Washington, DC: ICS Publications, 2001, 2007). Hereafter, references to Teresa's works will be from the ICS editions, together with a brief notation of the particular work that is being cited.

Carmel, *The Dark Night*, *The Spiritual Canticle*, and *The Living Flame of Love*.[2]

The present study will examine together the vision of spiritual direction offered by both Carmelite doctors. Their styles are very different. Teresa lacked formal training in theology and in writing, although she was well-read and she regularly consulted the leading theologians in Spain. She writes in an informal, conversational way that most readers find engaging (which is not to say that her works are always easy to read). John, on the other hand, was university-trained in the scholastic philosophy and theology of his day. His style in his books—as opposed to his poetry and letters—is often formal, academic, and analytical. Yet, despite these obvious differences, their basic theological and spiritual vision is largely the same. Teresa was fifty-two years old when she met the newly ordained, twenty-five-year-old John of the Cross. She was already advanced in prayer, author of her *Life*, and had begun the establishment of the Discalced Carmelite reform. She challenged the young Carmelite friar to join her reform, and she personally formed the young friar in its spirit. We do not know at what point in his spiritual journey John found himself at that moment, but we know that he had been considering transferring to the Carthusians in the hope of finding a life more conducive to silence and contemplative prayer. John immediately became one of the major collaborators in Teresa's work and soon became her confessor and, for a time, her spiritual director.

While these Carmelite doctors—both of them in their own way—have bequeathed to subsequent generations of seekers classic descriptions, analyses, and a theology of prayer and of mysticism, both were seeking to offer practical guidance to their readers about growth in prayer, especially in its advanced forms. But this, they insist, requires attention to broader issues of Christian living

---

[2] John of the Cross's collected works appear in one volume: Kieran Kavanaugh, OCD, and Otilio Rodriguez, OCD, trans/eds., *The Collected Works of St. John of the Cross*, rev. ed. (Washington, DC: ICS Publications, 1991). Hereafter, references to John's works will be from this edition, together with a brief notation of the particular work that is being cited.

and personal transformation outside moments of explicit praying.[3] This latter reality is too often missed when people come to their works seeking too narrowly their rich teaching on deep prayer and contemplation. Teresa and John wanted to provide down-to-earth assistance to real people—yes, especially to those more mature in the Christian journey, but also, more broadly, to sincere seekers at every stage of the Christian pilgrimage. They both believed that the guidance of others is necessary in the intentional Christian life, and they set out to provide it—in writing and in person to many people in their own lifetimes.

Teresa, whose works often explicitly refer to her personal experience, felt herself blessed to have had good spiritual direction, but she had also felt herself hindered by bad guidance, which caused her considerable suffering. She was anxious to prevent her readers from falling into the same difficulty while they pursued the growth that she was promoting through her writings.[4] John's works are almost entirely lacking in explicit references to his personal experience, but it is clear that he, too, had encountered bad directors directly or through the experience of those who subsequently reported that experience and its trials to him.[5] At the beginning of *The Ascent of Mount Carmel*, John offers a rather lengthy

[3] This is a point that I highlight in my *The Way of Transformation: Saint Teresa of Avila on the Foundation and Fruit of Prayer* (Washington, DC: ICS Publications, 2016).

[4] There are not many available resources in English on St. Teresa's teaching on spiritual direction, but see also Joel Giallanza, CSC, "Spiritual Direction According to St. Teresa of Avila," in *Spiritual Direction: Contemporary Readings*, ed. Kevin Culligan, OCD (Locust Valley, NY: Living Flame Press, 1983), 203–11.

[5] A number of further resources are available on John of the Cross's teaching on spiritual direction. See Kevin Culligan, OCD, "Qualities of a Good Guide: Spiritual Direction in John of the Cross' Letters," in *Carmelite Studies VI: John of the Cross*, ed. Steve Payne, OCD (Washington, DC: ICS Publications), 65–83; Kevin Culligan, OCD, *Toward a Model of Spiritual Direction Based on the Writings of Saint John of the Cross and Carl Rogers: An Exploratory Study* (PhD diss., Boston University Graduate School, 1979); Lucien-Marie Florent, OCD, "Spiritual Direction According to St. John of the Cross," in *Carmelite Studies I: Spiritual Direction*, ed. John Sullivan, OCD (Washington, DC: ICS Publications, 1980), 3–34; Gabriel of St. Mary Magdalene, OCD, *The Spiritual Director According to the Principles of St. John of the Cross* (Westminster, MD: Newman Press, 1952); Joel Giallanza, CSC, "Spiritual Direction According to St. John of the Cross," in *Spiritual Direction: Contemporary Readings*, ed. Kevin Culligan, OCD (Locust Valley, NY: Living Flame Press, 1983), 196–202; and Dennis Graviss, OCarm, *Portrait*

caution about bad directors before he lays out his own teaching for his readers.[6] They both set out, therefore, to offer their wisdom on this topic—insights that appear throughout their works.[7] This teaching is clearest in Teresa's *Life* (though distributed throughout) and in John's commentary on the third stanza of the *Living Flame of Love*. And it is this text that well-known Jesuit spiritual writer Thomas H. Green, SJ—who called John of the Cross "perhaps the greatest spiritual director the church has known"—reported that he reread every year in order to support his own ministry of spiritual direction.[8]

Both Teresa and John were, first of all, insistent on the need for spiritual guidance for anyone who seriously wanted to walk the Christian path and to grow in prayer. Among a collection of John's spiritual maxims are several focused on the importance of a spiritual director:

> 5. Whoever wants to stand alone without the support of a master and guide will be like the tree that stands alone in a field without a proprietor. No matter how much the tree bears, passers-by will pick the fruit before it ripens. . . .

> 7. The virtuous soul that is alone and without a master is like a lone burning coal; it will grow colder rather than hotter.

> 8. Those who fall alone remain alone in their fall, and they value their soul little since they entrust it to themselves alone.

> 9. If you do not fear falling alone, do you presume that you will rise up alone? Consider how much more can be accomplished by two together than by one alone. . . .

---

of the Spiritual Director in the Writings of Saint John of the Cross, 2nd rev. ed. (Rome: Edizioni Carmelitane, 2014).

   [6] *Ascent*, prologue, nos. 4–6, in *Collected Works*, 116–17.

   [7] Both Teresa and John offer insights into spiritual direction in various places throughout their works; but for Teresa, it is most concentrated especially in the context of speaking of her own experience of direction, good and bad, in the *Book of Her Life*. John's most prolonged and concentrated discussion of spiritual direction appears in the third book of his *The Living Flame of Love*. It is there that he famously speaks of bad directors as "blind guides."

   [8] Thomas H. Green, SJ, *The Friend of the Bridegroom: Spiritual Direction and the Encounter with Christ* (Notre Dame, IN: Ave Maria Press, 2000), 72.

11. The blind person who falls will not be able to get up alone; the blind person who does get up alone will go off on the wrong road.[9]

Both Teresa and John were themselves directors. In John's case, this is attested to by those who gave testimony for the process of his beatification—a process which began to unfold not long after his death (although it was delayed for a number of reasons). Perhaps no greater testimony to his skill can be offered than that of Teresa herself. In a letter to one of her prioresses who had taken offense that John referred to Teresa as his "daughter," Teresa calls John "the father of my soul" and urges the prioress: "Realize what a great treasure you have there in that saint. All the nuns in your house should speak and communicate with him on matters concerning their souls, and they will see how beneficial it is. They will find themselves making much progress in all that pertains to spirituality and perfection, for our Lord has given him a special grace in this regard."[10] In Teresa's own case, though the cultural limitations of the time would not have allowed her to refer to herself explicitly as a spiritual guide for others, especially for men, it is in fact quite apparent that she was. Particularly in her letters, it is clear that—with great practical experience and spiritual wisdom—she guided nuns, bishops, priests, and laypeople—among them, most notably her own brother.[11] Beyond these one-on-one relationships, Teresa's and John's more formal written works are a form of spiritual direction, since they wrote in order to guide those who were progressing in the spiritual life and in prayer but who too often lacked available resources to guide them.

In the present study, we will examine the insights of Teresa and John into spiritual direction, and specifically on the qualities of a

[9] *Sayings of Light and Love*, in *Collected Works of St. John*, 86.

[10] *Collected Letters*, II:146.

[11] See various letters to her brother, Lorenzo de Cepeda, especially Letters 177, 182, and 185 in *Collected Letters*, I: 473–78, 493–98, 504–10. See also Marcel Lépée, "Spiritual Direction in the Letters of St. Teresa," in *Carmelite Studies I: Spiritual Direction*, ed. John Sullivan, OCD (Washington, DC: ICS Publications, 1980), 61–80.

good director, including the three characteristics on which they
concur and emphasize: a director must be *learned* (that is to say,
have solid knowledge of Scripture and of the Christian spiritual
tradition), *experienced* in the spiritual path, and *discerning* (that is,
attentive to the Spirit at work as well as prudent in the relationship with the directee). Regarding these three characteristics, John
says clearly: "Besides being learned and discreet, a director should
have experience. Although the foundation for guiding a soul to
spirit is knowledge and discretion, directors will not succeed in
leading the soul onward in it when God bestows it, nor will they
even understand it if they have no experience of what true and
pure spirit is."[12] Teresa vacillates a bit about the relative importance of learning in the director (thinking that someone with such
knowledge can be consulted as needed), though she ultimately
affirms it as a critical quality:

> So it is very important that the master have prudence—I mean
> that he have good judgment—and experience; if besides these
> he has learning, so much the better. . . . And although it
> seems that learning is not necessary for such knowledge, my
> opinion has always been and will be that every Christian
> strive to speak if possible with someone who has gone
> through studies; and the more learned the person the better.
> Those who walk the path of prayer have a greater need for
> this counsel; and the more spiritual they are, the greater their
> need. Let not the spiritual person be misled by saying that
> learned men without prayer are unsuitable for those who
> practice it. I have consulted many learned men because for
> some years now, on account of a greater necessity, I have
> sought them out more; and I've always been a friend of men
> of learning.[13]

Of course, since these Carmelite doctors lived and wrote in
another time and culture, the continued value of their insights

[12] *Living Flame*, stanza 3, no. 30, in *Collected Works*, 685.
[13] *Life*, chap. 13, nos. 16–18, in *Collected Works*, I:130–31.

will only be fully apparent if we understand some basic elements of their context. Therefore, as we examine each of the three qualities in turn, we will point to some distinctive elements of their environment that help us to distinguish the enduring insight from its historical context.

Finally, before we begin, a few words must be said about the very term *spiritual direction*. In our day, many doubt the continued value of the term itself, because the relationship is concerned with more than what might narrowly be understood as *spiritual* and because *direction* sounds too, well, directive—that is, too passive on the part of the one who seeks the assistance of another and too authoritarian on the part of the one who offers it. Today, words like accompaniment, companionship or companioning, or friendship are often preferred. We cannot enter into that broader discussion within the limits of the present project. It must be noted that both John and Teresa were quite aware—as their writings and letters make evident—that the Christian life, spirituality, and the guidance being sought and offered had to be more than narrowly concerned with prayer (though they did view this as a particular focus for themselves as writers, since they felt other resources were available for the initial and broader aspects of the Christian life). In any case, in this context, we will continue to use the terms spiritual direction, director, and directee—interchangeably with alternate terms—because they probably remain the most commonly used. It is true that they both also spoke of guidance and of spiritual *guides*. But, more often, John and especially Teresa refer to the *confessor*, not because direction always or even usually occurred explicitly in the context of the sacrament, but rather because the director was usually a priest, and the visit of a priest to celebrate the sacrament for cloistered nuns provided the opportunity to speak more broadly and deeply than simply about sin. Further, other terms frequently used by the two Carmelite doctors, such as *spiritual master* and *spiritual father*, suggest that their vision was, in fact, perhaps more directive than contemporary authors might espouse. But again this is largely a matter of context, as we will see in what follows.

Learned

Teresa of Avila was a bright, literate woman in a culture in which many thought that women were incapable of serious intellectual work. She did not have a formal academic education, but she was well-read in spirituality—though vernacular Spanish was only at that time becoming a language for publication, and she could not read Latin. Still, as her *Life* makes clear, she counted among her friends and consulted widely among some of the most well-known theologians of her day. More deeply, she was a person committed to the pursuit of the truth and critical about the danger of being self-deceived. Self-knowledge, she teaches, is an essential characteristic, at every period of the Christian life: "This path of self-knowledge must never be abandoned, nor is there on this journey a soul so much a giant that it has no need to return often to the stage of an infant and a suckling."[14] For her, an important role of her spiritual guides was to assist her in such self-critical awareness.

As Teresa's prayer deepened and especially as she began to experience mystical encounters with God, she was even more concerned to find a director who was learned—that is, who had received formal academic training in Scripture and in theology (and with it, the general tradition of Christian spirituality). She began to fear that her experience of prayer or her interpretation of it might lead her astray and perhaps even into demonic hands. She therefore wanted an educated guide to keep her on the right path. But her concern to find a learned director was more fundamental. Teresa states: "My opinion has always been and will be that every Christian strive to speak if possible with someone who has gone through studies; and the more learned the person the better. Those who walk the path of prayer have a greater need for this counsel; and the more spiritual they are, the greater their need."[15]

Teresa goes on to remark how she had been harmed by half-learned men: "I have had a great deal of experience with learned

---

[14] Ibid., chap. 13, no. 15, in *Collected Works*, I:129–20.
[15] Ibid., chap. 13, no. 17, in *Collected Works*, I:131.

men, and have also had experience with half-learned, fearful ones; these latter cost me dearly."[16] In the *Life*, she says:

> Half-learned confessors have done my soul great harm when I have been unable to find a confessor with as much learning as I like. I have come to see by experience that it is better, if they are virtuous and observant of holy customs, that they have little learning. For then they do not trust themselves without asking someone who knows, nor do I trust them; and a truly learned man had never misguided me. Those others certainly could not have wanted to mislead me, but they didn't know any better.[17]

John of the Cross had studied at the University of Salamanca, which was, at the time, one of the great universities in Spain as well as Europe more broadly. He, too, was adamant about the need for theological knowledge. John insists that the director be "learned and discreet," and indeed, "the foundation for a guiding soul . . . is knowledge and discretion."[18] Without these qualities, John warns, spiritual directors become what he derisively calls "blind guides."[19] In this, they would be like the "consolers" of Job who thought they spoke with divine wisdom but were tragically in error, causing suffering to poor Job rather than benefit. Moreover, such directors, he says, would be like the builders of the Tower of Babel who were pursuing a project without understanding the necessary language by which they could gather the right materials and build securely.[20]

An understanding of the context is particularly important here. The sixteenth century was a time of widespread illiteracy in Spain and throughout Europe. This was especially true of the poor and working classes; but, even among upper-class families, women were often illiterate. Because of the inability of many to read, as well as the state of a Church that was in need of reform, religious

---

[16] *Interior Castle*, Fifth Dwellings, chap. 1, no. 8 in *Collected Works*, II:339.
[17] *Life*, chap. 5, no. 3 in *Collected Works*, I:71.
[18] *Living Flame*, stanza 3, no. 30, in *Collected Works*, 685.
[19] Ibid., stanza 3, nos. 29–62, in *Collected Works*, 684–98.
[20] *Ascent*, prologue, no. 4, in *Collected Works*, 116.

education was spotty, often of low quality, and sometimes largely lacking. But, at the same time, a spirit of change and of spiritual fervor was surging in Spain, and many people longed for a deeper spiritual life than the simple saying of prayers, devotions, and rituals. Many were attracted to a practice of more contemplative prayer being promoted especially by groups of reformed Franciscans. Their method (the "prayer of recollection") enabled many people to enter into a deeper and richer life of prayer, but it also led many into serious confusion and to beliefs outside the boundaries of Christian doctrine about God's relationship with us and the authentic shape of the human response to God. Many cases of misguided mystics and charlatans became widely known—and they came to the attention of the Spanish Inquisition. Teresa and John were certainly well aware of the vigilance of the Inquisition; but, more broadly, we have no reason to doubt their stated desire to submit their writing to the teachings of the Church. John of the Cross says as he begins the *Ascent*:

> Taking Scripture as our guide we do not err, since the Holy Spirit speaks to us through it. Should I misunderstand or be mistaken on some point, whether I deduce it from Scripture or not, I will not be intending to deviate from the true meaning of Sacred Scripture or from the doctrine of our Holy Mother the Catholic Church. Should there be some mistake, I submit entirely to the Church, or even to anyone who judges more competently about the matter than I.[21]

In a similar way, Teresa begins *The Way of Perfection*, saying:

> In all that I say in this book I submit to what our Mother the Holy Roman Church holds. If there should be anything contrary to that, it will be due to my not understanding the matter. And so I beg the learned men who will see this work to look it over carefully and to correct any mistake there may be as to what the Church holds, as well as any other mistakes in other matters.[22]

---

[21] Ibid., prologue, no. 2, in *Collected Works*, 115.
[22] *Way of Perfection*, foreword, in *Collected Works*, II:38.

When cautioned by friends that she might become the object of the inquisition's attention, Teresa reported that she laughed and said: "If anyone were to see that I went against the slightest ceremony of the Church in a matter of faith, I myself knew well that I would die a thousand deaths for the faith or for any truth of Sacred Scripture."[23]

In the context in which they lived and wrote, Teresa and John were understandably concerned to find directors who could help those who sought their guidance to remain within the bounds of sound doctrine. It is no surprise, then, that they viewed the direction relationship to involve elements of teaching and more explicit directing than contemporary models of spiritual guidance might promote. Different times and cultures require different forms of guidance or emphases.

We live in a different time. The people who seek direction today are themselves quite capable of reading about spirituality and theology. In fact, if they are seeking spiritual companionship, they are probably already predisposed to seek a greater knowledge and guidance about the Christian spiritual tradition on their own. There is no Inquisition looking over our shoulders. Perhaps, in a healthy way, we are less concerned about slipping into heresy. Instead, we can see that "learning," today, would enable the spiritual guide to draw more fully—beyond his or her personal experience alone—on tips, ideas, images, cautions, patterns, and possible pitfalls from the long and diverse spiritual tradition of the Church. And yet, at the same time, many Christians come to a personal conversion and a subsequent desire for deep prayer in their adult years. Their religious education, beyond the basics, may be almost a distant memory. We live in an age of subjectivism in which we are unavoidably tempted to move in the direction of simple personal feelings and emotional experiences of the divine—in which Christians are inclined to view even basic doctrinal beliefs as matters of personal opinion. Especially as the life of prayer deepens, it is easy to assess the quality of our prayer by the felt experience of it; and the felt experience can come to be interpreted as

---

[23] *Life*, chap. 33, no. 5, in *Collected Works*, I:286–87.

the arbiter of truths about God, the person of Christ, the nature of our relationship with God, and the importance of the Church and the sacraments. Among some in our day, there is a fascination with apparitions and other extraordinary phenomena as well as the demonic (which has its parallels in sixteenth-century Spain). In this context, Christians who seek to grow explicitly in the Christian life and in prayer might benefit from more knowledgeable assistance so as not to stray from the time-honored bounds of our understanding of Scripture and tradition. These—together with even our dogmas and doctrines—can be food for prayer and an authentic relationship with God. And they provide guideposts and boundaries for those who would truly be Christian in belief and in living.

Most probably, in our time, a "learned" director need not have an academic degree in theology, spirituality, or Scripture. But a solid grasp of the basic lines of these disciplines remains important. No wonder that contemporary certification and formation programs for spiritual directors usually include a more academic component that involves such areas as biblical theology and the history of Christian spirituality—its major figures and movements, and the like. Christians who come for direction ought to be able to receive counsel or at least gentle challenge if it seems that their interpretation of their personal experience and their discernment of the movement and direction of the Spirit in their lives is straying from fundamental beliefs about who God is or how God acts in history. This was the very concern of Teresa and John in their own time; and, recognizing that our context is quite different, it remains an important caution.

Experienced

Both Teresa of Avila and John of the Cross were particularly concerned about the guidance of people advancing along the path of prayer. They believed that many such people lacked adequate guidance to help them remain on the path and avoid possible pitfalls. They were concerned especially with prayer beyond the basics, moving into contemplative practice and into the kind of gifted, wordless prayer for which the word *contemplation* was traditionally reserved. Guidance of men and women far along this road required a director who could function something like a professional guide on a challenging wilderness trail—offering counsel and encouragement as well as advice on how to avoid wrong turns and possible falls. "Experienced" as a quality for a spiritual director, then, indicates a person who himself or herself has walked for some time on the journey, having experienced some of the important trials and graces of growing in Christian life and prayer, and thus having arrived at some level of spiritual maturity. Experience, then, is also a kind of knowledge; but, in this case, it is a practical, life-based knowing.

In her *Life*, Teresa details some of the trials she experienced at the hands of misguided directors who, though sincere, discouraged her and gave her unhelpful counsel. She says in a general way:

> Beginners need counsel so as to see what helps them most. For this reason a master is very necessary providing he has experience. If he doesn't, he can be greatly mistaken and lead a soul without understanding it nor allowing it to understand itself. . . . I have come upon souls intimidated and afflicted for whom I felt great pity because the one who taught them had no experience; and there was one person who didn't know what to do with herself. Since they do not understand spiritual things, these masters afflict soul and body and obstruct progress. One of these souls spoke to me about a master who held her bound for eight years and wouldn't let her go beyond self-knowledge; the Lord had already brought her to the prayer of quiet, and so she suffered much tribulation.[24]

The introduction of true contemplative prayer—given as a gift from God—is often quite subtle, John of the Cross notes. The signs are easily missed. In fact, he believed that many people are called

---

[24] Ibid., chap. 13, no. 14, in *Collected Works*, I:129.

by God to that deeper, wordless prayer; but, lacking adequate direction or even actively misdirected, they would never know it or could even be directed away from it. Finding a director who was aware of these signs and hopefully who had even experienced them for himself or herself was important for someone seeking to grow into deeper prayer. Some of John's most critical words are directed at spiritual guides who lack the experiential knowledge to guide people at this critical transition (or lack at least the humility to recommend a new director):

> These spiritual masters, not understanding souls that tread the path of quiet and solitary contemplation, since they themselves have not reached it and do not know what it is to part with discursive meditation, think these souls are idle. They hinder them and hamper the peace of restful and quiet contemplation that God of his own was according them, by making them walk along the path of meditation and imaginative reflection, and perform interior acts. . . . They do a great injury to God and show disrespect toward him by intruding with a rough hand where he is working.[25]

Again, Teresa and John are particularly concerned about the guidance of persons of more advanced prayer, but their basic premise here remains critically important. At the very least, they are suggesting that spiritual guides must themselves be committed to prayer and to growth in the Christian life. They must have a personal relationship with God in Christ and possess personal experience of the discipline required and possible practical helps and pitfalls in growing in the relationship. At the same time, the three qualities function together. The guide does not necessarily need to have personal experience of the most advanced movements of prayer—each person's journey and experience is unique (which is not to say that there are not broad patterns or typical movements and transitions). The other two recommended qualities—knowledge and discernment—can assist even where personal experience is lacking.

---

[25] *Living Flame*, stanza 3, nos. 53–54, in *Collected Works*, 695.

John of the Cross cautions strongly—in a general way, but relevant especially in this regard—that directors must be able to recognize and be willing to recommend a new director when they are not able to assist the person at their particular place in their journey. Different directors have skills and experience for some but perhaps not for others. With that in mind, John warns against directors who are possessive and cling to their directees, rather than recommending another director when their own skills and experience are no longer sufficient:

> Granted that you may possess the requisites for the full direction of some soul (for perhaps it does not have the talent to make progress), it is impossible for you to have the qualities demanded for the guidance of all those you refuse to allow out of your hands. God leads each one along different paths so that hardly one spirit will be found like another in even half its method of procedure. . . . You tyrannize souls and deprive them of their freedom, and judge for yourself the breadth of the evangelical doctrine. Therefore you endeavor to hold on to your penitents. . . . And this is not jealousy for the glory of God, but a jealousy motivated by your own pride and presumption or some other imperfection, for you should not assume that in turning from you this person turned from God.[26]

Using a very apt image, he warns:

> Not everyone capable of hewing the wood knows how to carve the statue, nor does everyone able to carve know how to perfect and polish the work, nor do all who know how to polish it know how to paint it, nor do all who can paint it know how to put the finishing touches on it and bring the work to completion. One can do with the statue only what one knows how to do, and when craftsmen try to do more than they know how to do, the statue is ruined.
> Let us see, then: If you are only a hewer, which lies in guiding the soul to contempt of the world and mortification of its

[26] Ibid., stanza 3, no. 59, in *Collected Works*, 697.

appetites, or a good carver, which consists in introducing it
to holy meditations, and know no more, how can you lead
this soul to the ultimate perfection of delicate painting, which
no longer requires hewing or carving or even relief work, but
the work that God must do in it? . . . What, I ask, will the
statue look like if all you do is hammer and hew . . .?[27]

With this rich image, John is suggesting both the varied and sometimes subtle skills required of mature spiritual guides as well as
the need for the director to approach each particular directee with
prudent care and discernment—the last of the three qualities of
the director to which we now turn.

Discerning

Teresa and John speak of the third quality by a number of terms,
indicating layers of meaning. A good spiritual guide must be discreet, in the sense of being able to hold confidences. This may
seem obvious, especially today, but Teresa once suffered from a
director who spoke of their conversations to others in the effort
to get wider counsel for how to proceed. Although innocent in
intention, it resulted in word of their conversations to spread more
broadly.[28] Secondly, a good guide must be discerning of the movements of the Spirit—that is, able to discern the divine voice speaking to him or her as well as, and especially, able to assist the
directee in discerning the movement and direction of the Spirit in
his or her life and prayer. Finally, a director must be discerning or
prudent about the actual state or situation of the particular person
with whom the guide is walking. In that way, the director will be
able to sense when it would be helpful to ask, support, encourage,
nudge, or challenge at a particular moment. In other words, the
director must always meet the person where he or she is, focused
on the person rather than a message or spiritual agenda to be
pursued.

---

[27] Ibid., stanza 3, nos. 57–58, in *Collected Works*, 696–97.
[28] *Life*, chap. 23, no. 13, in *Collected Works*, I:206.

Again, Teresa herself experienced directors who lacked such basic discretion. She recalls how a friend introduced her to a priest who would for a time become her director:

> I was most embarrassed to find myself in the presence of so holy a man, and I gave him an account of my soul and my prayer; but I didn't want him to hear my confession. I told him I was very busy—and that was true. He began with a holy determination to guide me as though I were a strong person—for by rights I should have been so because of the prayer he observed I was experiencing—in order that I might in no way offend God. When I saw him at once so determined about little things that, as I say, I didn't have the fortitude to give up immediately and so perfectly, I was afflicted. Since I saw he was taking my soul's attachments as something I would have to die to all at once, I realized there was need for much more caution.
>
> In sum, I understood that the means he gave me were not the ones by which I could remedy my situation, because they were suited to a more perfect soul. As for myself, even though I was advanced in receiving favors from God, I was very much at the beginning with regard to virtues and mortification. Certainly, if I were to have had no one else but him to speak to, I believe my soul would never have improved.[29]

In the end, and most importantly, for Teresa and John, it is the Holy Spirit who is always the true director. A human guide is an instrument who himself or herself must be docile to that divine direction for the assistance of the directee. This is, more properly, the quality of being spiritually discerning. Teresa herself always felt that, even in the midst of consulting many wise and experienced persons, it was God who was her ultimate and most foundational guide: "His Majesty has always been my Master."[30] John's comments on the matter are clear and unequivocal:

[29] Ibid., chap. 23, nos. 8–9, in *Collected Works*, I:203–4.
[30] Ibid., chap. 12, no. 6, in *Collected Works*, I:122.

These directors should reflect that they themselves are not the chief agent, guide, and mover of souls in this matter, but the principal guide is the Holy Spirit, who is never neglectful of souls, and they themselves are instruments for directing these souls to perfection through faith and the law of God, according to the spirit given by God to each one. Thus the whole concern of directors should not be to accommodate souls to their own method and condition, but they should observe the road along which God is leading one; if they do not recognize it, they should leave the soul alone and not bother it. And in harmony with the path and spirit along which God leads a soul, the spiritual director should strive to conduct it into greater solitude, tranquility, and freedom of spirit.[31]

Conclusion

Teresa of Avila and John of the Cross, mystical writers and doctors of the Church, were, before all else, a Christian woman and man who set out to grow in the Christian life and prayer. By God's grace and their own effort, they advanced in the ways of holiness and contemplative prayer. But before they arrived at union with God, they themselves experienced the ups and downs of the Christian journey. Teresa was, by her own account, greatly helped by the people who guided her along the way. Although no historical record remains, we can only assume that the same can be said for John. They took it, in turn, as their call to assist others along the same path.

These two Carmelite doctors were collaborators in a reform of the Carmelite Order and in the establishment of the Discalced Carmelites. But this was a reform grounded in a change in vision, priorities, and lifestyle to feed the personal spiritual growth of its members in order to take their distinctive place in the life and ministry of the Church. As such, Teresa and John were concerned to promote, guide, and assist this growth in their sisters and broth-

---

[31] *Living Flame*, stanza 3, no. 46, in *Collected Works*, 691.

ers as well as in the laity associated with them. Their writings did—and continue to do—just that. But their own letters and contemporary testimonies about their lives also make clear that spiritual direction was an important and fundamental aspect of their personal outreach to others, whether formally or not.

In attempting to help others find spiritual guides adequate to the task of walking with them from the beginnings of the Christian journey through its fullest possible maturity in this life, Teresa and John offered important teaching on the qualities essential for such spiritual companions. In doing so, they offer enduring insights, though undoubtedly wrapped in the perspectives of their particular culture. Spiritual directors, they tell us, should be *learned*—in that they should have a basic knowledge of Scripture and of Christian theology, especially of our spiritual tradition. They should be *experienced*—in the sense of being persons of authentic faith who themselves have set out on the Christian journey and even attained some maturity in order to offer knowing guidance. And spiritual directors should be *discerning*—open, attentive, and wise in understanding the ways of real flesh-and-blood human beings and, to the degree possible, the ways of the Spirit. These three qualities were manifested in their own lives and guidance of others, as their writings and the contemporary testimonies of their lives make abundantly clear.

CHAPTER FOUR

Guide Them All:
St. Francis de Sales on
Cultivating the Love of God

Kevin Schemenauer

St. Francis de Sales is the author of one of the most read spiritual classics of the Christian tradition, *Introduction to the Devout Life*. The work stands out for de Sales's attentiveness to the spiritual needs of those who live in the world. In light of this reputation, one is not surprised to read that Francis de Sales has much wisdom and prudence to offer on the topic of spiritual direction. Unfortunately, we cannot ask the great saint to give us a course or workshop on spiritual direction, and he provides us with no manuscript that directly addresses how to guide souls. The method required for analyzing his approach to providing spiritual support is to gather clues from his life and synthesize insights from his writings and letters. One discovers in these resources that the spiritual direction of Francis de Sales focuses on guiding individuals busy in the world to grow in love of God and surrender to God's will.

Following the method available to us, I will proceed in three steps. First, I will provide some background on the saint's life, with an eye to those aspects that provide context for the goals of his direction. Second, I will describe the aims of his advice: guiding those busy in the world to love of God and surrender to God's will. In describing these goals, I will document how de Sales identifies these goals in his spiritual writings and letters of direction. Third, I will show more concretely how de Sales guides his directees to these goals. In particular, I highlight three themes: the call to total surrender to God, the need for gradual growth, and the cultivation of holy liberty. While discussing these three major themes, I will draw from examples of spiritual direction that we can access through his letters.

His Life

Francis de Sales was born in 1567, thirty miles from Geneva, four years after the conclusion of the Council of Trent.[1] His parents were committed Catholics, a conviction that seems to have sunk deep in the heart and mind of Francis from an early age. Francis received the education of a noble, studying away from home from the age of seven until he was twenty-four. In the end, he would receive a doctor of arts from the Collège de Clermont of Paris and a doctorate in civil and canon law from the University of Padua.[2] His father hoped his education would allow him to mediate the politically complex situation of the Duchy of Savoy, caught between the king of Spain, the king of France, the Holy Roman Emperor, and church leaders. Instead, his formation served him well as a priest and bishop. His sophisticated education, paired with his love for God and the people of Savoy, allowed him to moderate the Catholic and Calvinist divisions in his diocese and the even more sophisticated complexity of human souls.

The relationship between Catholic-Calvinist dialogue and de Sales's spiritual direction is not negligible. De Sales would have been a different man and a different spiritual director were he not forced to wrestle at a young age with the question of predestination. Twice during his formal education, he endured dark periods of sickness and despair, struggling with the mystery of his eternal

---

[1] For details on de Sales's life, I rely heavily on Joseph Boenzi's biography, *Saint Francis de Sales: Life and Spirit* (Stella Niagara, NY: DeSales Resource Center, 2013).

[2] Ibid., 23–45.

destiny. De Sales worried that if God had not destined him for heaven, he would not be able to live in his passionate love for God.[3] After deep personal reflection, which included an intense study of Scripture and the Christian tradition with an eye on the question of predestination, he concluded with the conviction of faith that for those who seek God's glory and do his will, God will raise them so that they might praise him in eternal beatitude. De Sales had a passionate love for God and abandoned himself entirely into God's hands.[4]

The tension between Calvinist and Catholic leaders was often intense in the Duchy of Savoy. As a young priest, de Sales counseled the bishop to oppose the Duke of Savoy's plan to militarily occupy the valley of Chablais, which was a Calvinist stronghold. De Sales offered to go on a mission to the region. The people of Chablais did not initially welcome de Sales. After preaching his first three sermons at a church in Thonon, the market center of the area, "the leading citizens of Thonon protested with an oath that neither they nor any of the people should ever listen to a Catholic sermon."[5] Three months later, Francis responded to this oath by writing out his sermons in pamphlet form and secretly distributing them among interested families. He reasoned that if the people could not listen to his addresses, they could read them instead. These pamphlets began his writing career. Despite dangerous terrain and personal threats, de Sales traveled throughout the region. While he was a compelling orator and an astute thinker, de Sales found he was able to diffuse the tension and cultivate conversion of heart more effectively through private conversations. No doubt, these early experiences of guiding individuals and writing about matters of faith and spiritual growth had a profound impact on the young priest.

Before de Sales was ordained as the bishop of Geneva, the diocese of his childhood and family, he made a twenty-day retreat to prepare for his ministry. During the retreat, he had a profound

---

[3] Ibid., 33.
[4] Ibid., 38.
[5] Ibid., 47.

religious experience that gave him the conviction that he existed only for the people of God. To facilitate his ministry, he instituted a rule for himself "to live without show but also without ostentatious poverty, to work hard, to give as much time as possible to prayer, and to see to the ongoing formation of the clergy through meetings and study or retreat days."[6]

When Francis became bishop of Geneva, he was concerned with fulfilling the declarations of the Council of Trent. Among the decrees of the council that he was careful to implement was the statute insisting that bishops visit every parish in their diocese. This command was a priority in his ministry and no easy task. While recently losing several priests and communities to Calvinism, the diocese still included 450 parishes, some of which were in remote, mountainous regions. Between 1605 and 1609, Francis visited all 450 parishes of the diocese, sometimes taking isolated, dangerous paths. While de Sales is commonly known for his *Introduction to the Devout Life*, one biographer notes that his image of de Sales is riding a horse to visit the faithful in his diocese.[7] These visits were not merely obligatory or administrative. As if he were extending his earlier mission to Chablais to the whole diocese, de Sales took the opportunity of these visits to provide ongoing formation for priests and to minister to the faithful.

An account of Francis's life would not be complete without a discussion of the religious community of the Visitation of Holy Mary, which he founded with the enduring aid of St. Jane de Chantal. His vision for the order was innovative and pastoral. Whereas women's religious communities of his day were enclosed and tended to promote rigorous ascetical and spiritual programs, de Sales envisioned a community that encouraged a deeper life of devotion without being quite so strict and closed off to the world. While mostly living in an enclosed community, the sisters would serve the poor in their community and have the freedom

---

[6] Ibid., 56–57.

[7] Henri Bordeaux, *Saint Francis de Sales: Theologian of Love*, trans. Sr. Benita Daley (New York: Longmans, 1929), 16–17.

to attend to family obligations or emergencies.[8] This flexible vision would eventually give way to canonical requirements for enclosure as the religious community spread, but the initial plans show de Sales's conviction that holiness and life in the world are compatible. Francis's contact with this religious community also would have a profound impact on his spiritual growth and his motivation to write about spiritual matters. The first community of the Visitation of Holy Mary lived in Annecy near the saint's residence, and he visited them often.

Understanding the saint's life provides some context for those writings that relate most directly to spiritual direction. I will focus on four primary sources: *Introduction to the Devout Life*, *Treatise on the Love of God*, *Spiritual Conferences*, and his letters. His *Introduction to the Devout Life* is the fruit of the spiritual direction letters he provided to Madame Louise Duchastel, a cousin to Francis by marriage. Madame Duchastel presented Francis's letters of spiritual direction to Fr. Jean Fourier, who happened to be serving as a rector at the college of Chambéry where Madame Duchastel was living at the time. Fr. Fourier's encouragement had a significant impact on de Sales since Fourier had served as a spiritual guide for de Sales going back to his student days at the Collège de Clermont in Paris. If not for the faith of his family, his respect for the Collège de Clermont, and his success in writing pamphlets in his mission to Chablais, this book, which has had such a dramatic impact on the Catholic faithful, would not exist. In addition to de Sales's letters to his cousin-in-law, we also have numerous other correspondences, collected in various volumes, from which we get glimpses of the saint's direction of souls.

De Sales wrote his *Treatise on the Love of God* as a sequel to *Introduction to the Devout Life*. "My purpose here," he notes, "is to speak to souls that are advanced in devotion."[9] De Sales explains that this work is a by-product of his service of souls, his twenty-four

---

[8] Boenzi, *Saint Francis de Sales*, 81.

[9] Francis de Sales, *Treatise on the Love of God*, 4th ed., trans. Henry Benedict Mackey, OSB, Library of St. Francis de Sales, vol. 2 (London: Burn Oates and Washbourne, 1884), 14.

years spent in holy preaching, and his relationship with the Visitation community.[10] The Visitandines also inspired de Sales's *Spiritual Conferences*, which he delivered to the religious community and which were subsequently transcribed and collected by his audience.

The Goals of Spiritual Direction

The driving goal for Francis de Sales's spiritual direction is to guide those who live busy lives to a greater love of God. His concern for those who are active is not just about others but is also related to his self-identity. Both in his early mission work and in his work as a bishop, he had regular contact with the faithful. In one of his letters to Jane de Chantal, he writes, "I have just come from teaching a catechism lesson where I played the comedian with the children and made the audience laugh a bit by making fun of masks and balls."[11] His vigorous ministry meant that he, too, was one who was active in the world. He regularly notes in his letters his regret that he could not write sooner or longer. He opens his *Introduction to the Devout Life* noting the difficulty he had in finding time to write.[12] He also shows awareness that he is offering a unique kind of spiritual guidance: "Almost all those who have hitherto written about devotion have been concerned with instructing persons wholly withdrawn from the world or have at least taught a kind of devotion that leads to such complete retirement. My purpose is to instruct those who live in town, within families, or at court, and by their state of life are obliged to live an ordinary life as to outward appearances."[13] De Sales does not contrast those who are ordained or religious with the laity as if one group concerns holy things and the other group concerns the

[10] Ibid., preface, 10.

[11] *Francis de Sales, Jane de Chantal: Letters of Spiritual Direction*, trans. Péronne Marie Thibert, selected and introduced by Wendy W. Wright and Joseph F. Power, OSFS (New York: Paulist Press, 1988), 149.

[12] Francis de Sales, *Introduction to the Devout Life*, trans. John K. Ryan (New York: Image Books, 1989), 34–35.

[13] Ibid., 33.

world. Instead, he distinguishes those who withdraw from the busyness of the world and those who do not.

He identifies his work and responsibilities as a bishop on the side of those who are busy in the world.[14] He even anticipates that some readers may challenge his ability to write on spiritual matters since he is not a religious but a bishop with limited leisure. De Sales responds, "It is primarily the duty of bishops to lead souls to perfection."[15] Moreover, de Sales's direction to consecrated women shows that no one can completely withdraw from the world since even religious encounter the burdens of caring for human needs and relating well with others.

Love of God is a theme that permeates and frames all that Francis does and writes. He addresses *Introduction to the Devout Life* to "a soul who out of desire for devotion aspires to the love of God."[16] Throughout the book, he names his reader Philothea, whom he describes as "a soul loving, or in love with, God."[17] He writes in the first section of his *Introduction*, "Genuine, living devotion, Philothea, presupposes love of God, and hence it is simply true love of God."[18] One sees the theme of love of God feature even more prominently in his second spiritual manuscript, *Treatise on the Love of God*, in which de Sales explains the anthropological and theological foundations for his emphasis on love of God.

De Sales's focus on love of God flows from his understanding of human nature and God's lavish love. The saint maintains that love presides over all other human passions and affections, which "proceed from love, as from their source and root."[19] We desire and enjoy because of what we love. We hope for what we love

---

[14] Wendy W. Wright and Joseph F. Power write, "His day was always full—there was correspondence to attend to, officials who came on business, there were liturgical and pastoral duties at all times, and always the Genevan bishop received whoever wished to see him about personal spiritual matters. . . . Women, men, poor, rich, ignorant, learned the spiritually impoverished and the richly endowed." Wright and Power, "Introduction," in *Francis de Sales, Jane de Chantal*, 29.

[15] De Sales, *Introduction to the Devout Life*, 36.

[16] Ibid., 35.

[17] Ibid., 35; see also *Francis de Sales, Jane de Chantal*, 142.

[18] De Sales, *Introduction to the Devout Life*, 40.

[19] De Sales, *Treatise on the Love of God*, 25.

and hate what harms love's focus.[20] Central to human life, then, is the love that reigns in one's will. De Sales proposes that, while one can freely make an election of what love reigns in one's will, as long as that love lives and reigns without being rejected or checked by the will, one remains its subject.

He maintains that the will naturally seeks the love of God. God's abundant offering of love helps cultivate this natural desire. For de Sales, the gospels proclaim the need for the love of God to reign. The love of God is the universal means of salvation, the greatest and first commandment.[21] For those who elect for love of God to reign in their will, "Neither death, nor life, nor Angels, nor principalities, nor powers, nor things present, nor things to come, nor might, nor height, nor depth, nor any other creature, shall be able to separate us from the love of God, which is in Christ Jesus our Lord" (Rom 5:38-39).[22]

While naturally ordered toward the love of God, the will, even more than the intellect, is weakened by sin, de Sales suggests.[23] Consequently, even God's greatest servants, "drawn away and tyrannized over by the necessities of this dying life, are forced to suffer a thousand and a thousand distractions, which often take them off the practice of holy love."[24] Maintaining love of God as the master of one's soul is a decisive spiritual challenge. De Sales argues that love of God "holds the scepter, and has the authority of commanding so inseparably united to it and proper to its nature, that if it be not master it ceases to be and perishes."[25] The decisive character of loving God is a starting point for spiritual direction. He assumes that the directee approaches the director with a desire to grow in the love of God.

This starting point also has implications for how de Sales understands the relationship between the director and the directee. Since

[20] Ibid., 24.
[21] Ibid., 83–84.
[22] As quoted in de Sales, *Treatise on the Love of God*, 140.
[23] Ibid., 58.
[24] Ibid., 146.
[25] Ibid., 29.

the goal is to grow in greater love of God, the presumption is that the director's love of God inspires the directee. The directee must have complete trust in the director. This trust, though, is not the clinical trust of a patient receiving one-way support from a professional. De Sales makes clear that he is inspired and challenged to grow by the example of those he guides. Even more, de Sales speaks to his directees with the love of a father or an intimate friend. In one letter to Jane de Chantal, shortly after she decided that de Sales should be her spiritual director, de Sales writes, "I didn't believe that anything could be added to the affection I felt for you, especially when I was praying for you. But now, my dear daughter, a new quality has been added—I don't know what to call it. All I can say is that its effect is a great inner delight which I feel whenever I wish you perfect love of God and other spiritual blessings."[26] While his affection is most strongly stated in his letters to Jane, expressions of warmth and love to his directees are more the norm than the exception. He writes, for example, to Angélique Arnauld: "I hope that God, in giving me the holy friendship of his children, will also give me his most holy friendship."[27]

As an expression of spiritual friendship, one sees in his letters his willingness to share personal struggles and his request for prayers and guidance. In one letter to Jane de Chantal, he writes:

> While I am on the subject of my soul, I want to give you some good news about it: I am doing and shall continue doing for it all that you asked me to do—have no doubts about this. Thank you for your concern for its welfare, which is undivided from the welfare of your own soul. . . . I am a little happier than usual with my soul in that I no longer see anything in it which keeps it attached to this world, and I find it more in tune with eternal values. . . . But, my daughter, how can it be that even with such good will, I still see so many imperfections growing in me?[28]

[26] *Francis de Sales, Jane de Chantal*, 131.
[27] Ibid., 169.
[28] Ibid., 150–51.

Since love of God is the goal not only of spiritual direction but also life itself, Francis is open in his relationships to see how he also can grow in love of God.

De Sales's focus is not the intellectual task of convincing directees that love of God should reign in their soul. His spiritual guidance is primarily concerned with the will: to diagnose loves that limit the reign of God's love; to encourage surrender to God's will; to show how the love of God illuminates other loves; to guide the directee to more effectively live in that love; and to cultivate a more profound love of God. These tasks are aided by the excessive abundance with which God gives his love to humanity and God's movement to awaken the soul to love of God.[29]

The goals of spiritual direction for Francis de Sales are to cultivate greater love of God, which requires the evangelization of the will. These two goals provide the framework for understanding the three central themes of de Sales's direction: total surrender to the will of God, patient growth, and holy liberty.

Total Surrender

De Sales proposes that lovers become like their beloved and seek to conform to and make real the beloved's will.[30] While this conformity of will must be limited in all love of created things, not so with love of God. One of the central ways that lovers of God manifest their love is through commitment to God's will. De Sales challenges his readers to total surrender to the will of God.

For de Sales, the phrases "love of God" and "seeking God's will" often are used synonymously. He writes in a letter to one of his younger sisters, "I beg you, my dear sister, to pray earnestly to our Lord for me, that from now on He will keep me in the pathways of His will so that I may serve Him sincerely and faithfully. You see, dearest sister, I want either to die or to love God."[31] To love is to stay on the pathway of God's will.

---

[29] De Sales, *Treatise on the Love of God*, 88.

[30] Ibid., 325.

[31] *Francis de Sales, Jane de Chantal*, 163.

Surrender to God's will is a constant theme in de Sales's direction. He often concludes his letters with the prayer, "May God
ever be our all."[32] One sees his emphasis on the theme in a letter
to Jane de Chantal: "We shall resign ourselves totally and without
reserve to our Lord's will, surrendering into His hands all our
consolations, both spiritual and temporal. Purely and simply, we
shall entrust to His providence the life and death of all those who
belong to us, letting Him arrange according to His good pleasure
who is to outlive the others; for we are confident that, provided
His sovereign goodness be with us, in us, and for us, we have all
we need and more."[33] In offering one's entire life to God, one has
all one needs.

This call to complete surrender is one reason why de Sales often
speaks of Christ's crucifixion. When explaining how to pray, de
Sales offers Christ's passion as a fruitful focus of meditation.[34] The
crucifixion is both a model of surrender and a motivation inspiring
individuals to love God with their whole being. Christ's suffering
and death also provide a witness and hope for those who are
enduring the struggles that accompany the surrender of self.[35] In
the conclusion of *Treatise on the Love of God*, de Sales proposes that
"in the glory of heaven above, next to the Divine goodness known
and considered in itself, Our Saviour's death shall most powerfully ravish the blessed spirits in the loving of God. . . . Mount
Calvary is the mount of lovers. All love that takes not its beginning
from Our Saviour's Passion is frivolous and dangerous."[36]

To surrender to God's will, de Sales encourages a holy indifference or detachment from one's own will and ambitions. In his
discussion of indifference, de Sales is drawing from the Jesuit
tradition of his university years. To understand his insight about
indifference, one needs to know what de Sales does not mean by
the word. Indifference, for de Sales, is not a lack of concern for

[32] Ibid., 177; see also 162 and 168.
[33] Ibid., 143–44.
[34] De Sales, *Introduction to the Devout Life*, 86–96; *Francis de Sales, Jane de Chantal*,
112, 115–17, 135, and 178.
[35] *Francis de Sales, Jane de Chantal*, 116–17.
[36] De Sales, *Treatise on the Love of God*, 554.

things or denial of truth. He clarifies his meaning in a letter to Madame de la Fléchère: "I have no use for people who have no likes or dislikes, and who, no matter what happens, remain unmoved; they are this way either from a lack of energy and of heart, or through an unconcern for the difference between good and evil."[37]

His discussion of humility and maintaining one's honor in his *Introduction to the Devout Life* provides a good case study for his working understanding of indifference. De Sales is aware that pride can lead individuals to be grasping or overly vigilant in maintaining one's good reputation. Indifference encourages us to overcome these prideful tendencies and to place one's honor in the context of loving God. To counteract the tendencies of pride, one needs a detachment from one's reputation so that one can diagnose those instances in which one is inclined to seek honor in goods that belong to others. De Sales writes, "Some men become proud and overbearing because they ride a fine horse, wear a feather in their hat, or are dressed in a splendid suit of clothes. Is anyone blind to the folly of all this? If there is any glory in such things it belongs to the horse, the bird, and the tailor."[38] In situations that might cause unjust harm to one's honor, the issue might be so minor that insisting on rectifying the matter would be a prideful distraction rather than the cultivation of love. To overcome this inclination to honor self and seek one's benefit inordinately, Francis calls his readers not only to accept self-abnegation but to learn to love it. This indifference to one's honor, however, does not imply that one should lack concern for one's reputation. De Sales highlights how respect is a necessary foundation for society and that those in a position of authority sometimes need to maintain a basic level of honor to serve those entrusted to their care. De Sales also warns against a false indifference that would be personally demeaning. He writes, "We often say that we are nothing, that we are misery itself and the refuse of the world, but we would be very sorry if anyone took us at our word or told

[37] *Francis de Sales, Jane de Chantal*, 160.
[38] De Sales, *Introduction to the Devout Life*, 132.

others that we are really such as we say."[39] Indifference is not a lack of concern for God and the world but places goods and one's will within the framework of God's will and love of God. De Sales proposes that one should show indifference or detachment to all things. He makes no exceptions: health, sickness, beauty, deformity, weakness, strength, spiritual dryness, consolations, sufferings: "briefly, in all sorts of events."[40]

Francis points to Abraham as a model of holy surrender: "The dear love of country, the sweetness of the society of his kindred, the pleasures of his father's house, did not shake his constancy; he departs boldly and with fervor, and goes whither it shall please God to conduct him."[41] Abraham's holy indifference toward migration is only surpassed by his willingness to sacrifice Isaac.[42] De Sales writes, "The indifferent heart is as a ball of wax in the hands of its God, receiving with equal readiness all the impressions of the Divine pleasure; it is a heart without choice, equally disposed for everything, having no other object of its will than the will of its God."[43] In their introduction to the *Letters of Spiritual Direction*, Wendy M. Wright and Joseph F. Power write, "Salesian teaching on indifference, that true liberty of the children of God, is summed up in Francis de Sales's oft-quoted maxim: 'ask for nothing, refuse nothing.'"[44] Indeed, one will search long and hard to find Francis asking of God anything other than assistance in conforming to his will.

This call to holy surrender impacts Francis's guidance on prayer. He presents as a model of prayer a statue that is content to stay in the niche where the master has set it. He imagines the motionless figure saying: "I am not here for my own interest and service, but to obey and accomplish the will of my master and maker; and this suffices me."[45] In discussing spiritual dryness, he employs

[39] Ibid., 135.
[40] De Sales, *Treatise on the Love of God*, 375.
[41] Ibid., 548.
[42] Ibid., 548–49.
[43] Ibid., 374.
[44] Wright and Power, "Introduction," in *Francis de Sales, Jane de Chantal*, 52.
[45] De Sales, *Treatise on the Love of God*, 263.

the image of courtiers who go unnoticed by the prince. If God does not speak to us, we must not leave but remain faithfully in his presence.[46]

De Sales's emphasis on surrender to God illuminates his recommendations concerning mental prayer. He proposes that to begin mental prayer, one should place one's self in God's presence, which entails withdrawing one's soul from every other object and being attentive to God's presence at that very moment.[47] From there, he suggests asking for God's assistance in prayer and then encourages that one meditate on some mystery of the faith. He highlights that if one experiences spiritual affections prompted by God, then one should give space to those affections and not insist on completing the planned reading or vocal prayer since the goal is conformity to God.[48] De Sales notes that prayer can aid one's submission to God's will. He notes that just as a child learns to speak by remaining close to his mother, so also one learns the will of God by staying close to Christ in prayer. He writes, "Since prayer places our intellect in the brilliance of God's light and exposes our will to the warmth of his heavenly love, nothing else so effectively purifies our intellect of ignorance and our will of depraved affections. It is a stream of holy water that flows forth and makes the plants of our good desires grow green and flourish and quenches the passions within our hearts."[49]

The spiritual yearnings of the heart were central to de Sales's spiritual direction. De Sales concluded all of his letters with the phrase "Live Jesus in our hearts." Wright and Power highlight the point: "The directee brought the nascent yearning of his or her heart and the director then helped that person to learn to identify those promptings, to 'lean toward' the center of the self, to distinguish movements of the heart that seemed to be from God from those which seemed to be aligned to purposes alien to God, and to propose possible practices that might encourage the free expression

---

[46] De Sales, *Introduction to the Devout Life*, 93.
[47] *Francis de Sales, Jane de Chantal*, 151–52.
[48] De Sales, *Introduction to the Devout Life*, 88–91.
[49] Ibid., 81.

of those God-born impulses as well as practices that might curb the impulses born of other sources."[50] For de Sales, the human person has a natural desire for God, and prayer cultivates this desire.

In addition to seeing God's will in spiritual promptings, de Sales also challenges his readers to conform to God's providential care. De Sales often speaks of everyday obligations and commitments as God's will. God communicates his will in the embodied character of one's life. In the pamphlet *On Christian Perfection*, he proposes that many make the mistake of focusing on great trials rather than on the trials of everyday life.[51] He argues that cultivating holiness in the concrete reality of one's life is the most important and the least understood point in the spiritual life: "What is the use of building castles in Spain when we have to live in France?"[52]

De Sales notes the temptation of seeking the goods that are necessary to others' lives rather than the virtues and skills essential to one's own life circumstances. He writes, "I am the sworn enemy of all those useless, dangerous, unwise desires, for even if what we desire is good, the desiring itself is pointless since God does not want that kind of good for us, but another, to which He expects us to strive."[53] In the cultivation of good habits, de Sales challenges his readers to prefer the virtue most conformable to their duties and to excellence rather than those more inclined to their tastes or the more noticeable: "Choose the best virtues, not the most popular, the noblest, not the most obvious, those that are actually the best, not the most spectacular."[54]

De Sales encouraged individuals to hold together, often in tension, the spiritual promptings of their hearts with the reality of their current commitments and situation.[55] Too often, individuals want to give priority to one over the other. One sees this tension

[50] Wright and Power, "Introduction," in *Francis de Sales, Jane de Chantal*, 13–14.
[51] *Francis de Sales, Jane de Chantal*, 105–106.
[52] Ibid., 112; see also de Sales, *Introduction to the Devout Life*, 122.
[53] *Francis de Sales, Jane de Chantal*, 162.
[54] De Sales, *Introduction to the Devout Life*, third part, sec. 1, p. 122.
[55] Wright and Power "Introduction," in *Francis de Sales, Jane de Chantal*, 40–43.

dramatically expressed by Jane de Chantal, who desires to enter religious life while she has responsibilities toward her young children and father-in-law.[56] Total surrender requires conformity to God's will manifested in spiritual affections and life commitments but also a willingness to live in the tension between the two.

Wright and Power highlight how this theme of total surrender also is necessary for the director's approach to directees. De Sales does not insist on a prepackaged spiritual program or prayer method but cultivates "the diverse movements of God" as these movements manifest "within the great variety of persons."[57] He notes that the means of attaining perfection depends not only on vocational calling but also on individual skills and opportunities. Just as individuals possess different natural gifts, so do they vary in supernatural gifts: "The divine sweetness rejoicing, and as one would say exulting, in the production of graces, infinitely diversifies them, to the end that out of this variety the fair enamel of his redemption and mercy may appear . . . on earth every one receives a grace so special that all are different."[58] Accordingly, each person requires unique guidance.[59]

One sees an application of how de Sales tailors direction in his *Letters to Persons in the World*, which includes two letters addressed to men preparing to leave for work at court. In one correspondence, he discerns in his conversation partner a man of deep and stable faith. He praises the man for maintaining his faith within the complexities of court: "My dearest son, though you may change place, occupations and society, you will never, I trust, change your heart, nor your heart its love. . . . The variety of the faces of court and world will make no change in yours. Your eyes will ever regard heaven, to which you aspire, and your mouth will ever demand the sovereign good which you hope to have there."[60] In another letter, de Sales is concerned about a man going

[56] Ibid., 42; see also *Francis de Sales, Jane de Chantal*, 135–37.

[57] Wright and Power, "Introduction" in *Francis de Sales, Jane de Chantal*, 51.

[58] De Sales, *Treatise on the Love of God*, 82.

[59] Ibid., 14.

[60] Francis de Sales, *Letters to Persons in the World*, trans. Henry Benedict Mackey, OSB (New York: Benziger Brothers, 1900), 187.

off to court. He concludes that while the man's faith is strong enough to go off to court, he should be cautious to avoid vanity and ambition, bad books, fond loves, gaming, and delicacies.[61] De Sales alters his guidance to the person he addresses.

De Sales also surrendered his time by making himself available for spiritual direction. As Wright and Power observe, "Salesian liberty, in terms of practice, becomes a freedom to serve. The Genevan bishop was famous for his generosity with time and advice. His episcopal apartments were daily open to all who sought his counsel. The poor, the powerless, the tedious and overly scrupulous, were received equally with (and sometimes to the chagrin of) the rich, powerful, and magnanimous of spirit. This personal generosity of service was a result of the Savoyard's profound internalization of the liberty of the children of God. Such a freedom rested upon a non-attachment to his own particular notions of results."[62] In total surrender to God, de Sales made himself available to those he was committed to serve.

Small, Patient Growth

His call to total surrender to God's will might suggest that de Sales's guidance is a rigorous direction accessible to the rare few. On the contrary, while de Sales frames direction with the goal of total surrender, he always calls his readers to small, patient growth. He argues that on earth, we cannot completely empty ourselves, but we can "little by little and step by step, acquire that self-mastery which the saints took years to acquire."[63] De Sales often repeats his insight that while we should seek perfection, "we mustn't try to get there in a day."[64]

De Sales's call for gradual growth does not imply lighthearted acceptance of sin. He writes, "Keep in mind these four things: that

---

[61] Ibid., 176–83.

[62] Wright and Power, "Introduction," in *Letters of Spiritual Direction*, 53.

[63] *Francis de Sales, Jane de Chantal*, 108; see also 160 and de Sales, *Introduction to the Devout Life*, 48.

[64] *Francis de Sales, Jane de Chantal*, 97; see also 155–56.

by sin you have lost God's grace, given up your place in paradise, chosen the eternal pains of hell, and rejected God's eternal love."[65] De Sales places sin in its proper place. Sin is a part of everyone's life and an obstacle to the love of God, not an end in itself. One should not be surprised that one is imperfect and should not become preoccupied with sin.[66] He writes, "We must hate our faults, but we should do so calmly and peacefully, without fuss or anxiety. . . . Nothing is more favorable to the growth of these 'weeds' than our anxiety and overeagerness to get rid of them."[67] One should recognize the sin and then move on. The goal is not merely to uproot every weed but to cultivate a garden full of God's love.

To encourage gradual growth, de Sales frequently highlights what he names the "little virtues"—patience, gentleness, meekness, and humility. The spiritual director does not arm the directee to slay evil dragons but directs souls to the Good Shepherd who will lovingly care for his sheep. In humility, one recognizes that all good things come from God. One learns to rely on God rather than one's self. In meekness, one encourages the conversion of others by serving as a positive model rather than destroying those who do evil. In gentleness, one invites others to live in God's love rather than demanding or forcing conformity. In patience, one endures the suffering of life.

The cultivation of these little virtues is no small task. In being attentive to growing in everyday life, one is forced to acknowledge and struggle with the challenges of one's life: "Only in heaven will everything be springtime as to beauty, autumn as to enjoyment, and summer as to love. There will be no winter there; but here below we need winter so that we may practice self-denial and the countless small but beautiful virtues that can be practiced during a barren season."[68] Spiritual growth proceeds more like the cycles of the seasons than a continual springtime. We can face

---

[65] De Sales, *Introduction to the Devout Life*, 49.
[66] *Francis de Sales, Jane de Chantal*, 170 and 179.
[67] Ibid., 161.
[68] Ibid., 148.

and endure the suffering of barren seasons, trusting in God's loving care and assistance.[69] Encouraging trust in God, and with attentiveness to those busy in the world, de Sales focuses on accepting the struggles that come our way rather than actively seeking suffering.[70]

Patience is a central virtue for a spirituality of gradual growth that endures struggles. Patience requires firm and enduring commitments and self-control.[71] One must be patient with people, injustices, and sickness. The kind of patience that de Sales highlights most frequently is patience with one's self. He notes that after a life of giving way to one's passions, one should not be surprised that the path of devotion is long and arduous.[72] Focus on one's faults can represent false expectations and also be counterproductive: "Huntsmen push into the brambles, and often return more injured than the animal they intended to injure."[73] One should not be surprised by one's faults but confront them calmly and peacefully. A small step on the journey of gradual growth requires that one first understands where one is on the path. De Sales cautions against trying to pray like the seraphim or focusing on the end of a long journey that has only just begun: "Be satisfied if now and then you gain some advantage over the tendencies you fight against."[74]

De Sales's insistence on small, gradual growth applies to the task of removing superfluity from one's life. He encourages readers to gently prune the superfluous vines of their life one shoot at a time rather than hacking away at them with an ax.[75] By pruning the vines, one does not shock the system of one's spiritual life but cuts away what is unnecessary in order to bear abundant fruit. De Sales also imagines this movement away from the superfluous

[69] Ibid., 163.

[70] Ibid., 169; see also *Introduction to the Devout Life*, 141.

[71] De Sales, *Introduction to the Devout Life*, 128.

[72] *Francis de Sales, Jane de Chantal*, 158.

[73] De Sales, *Letters to Persons in the World*, 184; see also *Francis de Sales, Jane de Chantal*, 161–62.

[74] *Francis de Sales, Jane de Chantal*, 158; see also 97–98, 161–62.

[75] Ibid., 155.

as a climb of Mount Tabor. We should, he writes, little by little leave "behind us the affections for the low things of earth and aspire to the happiness that has been prepared for us."[76]

Holy Liberty

The goal of cultivating the love of God also points de Sales to the theme of holy liberty. He frequently takes up the subject of freedom when advising on prayer. Responding to questions from directees about their struggles to fulfill personal prayer commitments when confronted with illness or interruption, de Sales cautions against two extremes: instability and constraint.[77] On one extreme, the devout soul allows one's commitment to prayer to constrain one's service to neighbor. They are anxious to complete their prayer as intended and lack the freedom to respond to God's will manifested in illness, an emergency, or the needs of those before them. De Sales proposes the devout soul need not be anxious about having one's prayer interrupted since prayer, acceptance of limitations, and service to neighbor all follow the will of God and cultivate love of God. He writes, "I'd like to think that when some legitimate or charitable cause takes you away from your religious exercises, this would be for you another form of obedience and that your love would make up for whatever you have to omit in your religious practice."[78] Holy liberty is the freedom to respond to God's will. This liberty requires a detachment from all things, even one's intended prayer routine.

Moments when things do not go one's way present prime opportunities to manifest or grow in holy liberty. These moments serve as reminders that the ultimate goal of one's spiritual pursuits is not perfect adherence to a personal plan but the love of God. De Sales models this holy liberty in the advice he provides for prayer. When he offers suggestions for prayer to Jane de Chantal, he defers to her freedom, stating that she can use or not use his

[76] Ibid., 163.
[77] Ibid., 139.
[78] Ibid., 134; see also 138–39.

advice depending on whether she finds them fruitful.[79] As a spiritual director, he is open to the idea that his suggestions might not be the best thing for his reader. De Sales's critique of constraint clarifies that one should not be scrupulous or anxious about one's plans and thereby make one's plans the ultimate good.

Concern about constraint does not imply that de Sales is encouraging spiritual laxity.[80] He frames his conversation of freedom also with the extreme of instability. Holy liberty is not the rationalization of a lack of discipline or self-control. One should have a good reason to stray from one's intended plan and do so only with the conviction that God wills the exception.[81] One should not deviate from commitments in a way that causes scandal or injustice, or that moves one away from vocational promises.[82] Obedience remains central for holy liberty. Freedom orders obedience toward a genuine commitment to God's will. De Sales emphatically and succinctly summarizes his ideas on holy liberty when he writes in capital letters: "DO ALL THROUGH LOVE, NOTHING THROUGH CONSTRAINT; LOVE OBEDIENCE MORE THAN YOU FEAR DISOBEDIENCE."[83]

Conclusion

De Sales had a deep faith from a young age. He lived in the Calvinist-Catholic tensions of his region and had a great love for the people of the Diocese of Geneva. De Sales's spiritual direction stands out for his commitment to those who live in the world and for his unwavering focus on cultivating the love of God. He begins with the assumption that the directee wants to grow in love of God, and he insists on total surrender to God's will. This commitment to complete surrender is lived out through small, everyday actions that cultivate the little virtues and lead to incremental growth in holiness. Through self-surrender and gradual growth,

[79] Ibid., 124–25.
[80] Ibid., 146.
[81] Ibid., 139.
[82] Ibid., 140.
[83] Ibid., 134.

the devout soul lives a holy liberty that remains obedient to spiritual commitments and responsive to life circumstances and responsibilities.

For de Sales, these themes of spiritual direction are more than a technique—they manifest the purpose of life. Accordingly, one sees these themes in de Sales's life and in the manner in which he provides spiritual direction. He does not insist on one spiritual program, but surrenders to how God is working on the soul before him. He does not use his own spiritual journey or location on that path as the standard for his directees, but patiently invites them to take the next step on their journey and grow through their everyday actions and commitments. He cultivates a holy liberty, obedient but responsive.

In de Sales's letters and writings, one sees a model for how spiritual directors can guide those busy in the world toward a more loving relationship with God. All activities and responsibilities provide opportunities to grow in love of God, and providing spiritual direction is no exception. Since spiritual directors also are individuals busy in the world who seek to grow in their love of God, de Sales's wisdom suggests how those providing spiritual direction can personally grow through their direction of others. Spiritual directors should make the love of God the primary goal of their life. Sometimes the best guidance is the model of holiness. Directors should surrender their direction to God. They should seek God's will and the directee's best interest in discerning who they advise and in how many or how few people they guide. Spiritual directors should seek small, gradual growth and be patient with themselves as spiritual directors. They should not be surprised when their direction lacks perfection, but should seek to gradually improve their ability to guide others. They should cultivate holy liberty in their direction that is obedient to their commitments but also creatively responsive to individual needs and God's intervening grace. Finally, in guiding others, spiritual directors should encounter God's grace and grow in their love of God. In providing direction, as in all things, de Sales invites us to pray: Live Jesus in our hearts!

CHAPTER FIVE

Spiritual Direction and Private Revelations: Learning from the Life of St. Faustina Kowalska

Robert E. Alvis

In the Roman Catholic tradition, a distinction is drawn between *revelation*, an order of knowledge concerning God's nature and plan for creation that is revealed by God and relevant to all humankind, and *private revelations*, communications from God or the saints to individuals for their personal benefit or for guidance in a specific place or time. As noted in the *Catechism of the Catholic Church*, it is not the role of private revelations "to improve or complete Christ's definitive Revelation, but to help live more fully by it in a certain period of history."[1]

Over the centuries, private revelations have enriched the faith lives of innumerable Catholics, including both direct recipients and those hearing about them secondhand. Such communications have offered assurance in the face of trials, insight into matters of religious belief and practice, and new expressions of piety. At the same time, private revelations have caused considerable consternation. Individuals claiming access to information from supernatural sources have displayed the capacity to overshadow, at

---

[1] *Catechism of the Catholic Church*, 2nd ed. (United States Catholic Conference—Libreria Editrice Vaticana, 1997), par. 67.

least in the short term, more mundane forms of authority such as the holding of a church office. Furthermore, the content of many private revelations has been deemed contradictory to established church teaching. For this reason, claims to private revelations have been subject to careful scrutiny by church officials in order to determine their ultimate source, be it divine, diabolical, imagined, or fabricated.

In most instances, the task of scrutinizing purported revelations has fallen to priests, who, particularly in their function as confessors, often have been the first to encounter claims of supernatural communication. Owing to the private nature of such conversations, the influence that priests have wielded in these situations usually has been shrouded in mystery. By virtue of the authority they have enjoyed in the eyes of those seeking their counsel, it is safe to assume that priests have shaped how the people under their care have interpreted their interior experiences. By virtue of their positions in the Church's governing structures, they also have had the capacity to raise the profile of those revelations they have determined to be genuine.

This chapter considers the role priestly confessors played in the life of Sr. Maria Faustina Kowalska, OLM, one of the most influential Catholic mystics of the past century and, as of April 30, 2000, a saint. Over the course of her relatively short life, Faustina experienced an extraordinarily large number of private revelations, and she turned to a series of confessors as she sought to make sense of these messages. Her confessors responded in various ways, from patronizing dismissal to enthusiastic support. Fortunately for later historians, Faustina described these encounters in the journal she maintained in the years 1933–38.[2] She also corresponded with a number of her confessors, and some of these letters survive. Taken together, these sources provide a rare and valuable glimpse into the relationship between confessor and mystic.

---

[2] One of Faustina's confessors, Fr. Michał Sopoćko, ordered her to maintain the diary and to record her mystical experiences. She complied, and over the course of six years she wrote 447 pages of text distributed over six notebooks.

The following analysis highlights the degree to which confessors shaped Faustina's own reactions to and interpretations of her experiences, sometimes leading her to ecstatic heights and other times to the depths of despair. It also demonstrates her confessors' capacity to lend credibility to Faustina's claims and to advance the work she believed God was calling her to undertake. Indeed, without their support it is hard to imagine how Faustina would have made much of an impact upon Catholic life.

While the support of confessors was important to Faustina, it was not all-determining. The strength of her conviction enabled her to persevere after dispiriting encounters with disbelieving priests. There is an important lesson in this for contemporary priests who find themselves counseling would-be mystics. Finally, Faustina's case serves as a salutary reminder of some of the risks faced by priests who choose to advocate publicly for such individuals under their care.

Private Revelations and Priestly Discernment

Certain priestly practices, such as performing the sacraments, have been governed by detailed rubrics, which have resulted in broadly similar outcomes across the Catholic world. By contrast, the counseling of individuals who believe they are receiving private revelations is a kind of work that evades easy instruction. It requires careful discernment of data specific to each case.

While precise rubrics may have been lacking, an array of norms have informed how priests were to respond to such cases. One of the best resources concerning the norms in place during Faustina's life can be found in Augustin Poulain's *The Graces of Interior Prayer*, a work first published in 1910.[3] In his service as a confessor, Poulain, a Jesuit priest based in France, met many Catholics who shared with him the extraordinary phenomena they were experiencing in their interior lives. Drawing upon these encounters and his familiarity with the Church's rich mystical tradition, Poulain

[3] Augustin Poulain, *The Graces of Interior Prayer: A Treatise on Mystical Theology*, trans. Leonora L. Yorke Smith (London: Routledge & Kegan Paul, 1951).

recorded his insights on such matters as one part of a larger study on mystical theology. The book received a warm reception in the Catholic world, including from Pope Pius X, and was republished many times over in a variety of languages. It has long been regarded as a classic text of the genre.

Poulain's reflections on private revelations are marked by an abundance of caution. He affirms that genuine revelations from God are gifts that can benefit the welfare of faithful Christians. They are by no means essential to understanding the gospel and adhering to its dictates, however, and "**belief** in them is **not required** by the Church even when she approves them." Such approbation merely signals that nothing in a given revelation is "contrary to faith or morals."[4] At the same time, Poulain warns that most purported revelations do not come wholly from God and are "a source of danger."[5] Even genuine revelations can be tarnished by degrees of error and human intervention, consciously or unconsciously. A more serious danger lies in false revelations, for which he identifies five common causes: simulation, an overactive imagination, faulty memory, the work of the devil, and invention of falsifiers.[6]

Having outlined the stakes involved, Poulain offers specific counsel to those tasked with determining the veracity of purported revelations. He recommends seven inquiries into the lives of those claiming revelations: their physical, intellectual, and moral qualities; their educational background (to exclude the possibility that the revealed knowledge they claim might have been the result of formal study); the virtues they possess, both before and after receiving revelations (genuine revelations can enhance sanctification); the "extraordinary graces of union with God" they have experienced; previous revelations and predictions made on the basis of the same; great trials they have suffered ("crosses" invariably accompany "extraordinary graces"); and the precautions they

---

[4] Ibid., 320. Boldface in the original here and in footnote 10.
[5] Ibid., 348.
[6] Ibid., 340–45.

have taken to avoid illusions.[7] Poulain further recommends nine forms of scrutiny of purported revelations: whether they have been preserved in authentic texts; their conformity with church teaching; their conduciveness to moral living; their usefulness for the salvation of the soul; the dignity of the circumstances surrounding them; the sentiments engendered in the persons receiving them; whether they have inspired bold enterprises; whether they have stood the test of time; and whether God appears to have favored the undertakings inspired by them.[8]

Poulain shares a special piece of advice concerning revelations received by women: "The revelations of women are probably false when they lead to a wish to direct **clergy and princes** and to teach them, speaking with an air of authority. For this is not the part that women should play in the Church—at least, not as a regular practice."[9] In his rules for spiritual directors, Poulain advises them to move slowly, to avoid showing admiration or distrust for the visionary, to maintain appropriate boundaries, and to engage in regular prayer.[10]

Poulain's skeptical reserve toward claims of private revelations no doubt was shared by a great many priests and prelates in his day. Catholic officials were well aware of the all-too-human motivations that could lead one to invent or imagine messages from holy sources, and past experience showed how false claims to revelations could sow confusion among the faithful and bring embarrassment on the Catholic Church as a whole. The number of modern mystics whose private revelations have gained a measure of public approbation from church officials is relatively modest, and it is no doubt dwarfed by a much larger number of individuals, most now lost to the historical record, who shared their inner lives with priests only to be advised to reject such phenomena or to maintain silence on the matter.

---

[7] Ibid., 351–60.
[8] Ibid., 360–72.
[9] Ibid., 371.
[10] Ibid., 380–89.

At the same time, the possibility of private revelations was widely accepted among the clergy, and the enthusiasm surrounding high-profile instances of the same in the modern era—the messages revealed at Lourdes and Fatima, for example—reinforced their importance in the life of the Catholic Church. In this context, encounters with individuals making credible claims to private revelations could be viewed as a remarkable privilege. For ambitious priests, managing the public profile of a recognized mystic enhanced their influence, which they could apply toward their own favored goals. Mystics who were young, female, and/or undereducated proved especially susceptible to such management, owing to their weaker command of the Catholic theological tradition and the submissiveness they were expected to demonstrate toward priests. In their analysis of the Italian mystic St. Gemma Galgani (1878–1903), Rudolf M. Bell and Christina Mazzoni illustrate how the Passionist Fr. Germano Ruoppolo di San Stanislao, Gemma's confessor and later a leading advocate of her canonization, carefully framed her experiences in ways that served the interests of the Passionist order.[11] In his study of the brief public career of Claire Ferchaud, a young French woman whose claims to private revelations generated national interest for a number of months in 1916–17, Raymond Jonas describes how Fr. Jean-Baptiste Lemius manipulated her to promote his own religious project and professional advancement.[12]

Faustina's Interior Life to 1932

Helena Kowalska was born on August 23, 1905, to an impoverished farming family in the village of Głogowiec in Russian-controlled Poland. Raised in an intensely religious household, she reports hearing "God's voice in my soul" for the first time at age

---

[11] Rudolf M. Bell and Christina Mazzoni, *The Voices of Gemma Galgani: The Life and Afterlife of a Modern Saint* (Chicago: University of Chicago Press, 2003), 159–92.

[12] Raymond Jonas, *The Tragic Tale of Claire Ferchaud and the Great War* (Berkeley: University of California Press, 2005), 62–83.

seven.[13] After just two years of formal education, she went to work, primarily as a domestic, in order to help support her family. Feeling called to religious life at age fifteen and again at eighteen, she informed her parents of her wish to join a convent. Her parents refused on both occasions, recognizing that they could not afford the dowry typically expected of female postulants.[14]

Kowalska ultimately decided to defy her parents after a mystical encounter with Christ in July 1924. While she was attending a dance in a park in the city of Łódź, Christ appeared to her, covered in wounds and offering words of reproach: "**How long shall I put up with you and how long will you keep putting Me off?**" Deeply troubled, Kowalska made her way to the Cathedral of St. Stanisław Kostka to pray for guidance. While there she heard a voice that issued the following command: "**Go at once to Warsaw; you will enter a convent there**." She screwed up her courage, boarded a train, and in her "one dress, with no other belongings," arrived in Warsaw.[15]

With so few resources at her disposal, Kowalska struggled to find a congregation that would accept her. She finally gained provisional acceptance—provided she could raise the funds needed to pay for her wardrobe—from the Congregation of the Sisters of Our Lady of Mercy, a community whose primary work involved the rehabilitation of women in morally compromised circumstances. Kowalska eventually raised the necessary amount, and in August 1925 she began her postulancy. She was accepted into the novitiate in April 1926, at which time she received her name in religion, Maria Faustina.[16]

Faustina felt disappointed with her congregation almost from the start and entertained thoughts of leaving. In keeping with the

[13] Maria Faustina Kowalska, *Diary: Divine Mercy in My Soul* (Stockbridge, MA: Marian Press, 2014), par. 7.

[14] Sophia Michalenko, *The Life of Faustina Kowalska: The Authorized Biography* (Ann Arbor, MI: Servant Books, 1999), 17–21.

[15] Kowalska, *Diary*, pars. 9–10. In published versions of her diary, boldface is used to signal words spoken by God to Faustina.

[16] Every member of her congregation took the name Maria as her first name, followed by a second name that would serve as her routine source of identification.

practices of many congregations, its members were divided into two groups: the "first choir," which consisted of higher class, better educated sisters who performed more prestigious work like teaching, and the "second choir," which encompassed sisters from the lower ranks of the social order who performed more menial tasks. Faustina found herself relegated to the second choir, and the division rankled her. More importantly, many of her fellow sisters fell well short of her lofty expectations of the vowed religious life: the striving after virtue and an intense life of prayer and self-mortification. The gulf between her ideals and the realities of her congregation led to her estrangement from many of her peers. "From the very moment I entered the convent," she writes, "I have been charged with one thing; namely, that I am a saint. But this word was always used scoffingly. At first, this hurt me very much."[17]

As she settled into her life in religion, Faustina had to contend with a growing array of mystical experiences. Early on she had a vision of souls suffering in purgatory and heard the voice of God announce, "**My mercy does not want this, but justice demands it.**"[18] The intertwined themes of humanity's sinfulness and God's mercy would surface time and again in many subsequent revelations. Toward the end of her first year in the novitiate, Faustina fell into an extended period of spiritual despair, in which she felt "rejected by God." In the midst of her turmoil, she stumbled upon the idea of *trust* in God's mercy. In her account of this difficult time, she recounted her following plea to Jesus: "Jesus, who in the Gospel compare Yourself to a most tender mother, I trust in Your words because You are Truth and Life. In spite of everything, Jesus, I trust in You in the face of every interior sentiment which sets itself against hope."[19] The importance of trust would continue to figure prominently in her future interior life. In these years, she also came to embrace the venerable Catholic idea that she was one of a select few destined to suffer for the redemption of others. On

[17] Kowalska, *Diary*, par. 1,571.
[18] Ibid., par. 20.
[19] Ibid., par. 24.

one occasion she was mystically transported to the judgment seat of God, and God alerted her to her fate: "**You will go back to earth, and there you will suffer much, but not for long; you will accomplish My will and My desires.**"[20]

On February 22, 1931, Faustina had the first of a series of visions that convinced her she was being called by Christ to something considerably larger than expiatory suffering. Indeed, her new challenge was to institute significant changes in the public life of the Catholic Church. In the evening when she was in her cell, Jesus appeared to her clothed in a white garment. "One hand [was] raised in a gesture of blessing, the other was touching the garment at the breast. From beneath the garment, slightly drawn aside at the breast, there were emanating two large rays, one red, the other pale." As she marveled at this vision, Jesus issued the following command: "**Paint an image according to the pattern you see, with the signature: Jesus, I trust in You. I desire that this image be venerated, first in your chapel, and [then] throughout the world.**" He then explained the power of the image: "**I promise that the soul that will venerate this image will not perish. I also promise victory over [its] enemies already here on earth, especially at the hour of death.**" Jesus went on to explain the connection between this image and a new feast day to be included in the Church's liturgical calendar: "**I want this image . . . to be solemnly blessed on the first Sunday after Easter; that Sunday is to be the Feast of Mercy.**"[21]

The intensity of her mystical experiences and the immense assignment she felt called to undertake left Faustina overwhelmed and awash in self-doubt. Compounding her frustrations was her inability to find a priest who took her seriously and could shed light on the developments in her interior life. One confessor, seeing how troubled she was, assigned her a penance designed to lighten her spirits. "I was ordered to say the *Te Deum* or the *Magnificat*, or to run fast around the garden in the evening, or else to laugh out

---

[20] Ibid., par. 36.
[21] Ibid., pars. 47–49.

loud ten times a day."[22] When she told another priest about her vision of Christ and his order that she paint it, the priest dismissed its significance with the following advice: "That refers to your soul. . . . Certainly, paint God's image in your soul."[23]

Faustina summarizes her encounters with confessors in these years as follows: "Confessors could neither understand me nor set my mind at peace concerning these matters." She then catalogs three mistakes confessors commonly make, which seem to draw from her own experience. A soul can be led to doubt "when the confessor has little knowledge of extraordinary ways and shows surprise if a soul discloses to him the great mysteries worked in it by God," she laments. Also deleterious is when "the confessor does not allow the soul to express itself frankly, and shows impatience." She concludes: "It also happens sometimes that the confessor makes light of little things. There is nothing little in the spiritual life."[24]

Faustina was also tormented by the skepticism of her superiors and fellow sisters when she shared glimpses of her interior life. She wrote, "My Superiors did not believe what I said and treated me with pity as though I were being deluded or were imagining things."[25] Some of her fellow sisters "began to speak openly about me and to regard me as a hysteric and a fantasist, and the rumors began to grow louder. One of the sisters came to talk to me in private. She began by pitying me and said, 'I've heard them say that you are a fantasist, Sister, and that you've been having visions. My poor Sister, defend yourself in this matter.' "[26]

The skeptical responses of her confessors, superiors, and fellow sisters led Faustina to doubt the divine origin of her experiences and to attempt to put them behind her. "Believing myself to be deluded," she writes, "I resolved to avoid God interiorly for fear of these illusions."[27] Yet the encounters continued. At one point,

[22] Ibid., par. 68.
[23] Ibid., par. 49.
[24] Ibid., pars. 111–12.
[25] Ibid., par. 38.
[26] Ibid., par. 125.
[27] Ibid., par. 38.

God reminded her: "**You shall not get away from Me, for I am everywhere. You cannot do anything of yourself, but with Me you can do all things.**"[28] After struggling to make headway with the painting, Faustina was tempted to ignore the command to execute it, only to face a terrifying new vision: "Suddenly, I saw the Lord, who said to me, **Know that if you neglect the matter of the painting of the image and the whole work of mercy, you will have to answer for a multitude of souls on the day of judgment.** After these words of Our Lord, a certain fear filled my soul, and alarm took hold of me. Try as I could, I could not calm myself."[29] Such experiences reinforced Faustina's conviction that God had specific, unyielding expectations of her, despite her apparent lack of the means to achieve them.

A Turning Point

Faustina's reminiscences of her early years in her congregation make for discouraging reading. She was regarded as overly zealous and deluded by many of her peers, and she believed she was being called by God to major undertakings that she was unable to accomplish. Her situation brightened considerably toward the end of 1932 and into 1933, thanks in large part to encounters with a series of sympathetic confessors. Their words and actions boosted her confidence, improved her standing in her congregation, and supplied the means to advance her objectives.

The first of these encounters took place in November 1932 when she moved to Warsaw to begin her "third probation," a five-month period of preparation before final vows. During a spiritual retreat in Walendów led by Fr. Edmund Elter, SJ, Faustina dared to share what was going on in her interior life with the priest, and she was overjoyed by his response. "Sister, be completely at peace," he noted. "Jesus is your Master, and your communing with Him is

[28] Ibid., par. 429.
[29] Ibid., par. 154.

neither daydreaming nor hysteria nor illusion. Know that you are on the right path."[30]

On the eve of making final vows in April 1933, Faustina traveled to Kraków for another spiritual retreat. She described her mystical experiences with the retreat leader, Fr. Józef Andrasz, SJ. He, too, offered words of encouragement and advice: "It is not right for you to turn away from these interior inspirations, but you must absolutely—and I say, absolutely—speak about them to your confessor; otherwise you will go astray despite the great graces you are receiving from God."[31] Faustina records her elation over this encounter: "This priest . . . untied my wings so that I could soar to the highest summits."[32] Andrasz remained in contact with Faustina for the rest of her short life, and after her death he endeavored to promote awareness of her experiences.

After making final vows, Faustina was assigned to a convent in Vilnius, where in the summer of 1933 she encountered her most consequential confessor, Fr. Michał Sopoćko, a priest of the Archdiocese of Vilnius and a lecturer at the local Stefan Batory University. Periodically, he heard the confessions of the sisters in her convent, and Faustina opened up to him about her mystical life. Sopoćko was at first skeptical, and he requested that she be examined by a local psychiatrist, Dr. Helena Maciejewska. After Maciejewska concluded that Faustina was not suffering from a mental disturbance, Sopoćko grew more receptive to what the nun was telling him. Before long, he emerged as a true believer in her private revelations and a critical ally in the work she felt called to undertake.

Like Elter and Andrasz before him, Sopoćko assured Faustina of the divine origin of her mystical encounters. Drawing on his familiarity with Catholicism's mystical tradition, he also provided her with terms and categories that shaped her understanding of what she was experiencing. In a journal entry from 1935, for instance, Faustina notes how Sopoćko explained to her the "three

---

[30] Ibid., par.174.
[31] Ibid., par. 52.
[32] Ibid., par. 257.

degrees in the accomplishment of God's will": (1) the faithful observation of "rules and statutes"; (2) the acceptance and faithful fulfillment of "interior inspirations"; and (3) the soul's complete abandonment to "the will of God." Sopoćko confirmed that she had reached the second degree of this process but was still short of the third. This explanation proved to be deeply meaningful to Faustina: "These words pierced my soul. I see clearly that God often gives the priest knowledge of what is going on in the depths of my soul."[33]

As a humble second-choir nun, Faustina had come to learn how difficult it was, on her own, to fulfill the obligations she believed God had placed on her. Sopoćko, by contrast, had the credibility and means to make things happen. Having concluded that Christ's command concerning the painting was genuine, in 1934 Sopoćko commissioned artist Eugeniusz Kazimirowski to commit Faustina's vision to canvas, and he persuaded Faustina's superior, Mother Irena Krzyżanowska, to allow Faustina to pay periodic visits to Kazimirowski in order to describe how Christ had appeared to her.[34] Krzyżanowska's consent is an example how Sopoćko's faith in Faustina strengthened her credibility in the eyes of her fellow sisters and superiors.

With the completed painting in hand, Sopoćko was then challenged to attract a devotional following to the image and the larger message it represented. Here, he had to tread carefully. Faustina's visions had yet to receive formal recognition, and Sopoćko understood how cautious the Catholic Church could be in such cases. At this point, he did not have the confidence to ask his archbishop for permission to display the painting in a public location. In the spring of 1935, however, Sopoćko sensed a providential opening. He had been asked to preach during three Masses at Ostra Brama,

---

[33] Ibid., par. 444.

[34] When Faustina saw the finished painting in June, she was disappointed, for it fell short of the image of Christ she had seen, but she soon came to accept it. She writes: After returning to the convent, "I said to the Lord, 'Who will paint You as beautiful as You are?' Then I heard these words: **Not in the beauty of the color, nor the brush lies the greatness of this image, but in My grace.**" Kowalska, *Diary*, par. 313.

the most important Catholic shrine in Vilnius, on the weekend after Easter. In Faustina's 1931 vision, the Sunday after Easter happened to be the day that Christ had targeted for a new feast day devoted to God's mercy. Sopoćko arranged for Kazimirowski's painting to be displayed in Ostra Brama throughout the weekend.[35] Faustina was permitted to attend one of the Masses at the shrine, much to her elation. In her journal she notes, "It was a great joy for me to see others returning to the source of happiness, the bosom of The Divine Mercy."[36]

A New Congregation

During her assignment in Vilnius, for the first time in her life Faustina could rely upon a sympathetic confessor who was deeply invested in her mystical experiences and willing to use his clout to advance her agenda. This greatly bolstered her confidence. It may also have inspired her to realize her long-standing wish to affiliate with a different congregation more suited to her ideals.

Faustina first enunciated the idea that God was calling her to found a new congregation in a diary entry on June 9, 1935. She writes, "As I was walking in the garden in the evening, I heard these words: **By your entreaties, you and your companions shall obtain mercy for yourselves and for the world.**" Faustina sensed that she was being called to help create and participate in a new congregation, the purpose of which would be to "proclaim the mercy of God to the world and, by its prayers, obtain it for the world."[37]

The Catholic Church of Faustina's day treated religious vows with the utmost seriousness. Abandoning the final vows one had made to a congregation was no small matter, and winning approval for a new congregation was a complicated process. Having gained Sopoćko's trust, Faustina dared to share with him her inspiration concerning the new congregation. Once again, he proved to be receptive and encouraging. He affirmed that God often

[35] Michalenko, *The Life of Faustina*, 96.
[36] Kowalska, *Diary*, par. 421.
[37] Ibid., pars. 435–36.

chooses humble people like her to pursue great initiatives. His words eased her fears and hesitation, and at the end of their conversation she had a vision of Christ that dispelled all doubt concerning her future course. He said, "**I desire that there be such a Congregation.**"[38]

The dream of a new congregation consumed much of Faustina's attention in the last years of her life. She recorded numerous mystical experiences pertaining to it, and she reflected in great detail about its defining characteristics. In contrast to her present congregation, admission would not depend on being able to afford a dowry and there would be no distinction in rank. Rather, the primary criterion for entry would be a woman's character. Members would be expected to possess a strong will, to despise the world, and to be governed by the virtue of love in all things. Their purpose would be "to stand between heaven and earth, begging God constantly for mercy on the world and that priests be empowered so that their words be not empty and that they . . . might keep themselves completely stainless."[39]

In one vision, Faustina saw a ruined building that, as she understood it, was to house the new congregation.[40] After describing the building to Sopoćko, he was determined to find it. Eventually he arranged to take Faustina to view a certain dilapidated house in Vilnius in order to determine whether it was the structure she had seen in her vision. Faustina confirmed that it was. "The moment I touched the boards which had been nailed together in place of the doors, a strength pervaded my soul like a flash, giving me unshakable certitude," she writes. "I went away quickly from that place, my heart full of joy, for it seemed to me that there was a certain force chaining me to that place."[41] Sopoćko made arrangements to purchase and restore the house so that it might function in the future as a convent.

While Sopoćko could buy a building, he could not found a new congregation. This required a higher authority. One measure of

38 Ibid., par. 436–37.
39 Ibid., par. 537.
40 Ibid., par. 559.
41 Ibid., par. 573.

Faustina's mounting confidence was her decision to speak to the archbishop of Vilnius, Romuald Jałbrzykowski, of her revelations in the hope that he might support her. She did so in August 1935, when the archbishop visited her convent and heard her confession. His response disappointed her deeply: "As regards your leaving the Congregation and thinking of another one, do not entertain such thoughts, for this would be a serious interior temptation."[42] Crestfallen, Faustina turned to Jesus in prayer, and she emerged reassured that the archbishop would be made to understand.

Faustina had another opportunity to speak to Archbishop Jałbrzykowski on January 8, 1936. She explained once again that Jesus was calling for the creation of a new congregation that would "entreat the mercy of God for the world." His response suggests that he sought to put her off as diplomatically as he could: "As regards this congregation, wait a while, Sister, so that all things may arrange themselves more favorably. This thing is good in itself, but there is no need to hurry. If it is God's will, it will be done, whether it be a little sooner or a little later." Faustina was frustrated and perplexed that a prelate of Jałbrzykowski's stature should disregard what she understood to be God's will. She describes subsequent mystical experiences that seem to reflect her inner turmoil. She heard a voice that said, **"They will oppose you in many things, and through this My grace will be manifest in you, and it will be evident that this matter is My doing."**[43] She also sensed that Jesus was displeased with the archbishop for not trusting her, and she pleaded with Jesus on his behalf.[44]

Deference and Agency

Faustina's willingness to talk about her ambitious plans with her archbishop, and then to bring the matter up again after he dismissed them, are telling indications of the assertiveness she was able to summon in her interactions with clerics. It is clear

---

42 Ibid., par. 473.
43 Ibid., pars. 585–86.
44 Ibid., par. 595.

from her writings that Faustina understood and generally exhibited the deference the Church expected lay Catholics, and especially women, to show toward their confessors. Reflecting upon her early attempts to make sense of her mystical experiences, she writes, "For many very good reasons, I learned that a woman is not called to discern such mysteries."[45] She repeatedly emphasizes the importance of having a wise confessor, and she notes the following concerning Sopoćko: "My confessor is an oracle for me. His word is sacred to me."[46] At the same time, her mystical experiences convinced her both that God was calling her to undertake major works that could save countless souls from damnation, and that she would be held accountable if these works failed to come to fruition. With so much at stake, she simply had to win over capable allies to her cause, and the most obvious candidates were the priests in whom she confided.

This helps explain Faustina's boldness during her first encounters with Sopoćko in the summer of 1933, which he described in written testimony in 1948. Upon seeing him, Faustina believed that she recognized him from an earlier vision, and a voice in her soul identified him as the one who would assist her in her work.[47] Faustina promptly informed the priest that God had told her that he was to help her realize the grand designs God had entrusted to her. The audacity of her claims made Sopoćko uncomfortable, and he ordered that she find a different confessor. Faustina sought him out again not long thereafter, insisting that she would endure whatever she had to in order to retain his counsel and support. Impressed by her persistence, Sopoćko relented.[48]

Sopoćko eventually directed Faustina to keep a diary, which she was given to understand that he might read from time to time. The diary offered her another means of influencing her confessor,

---

[45] Ibid., par. 123.

[46] Ibid., par. 293.

[47] In this experience, the voice in her soul said, "**This is the visible help for you on earth.**" Kowalska, *Diary*, par. 53.

[48] M. Elżbieta Siepak, *Wspomnienia o świętej Siostrze Faustynie Kowalskiej ze Zgromadzenia Matki Bożej Miłosierdzia*, 2nd ed. (Kraków: Wydawnictwo Misericordia, 2015), 53–54.

and some of her entries seem designed, at least in part, to encourage his perseverance in the challenging work she believed he was being called to undertake. When Sopoćko displayed the aforementioned painting in the Ostra Brama shrine, for instance, Faustina describes the following vision she had while attending Mass there: The painting "came alive and the rays pierced the hearts of the people gathered there."[49] After Sopoćko took her to view the dilapidated house in Vilnius, Faustina recorded the following affirmation: "I am delighted that God is acting in this way through my confessor. . . . God is giving him so much light."[50]

After she was transferred from Vilnius in March 1936, Faustina exchanged letters with Sopoćko for the remaining two years of her life, and the surviving correspondence offers a valuable perspective on their relationship. She was the more active correspondent, writing nineteen letters to his seven. While always gracious, Faustina displayed flashes of impatience in her letters, politely pressing her confessor for information concerning his efforts to promote the image of her vision of Christ, the feast day devoted to God's mercy, and the founding of a new congregation. "I am eager to know more, dear Father, about your affairs and your efforts concerning the various works of God," she writes in a letter on March 24, 1937.[51] Sopoćko repeatedly stressed the importance of proceeding cautiously and deliberately with projects of such magnitude. Faustina, by contrast, was inclined to bold steps. In a July 5, 1936, letter she floated the idea of her traveling to Rome to petition the pope directly concerning the founding of a new congregation.[52] In letters dated November 19, 1936, and April 11, 1937, she suggested that she could write Archbishop Jałbrzykowski, who had been resisting Sopoćko's efforts.[53] Sopoćko discouraged these ideas, believing they could backfire.

[49] Kowalska, *Diary*, par. 417.

[50] Ibid., par. 573.

[51] M. Beata Piekut, ed., *Listy świętej Siostry Faustyny* (Kraków: Wydawnictwo Misericordia, 2005), 76.

[52] Ibid., 42.

[53] Ibid., 62 and 79.

Another measure of Faustina's agency can be found in the relative stability of her private revelations over time. In the cases of Gemma Galgani and Claire Ferchaud described above, the messages they articulated appear to have evolved under the influence of domineering confessors. The same dynamic is not apparent in the relationship between Faustina and Sopoćko. Part of the explanation for this may be that Sopoćko simply had a gentler temperament and lacked the kind of agendas that drove the priests who were guiding Gemma and Claire. It also seems that the force of Faustina's convictions and the content of her private revelations persuaded Sopoćko that he was entangled in a divine enterprise. This disposed him to listen carefully to Faustina and to execute her ideas as faithfully as possible.

Final Years

The vibrancy of Faustina's interior life during her years in Vilnius coincided with her physical deterioration, which ultimately led to a diagnosis of tuberculosis. Her superiors determined in March 1936 that Faustina's fragile health necessitated a transfer to the more agreeable climate of southern Poland. Faustina was disappointed by this news, in part because it would deprive her of regular contact with Sopoćko, not to mention Mother Irena Krzyżanowska, the superior of the convent in Vilnius who gradually had come to believe in the divine origins of Faustina's visions. In her diary she recorded her fear that she "would be alone again and would not know what to do."[54] These words proved to be prophetic.

Faustina stayed for a short time in a convent in Walendów. While there she went to confession with a priest named Bukowski, and during their conversation she described some of her mystical experiences, including those related to the founding of a new congregation. Bukowski reacted in alarm. Shouting loudly, he warned: "Sister, this is an illusion. The Lord Jesus cannot be demanding this. You have made your perpetual vows. All this is an

---

[54] Kowalska, *Diary*, par. 627.

illusion. You are inventing some sort of heresy!" He then gave her the following instruction: "You must not follow any inspiration. You should get your mind off all this. You should pay no attention to what you hear in your soul and try to carry out your exterior duties well." Faustina was devastated by the encounter. She writes: "Great darkness fell upon my soul. I feared lest I hear some inner voice."[55]

Bolstered by fresh revelations, Faustina soon regained confidence in the interior messages she had been receiving. Finding sympathetic ears and powerful allies continued to be a struggle, however. Not long after she had settled in at her congregation's convent in Łagiewniki, just south of Kraków, Archbishop Jałbrzykowski paid a short visit to the community on September 14, 1936. During a brief encounter, Faustina reminded the archbishop of her proposal for a new congregation. He once again counseled patience: "The Lord Jesus will arrange the circumstances in such a way that everything will turn out all right."[56] When Faustina inquired with Mother General Michaela Moraczewska on October 31, 1936, about the possibility of leaving the congregation in order to found a new one, her superior answered: "If Jesus demands of you that you leave this Congregation, let Him give me some sign that this is His will. Sister, pray for such a sign, because I am worried lest you should fall prey to some illusion."[57] A month later, Faustina recorded the following bitter words in her diary: "I see my superiors' disbelief and doubts of all kinds and, for this reason, their apprehensive behavior towards me."[58]

The discouraging reactions of priests and superiors to her mission, along with frank assessments of her own lack of influence, occasionally led Faustina to abandon hope. On January 14, 1937, she recorded the following conversation with Jesus: "You see very well that I am not in good health, that I have no education, that I have no money, that I am an abyss of misery, that I fear contacts

---

[55] Ibid., pars. 643–44.
[56] Ibid., par. 693.
[57] Ibid., par. 750.
[58] Ibid., par. 786.

with people."[59] Invariably, however, new mystical encounters and
the spiritual joys that accompanied them would remedy her despair. In making sense of her tumultuous interior life, Faustina
repeatedly circled back to the conclusion that God and Satan were
at war in her soul. "Although the temptations are strong, a whole
wave of doubts beats against my soul, and discouragement stands
by, ready to enter into the act. The Lord, however, strengthens my
will, against which all the attempts of the enemy are shattered as
if against a rock."[60]

In the final two years of her life, Faustina occasionally had
the opportunity to speak with Fr. Józef Andrasz, one of the first
priests who gave credence to her interior experiences. Faustina's
descriptions of these encounters suggest that, as gently as he
could, Andrasz sought to soften her ambitions regarding a new
congregation. On August 15, 1937, he counseled: "As regards the
matters in question, be absolutely obedient to the Archbishop
[Jałbrzykowski]. . . . Sometimes, a little bitter truth is necessary."[61] They met again on February 27, 1938, as Faustina's physical
condition was growing increasingly dire, and he offered the following words: "As for yourself, try to be a good religious here—
although things may turn out that way also—but try to be a good
religious right here."[62]

In these final years, Faustina was encouraged by letters and
visits from Sopoćko, who remained as committed as ever to her
cause. In 1936, he published a series of articles about her visionary
experiences in a periodical sponsored by the Archdiocese of Vilnius, which included a reproduction of Kazimirowski's painting.[63]
Faustina was elated to receive a copy of one of the articles in
August 1936, and before long she experienced another remarkable
vision: "I suddenly saw the Lord Jesus in a great brightness, just
as He is painted, and at His feet I saw Father Andrasz and Father

[59] Ibid., par. 881.
[60] Ibid., par. 1,086.
[61] Ibid., par. 1,243.
[62] Ibid., par. 1,618.
[63] Michał Sopoćko, *Jezus Król Miłosierdzia: Artykuły z lat 1936–1975* (Warsaw:
Wydawnictwo Księży Marianów, 2005), 33–52.

Sopoćko. Both were holding pens in their hands, and flashes of light and fire, like lightning, were coming from the tips of their pens and striking a great crowd of people who were hurrying I know not where."[64] This vision offered a powerful affirmation of the two confessors who supported Faustina the most in her life as a mystic.

Conclusion

After a grueling struggle with tuberculosis, Faustina finally succumbed on October 5, 1938. At that point, her many mystical experiences had yielded few concrete results. An image of her vision of Christ had been painted, but only a modest number of people had ever seen it.[65] Sopoćko published a pamphlet in 1937 that contained a specific set of prayers that, according to Faustina, Christ had dictated to her, but the prayers had yet to become widely known.[66] Her call for the creation of a Catholic feast day devoted to God's mercy and the founding of a new women's congregation had generated no significant momentum.

Faustina's actual accomplishments, though, were considerably greater than this brief résumé suggests. In winning over Andrasz and Sopoćko, she gained influential allies who continued to pro-mote her causes for the remainder of their lives. In the decades following her death, they helped build a growing devotion to the image of the Divine Mercy and the prayer that accompanied it, first in Poland and then abroad. While living in Kraków in the early 1940s, a young seminarian named Karol Wojtyła discovered the devotion, and he became its most consequential advocate in his later career as archbishop of Kraków and then as Pope John Paul II. On April 30, 2000, he canonized Faustina and introduced

---

[64] Kowalska, *Diary*, par. 675.

[65] After the painting was completed, Sopoćko initially had it hung in the corridor of a Bernardine convent in Vilnius. As noted earlier in the chapter, the painting was briefly displayed in the Ostra Brama shrine in 1935. In 1937, it was relocated to St. Michael's Church in Vilnius, where Sopoćko served as rector.

[66] Faustina detailed the content of the prayers in a letter to Sopoćko on October 12, 1936. Piekut, *Listy świętej*, 57–61.

Divine Mercy Sunday into the liturgical calendar of the Catholic Church.

Aside from Andrasz and Sopoćko, most of the priests in whom Faustina confided remained decidedly cool to her remarkable claims. This skepticism was consonant with a common wisdom among Catholic clergy, who were well aware that spurious revelations could lead the faithful astray and bring discredit upon the Church as a whole. In *The Graces of Interior Prayer*, Augustin Poulain recommends no less than seven inquiries into the lives of would-be mystics and nine inquiries into purported revelations in order to determine the veracity of the same. Sopoćko himself was initially skeptical, which led him to have Faustina evaluated by a psychiatrist.

If it is wise for priests to doubt claims to private revelations, such skepticism cannot be absolute. The Catholic Church long has acknowledged the principle that God sometimes communicates to individuals messages intended for the broader community of faith. Priests are often the first ones to encounter would-be mystics, and their responses can determine whether a purported revelation finds a wider hearing. Andrasz and Sopoćko ultimately determined that Faustina possessed the qualities of a genuine visionary. In affirming her experiences, they bolstered her confidence in the integrity of her interior life and raised her stature within her congregation. They also had the means to give tangible shape to her visions. Without the support of these sympathetic confessors, it is difficult to imagine how Faustina could have made a significant mark on the wider Church.

From a Catholic standpoint, priestly engagement with would-be mystics is a high-stakes endeavor. Affirming spurious revelations has the potential to sow confusion and embarrass the Church. On the other hand, rejecting genuine revelations carries its own risks. In a certain sense, it can be seen as standing in the way of God. In this regard, Faustina's example offers some assurances. Her encounters with a series of skeptical priests left her deeply discouraged, and yet she persisted. After each discouragement, fresh mystical experiences convinced her that God would not let her rest until her mission was completed. This pattern suggests that genuine revelations are not so easily thwarted.

By aligning themselves with purported mystics, priests also run risks on a personal level. Mystical claims invariably generate controversy, and priests who vouch for the veracity of the same can face hostile scrutiny. As Sopoćko went public with his advocacy of the Divine Mercy devotion and Faustina's role therein in the late 1940s and early 1950s, he paid a heavy price, at least in the short term. He was criticized by opponents of the devotion, was silenced by his archbishop, and had to endure the humiliating prohibition of the Divine Mercy devotion by the Vatican starting in 1959. His reputation was gradually rehabilitated, in tandem with the devotion itself, in the years before his death in 1975. Pope Benedict XVI beatified Sopoćko in 2008.

Another risk is the temptation to manipulate the message of a would-be mystic to conform to a confessor's personal agenda. The temptation has been especially high in instances where priests have directed undereducated female mystics, on account of the higher status and authority priests typically possess in such relationships. As noted above, Gemma Galgani and Claire Ferchaud both found themselves being directed by forceful confessors who seemed determined to channel the mystical experiences of these women toward preordained ends. There is little evidence of such manipulation in Faustina's case. This humble nun and her primary confessor were convinced that God had chosen them to help advance a devotional program with ramifications for the Catholic Church around the globe. Before the magnitude and audacity of such a charge, they could only tremble.

CHAPTER SIX

Blessed by the Cross:
The Spiritual Correspondence of
St. Teresa Benedicta of the Cross

Fr. Thomas Gricoski, OSB

Should we strive for perfect love, you ask? Absolutely. For
this we were created. Perfect love will be our eternal life. . . .
Jesus became incarnate in order to be our way. What can we
do? Try with all our might to be empty: the senses mortified;
the memory as free as possible from all images of this world
and, through hope, directed toward heaven; the understanding stripped of natural seeking and ruminating, directed
to God in the straightforward gaze of faith; the will (as I have
already said) surrendered to God in love.[1]

St. Teresa Benedicta of the Cross (1891–1942) is an unlikely and
challenging model for spiritual directors. Born Edith Stein, Teresa
Benedicta never wrote a treatise on spiritual direction. She had no
spiritual directees in the traditional sense. But through her letters
she responds to numerous requests for spiritual direction. She
received requests for life advice, spiritual direction, and vocational

---

[1] Edith Stein, *Self-Portrait in Letters, 1916–1942*, ed. Lucy Gelber and Romaeus
Leuven, trans. Josephine Koeppel, The Collected Works of Edith Stein, vol. 5 (Washington, DC: ICS Publications, 1993), 317, Letter 311.

discernment from students, friends, and admirers. At least one-third of her letters contain some kernel of spiritual direction for their recipients. The spiritual advice of Edith Stein is clear and consistent: Take up your cross. The cross was no mere motto for Teresa Benedicta, since she lived what she taught, and gave her life as a martyr at Auschwitz in 1942. This chapter elaborates the cruciform spirituality of Teresa Benedicta as a model for spiritual directors.

This study of Edith Stein's practice of spiritual direction via correspondence yields three primary conclusions. First, spiritual direction can be an informal and occasional matter between friends or acquaintances, where one person helps another in their relationship with God. Second, those who lead a spiritual and holy life will attract the attention of those who wish to live with a similar spiritual intensity and clarity. And third, spiritual direction is not primarily about offering consolation or even teaching advanced forms of prayer, but ultimately leads one to imitate Christ's selfless love, in prayer and deed.

This chapter has two sections. First, I sketch Stein's biography as a profile in spiritual development. Stein's faith story moves from Judaism, to atheism, to Catholicism, to Carmelite mysticism, and finally to self-offering and martyrdom. The moments of providential and occasional guidance will be added to the elements of formal spiritual direction in her story. Second, I give examples of Stein's spiritual direction through written correspondence. Links to her spiritual and theological writings indicate the cruciform spirituality from which Stein spoke and assisted others. The spiritualities of St. John of the Cross and St. Teresa of Avila influenced her profoundly. In dialogue with her Carmelite forebears, the saint learned and practiced a true science of the cross. This spiritual life made her a beacon for other seekers, as well as prepared her for heroic sanctity and martyrdom. The external acceptance of suffering is enabled only by an interior faith. Stein integrated Teresa of Avila's spirituality of interiority into her philosophical vision of the human soul. The life and writings of John of the Cross inspired Stein to make the cross of Christ the focal point of her life.

These influences combined in a philosophical mind to produce a keenly aware mystic who attracted the attention of many women and men looking for direction in their lives.

Conversion to the Cross

Stein attributed her spiritual path to so many providential encounters: a grandfather's piety, an older sister's skepticism, a professor's lecture on mysticism, a grieving widow's strength, an anonymous woman's reverence before the Blessed Sacrament, hearing a devout hymn, the chance finding of a book, and several other pivotal moments. The story of these pivotal moments of gradual conversion stands as a test case for the value of occasional and informal spiritual encounters. In such chance encounters the fingerprints of Divine Providence are more easily discerned, because one was not expecting to find God there.

Edith Stein was born in 1891, the eleventh and last child of a pious Prussian Jewish family in Breslau, Silesia (present-day Wrocław, Poland). The day of her birth provided the first clue that this child was destined for something great and holy: Edith was born on Yom Kippur, the Day of Atonement. The customs for this day are described in the Pentateuch: a day of fasting and penance, the high priest entering the holy of holies to sprinkle blood on the mercy seat, the rite of the scapegoat, and many hours spent in prayer.[2] Later in life, when the Second World War was escalating, Sr. Teresa Benedicta asked permission from her mother superior to "allow me to offer myself to the heart of Jesus as a sacrifice of atonement for true peace."[3] By 1938, she had already begun to see herself as interceding for the salvation of others, calling herself a "very poor and powerless little Esther."[4] Queen Esther was estranged from Hebrew practices by living in the household of the

---

[2] Cf. Lev 16:1-34; 23:26-32; 25:9; Num 29:7–11; Heb 6:19; 9:7.

[3] Stein, *Self-Portrait in Letters*, Letter 296.

[4] Ibid., Letter 281. "I keep having to think of Queen Esther who was taken from among her people precisely that she might represent them before the king. I am a very poor and powerless little Esther, but the King who chose me is infinitely great and merciful. That is such a great comfort."

Persian king Ahasuerus. By her conversion to Catholicism, Edith suffered a degree of estrangement from her family, particularly her mother. Edith saw this estrangement, however, as serving a higher purpose: to appeal to Christ the King for the salvation of her people.

Such biblical self-understandings flower within a pious religious culture. As the youngest child in the Stein family, Edith was to ask the four questions at the Seder meal every Passover: Why is this night different from all other nights? In her autobiography, Stein describes growing up in a fairly observant Jewish household. She recalls the piety of her maternal great-grandfather, who sang the prayers at synagogue and had a room devoted to prayer in his home.[5] Her mother grew up in an observant Jewish home and attended a Jewish school set up by Edith's grandfather. Edith notes that her family observed all of the Jewish religious prescriptions, but did not engage in intensive daily Talmudic studies at home.[6] The Stein family practiced their Judaism while also working to integrate into German society.

Stein wrote her autobiography, *Life in a Jewish Family*, during the rise of National Socialism precisely to show how normal and well-integrated Jews were in German society. The work is meant to dispel anti-Jewish myths, to open a window into a typical German Jewish family.[7] Stein's father, Siegfried, ran a lumber business. He died of heatstroke while inspecting a forest in 1893, when Edith was two years old. Stein's mother, Auguste, decided to run the business herself and provide for her family. Stein's oldest brother, Paul, was a banker; Else was a teacher; Arno worked in the family business; Rosa (who died alongside Edith at Auschwitz-Birkenau) converted to Catholicism and worked for the Carmelite nuns; Erna became a physician; Edith was a philosopher, teacher, speaker on women's topics, Carmelite nun, and martyr.

---

[5] Edith Stein, *Life in a Jewish Family: Her Unfinished Autobiographical Account*, ed. Lucy Gelber and Romaeus Leuven, trans. Josephine Koeppel, The Collected Works of Edith Stein, vol. 1 (Washington, DC: ICS Publications, 1986), 27.

[6] Ibid., 30–31.

[7] Ibid., 23–25.

At least one of Stein's older siblings veered away from their religious upbringing. Edith describes Else and her husband, Max, as "totally without belief, religion had no place whatsoever in their home."[8] At age fourteen, Edith was sent to live with her sister and brother-in-law to help take care of the children and to learn how to manage a household. She stayed for ten months with her sister, during which time she "read much that was not good for me."[9] Stein writes that during this time she "deliberately and consciously gave up praying."[10] Although it is normal for a teenager to question her faith, it is arguable that the secular environment of her sister's home influenced Edith's decision to stop praying. Her lack of prayer may indicate a lack of faith, because the transition did not derive from mere disinterest but rather resulted from a "deliberate and conscious" decision. She does not seem to have busied herself with active atheism. Nonetheless, her newfound unbelief would persist for at least thirteen years. It would take several providential encounters before Edith would profess faith in God again. A childhood faith was rather easily supplanted, while adolescent atheism was harder to uproot.

The future scholar was not always interested in searching for the truth. Edith had been sent to live with her sister Else because she no longer wished to go to school. She had finished her studies at a school for girls in Breslau, equivalent to junior high school. Those who wished to enter university would prolong their studies by enrolling in a *Gymnasium*, a preparatory school. Although her grades were excellent, Edith wished to end her education and not enter the *Gymnasium* or university.[11]

During her ten months at her sister's home in Hamburg, Edith changed her mind and decided to enroll in the *Gymnasium*. Around this time an earnest search for truth was kindled. Her future novice mistress, Sr. Teresia Renata Posselt, attributes this phrase to Teresa

[8] Ibid., 148.
[9] Ibid.
[10] Ibid.
[11] Ibid., 15–16.

Benedicta: "My longing for truth was a continuous prayer."[12] Her search for truth led her to the University of Breslau, where she studied psychology for two years. She was recommended to read a recent book about philosophy to help her grapple with the foundations of psychology. The book was Edmund Husserl's *Logical Investigations*, which is the seminal work of the new philosophical method of phenomenology. Edith was so impressed by Husserl's project that she transferred to the University of Göttingen where he was lecturing. Phenomenology was a new current in German philosophy because it asserted confidence in one's ability to know the truth. Husserl's primary assertion was the concept of intentionality—that consciousness always encounters an object. The object shows itself to consciousness, which must look at the object from multiple viewpoints in order to gain a fuller understanding.

Essential to the phenomenological method is an unrestricted interest in all phenomena, all that which appears to consciousness. Phenomenology does not limit itself to studying material phenomena, or scientific phenomena. The radical openness of phenomenology led its practitioners to consider interior phenomena, such as empathy, memory, and religious experience. By refusing to deny the possibility of religious experience, phenomenology works as a kind of Trojan horse for faith. A number of phenomenologists experienced religious conversions during their studies. Husserl himself and his wife, Malvine, were Jewish converts to Lutheranism.

In addition to possibly reading about Christian religious experience, Stein witnessed a small example of Christian worship. An anonymous woman's act of piety made a strong impression on Edith shortly before she defended her dissertation in philosophy in 1916. Edith and Pauline Reinach were touring the old city section of Frankfurt when they entered the cathedral:

---

[12] Teresia Renata Posselt, *Edith Stein: The Life of a Philosopher and Carmelite*, ed. Susanne M. Batzdorff, Josephine Koeppel, and John Sullivan (Washington, DC: ICS Publications, 2005), 63.

> We stopped in at the cathedral for a few minutes; and, while
> we looked around in respectful silence, a woman carrying a
> market basket came in and knelt down in one of the pews to
> pray briefly. This was something entirely new to me. To the
> synagogues or to the Protestant churches which I had visited,
> one went only for services. But here was someone interrupt-
> ing her everyday shopping errands to come into this church,
> although no other person was in it, as though she were here
> for an intimate conversation. I could never forget that.[13]

The common act of Catholic piety impressed Edith with the
sense of an interior and intimate conversation. The possibility of
such an interior conversation must have intrigued the young philosopher who had spent years introspecting and examining her
consciousness. The subject of Stein's doctoral project is the question of empathy, particularly what it means to share someone's
experience in a secondhand way. A mother who winces when she
sees a young child scrape her knee is experiencing the child's pain
empathetically. Edith was perhaps experiencing this anonymous
woman's sense of intimacy and communion with an interior inter-
locutor. The phenomenological method not only attracted a
woman who was keen on introspection and carefully paying attention to interior consciousness. It also seems to have deepened
Stein's awareness of her own interiority and, through empathy,
the interior lives of others. Being aware of one's interior reality is
essential to the spiritual life; similarly, empathy is an essential skill
for spiritual directors.

Stein's empathy for a friend prompted the pivotal moment of
Stein's conversion to faith in Christ. In November 1917, Stein received the news that her friend and colleague Adolf Reinach had
been killed on the front in Flanders. Adolf Reinach was husband
to Anna and brother to Pauline. Pauline and Adolf were both
friends with Edith through their scholarly work, but Edith was
only acquainted with Adolf's wife, Anna. In Stein's biography,
Posselt writes that when Stein prepared to go to visit Anna "she
feared to find Frau Reinach, whom she had only known as this

[13] Stein, *Life in a Jewish Family*, 401.

fine man's radiantly happy wife, transformed into a broken, despairing widow."[14] This empathetic anticipation of Anna's grief gave way, however, to Edith's surprise at Anna's fortitude.

According to Posselt's interpretation, Anna indicated that the cross of Christ was the source of her strength, that she did not regard her husband's death as a cruel twist of fate, but rather accepted the death as "part of her Master's holy Cross."[15] The details of this pivotal encounter were only recorded in a letter from a priest to Stein's novice mistress some eight years after the martyr's death. The priest was Fr. Johannes Hirschmann, SJ, who belonged to the Jesuit residence at Valkenburg, in the Limburg region of the Netherlands, about twenty miles away from the Carmel in Echt to which Teresa Benedicta had fled in 1938. Hirschmann writes to Posselt in 1950 to relate Teresa Benedicta's words during a conversation they had in the parlor in Echt: "This was my first encounter with the Cross and the divine power it imparts to those who bear it. For the first time I saw before my very eyes the Church, born of Christ's redemptive suffering, victorious over the sting of death. It was the moment when my unbelief was shattered, Judaism paled, and Christ radiated before me: Christ in the mystery of the Cross."[16]

When encountered for the first time, or at least when one attempts to grapple with its logic, the mystery of Christ crucified is indeed "a stumbling block to Jews and foolishness to Gentiles" (1 Cor 1:23). For Stein, as an unbelieving Jewish philosopher, the cross of Christ could be both a stumbling block and foolishness. Rather than turn away, however, she peered closer. It would be four more years until Edith would request baptism.

Hedwig Conrad-Martius describes the atmosphere of religious conversion that lived in the background of the phenomenological circle.[17] The Reinachs were Jewish converts to Christianity. Only

---

[14] Posselt, *Edith Stein*, 59.

[15] Ibid., 59.

[16] Ibid., 59–60.

[17] Edith Stein, *Briefe an Hedwig Conrad-Martius (Mit einem Essay über Edith Stein)*, ed. Hedwig Conrad-Martius (München: Kösel-Verlag, 1960), 67. "Husserl, who was baptized Lutheran in his younger years [age twenty-eight], was Jewish. Adolf Reinach

a year before his death, Adolf and Anna Reinach were baptized by a Lutheran minister. Adolf found meaning in wartime tragedies through his faith: "They serve to bring men closer to God."[18] It was at Hedwig's home, however, that Edith would experience the decisive encounter that led her quickly to request baptism at the nearest Catholic parish.

In addition to the practice of Christianity, Edith Stein may have also become acquainted during these years with the contemplative and mystical spiritual practices that would attract her later to enter Carmel. Rudolf Otto (1867–1937) taught theology at Breslau and Göttingen, although he and Stein do not seem to have crossed paths. Stein would have likely been familiar, however, with Otto's influential work on religious experience and the sacred or "numinous" dimension of reality. Husserl lectured on Otto's *The Idea of the Holy* in 1918 at Freiburg while Stein was there working with Husserl.[19] She also cites at least one work by the American philosopher of religion William James, and so it is possible she read his *Varieties of Religious Experience*, first published in 1902. Both James and Otto mention John of the Cross, the Spanish Carmelite mystic with whom Stein would later find spiritual kinship.[20]

The decisive spiritual encounter in Edith's conversion came through reading another book, Teresa of Avila's autobiography,

---

was Jewish. He was baptized Lutheran with his Jewish wife on furlough during the First World War. His wife, who was among our very close friends, later converted to Catholicism. Max Scheler, who in that time often came from Bonn to philosophize with us in Göttingen for a week, was a [Catholic] converted Jew. A great number of Husserl's students at that time were Jewish."

[18] Sylvie Courtine-Denamy, *Three Women in Dark Times: Edith Stein, Hannah Arendt, Simone Weil, or, Amor Fati, Amor Mundi*, trans. G. M. Goshgarian (Ithaca, NY: Cornell University Press, 2000), 14, http://archive.org/details/threewomenindark00cour_0.

[19] "Edith Stein's Conversion Was No Coincidence," *ZENIT English* (blog), February 8, 2007, https://zenit.org/articles/edith-stein-s-conversion-was-no-coincidence/. The article quotes Fr. Ulrich Dobhan, OCD, Carmelite Provincial in Germany.

[20] For an overview of the connections between Stein and John of the Cross, see Harm Klueting, "Edith Stein and John of the Cross: An Intellectual and Spiritual Relation from Husserl's Lecture in 1918 to the Gas Chamber of Auschwitz in 1942," in *Intersubjectivity, Humanity, and Being. Edith Stein's Phenomenology and Christian Philosophy*, ed. Mette Lebech (Bern: Peter Lang, 2015); Steven Payne, "Edith Stein and John of the Cross," *Teresianum* 50, no. 1 (1999): 239–56.

which she discovered during a stay in the home of her friends Theodor and Hedwig Conrad-Martius in the summer of 1921. Posselt again gives us her recollection of Stein's story: "I picked at random and took out a large volume. It bore the title *The Life of St. Teresa of Avila*, written by herself. I began to read, was at once captivated, and did not stop till I reached the end. As I closed the book, I said, 'That is the truth.'"[21] A short time later, Edith went out to purchase a Catholic catechism and missal. After studying these materials, she attended her first Catholic Mass, at the parish church near Hedwig's home, in Bad Bergzabern. Because of her study of the missal, she found the Mass familiar. After Mass she approached the priest, seventy-year-old Eugen Breitling, and "without more ado asked him for baptism."[22] The priest was surprised and indicated that there would need to be a period of instruction before one could be baptized. Since Stein had been studying on her own, she reportedly said, "Please, Father, test me."[23]

This climactic story of Stein's conversion comes to us through her novice mistress. Stein herself did not write about these events and only spoke of them to a few confidants. Although she would find that others were sharing their spiritual life and asking for advice from her, Edith was reluctant to communicate her most intimate interior experiences. Her spiritual writings are surely written from a place of personal experience, but they are not first-person narrations of her interior life. Her family was perhaps most curious about Edith's conversion, and they seem to have received the least insight from Edith. When asked about her conversion to Catholicism, or why she wanted to become a Carmelite nun, she would say to her family "*secretum meum mihi*," "my secret belongs to me."[24] This reticence, however, was not brought about by her

[21] Posselt, *Edith Stein*, 63.

[22] Ibid., 64.

[23] Ibid., 64.

[24] Susanne M. Batzdorff, *Aunt Edith: The Jewish Heritage of a Catholic Saint* (Springfield, IL: Templegate, 1998), 117–18.

conversion. Even when she was a young woman her family had called her "a book sealed with seven seals."[25]

Edith and Fr. Breitling must have met several times until the date of baptism was set for January 1, 1922. She was thirty years old at the time of her baptism and First Communion. By a special dispensation, her Lutheran friend Hedwig served as her baptismal sponsor. Appropriately, and giving credence to the importance of Teresa of Avila for her conversion, Edith chose the baptismal name Teresa Hedwig.[26] A month later on Candlemas, February 2, she received the sacrament of confirmation in the house chapel of the bishop of Speyer, Ludwig Sebastian. It was around this time that Edith met her first spiritual director, vicar general of the diocese, Canon Joseph Schwind (1851–1927).

Edith's immediate desire was to enter Carmel and take up the contemplative life that she had discovered in the writings of Teresa of Avila. Two factors delayed her entry: Edith's consideration for her mother, who would feel this additional separation acutely, and Fr. Schwind's advice as spiritual director. Some months after her baptism and confirmation, Edith returned to Breslau to visit her mother in June, and then for a longer visit during the fall and winter of that year.[27] Posselt reports Stein's thinking about Carmel and her mother: "Initially when I was baptized on New Year's Day 1922, I thought of it as a preparation for entrance into the Order. But a few months later, when I saw my mother for the first time after the baptism, I realized that she couldn't handle another blow for the present. Not that it would have killed her—but I couldn't have held myself responsible for the embitterment it would have caused."[28] Posselt describes a melodramatic encounter when Edith knelt before her mother and announced, "I am

[25] Stein, *Life in a Jewish Family*, 63.

[26] Posselt, *Edith Stein*, 294.

[27] Edith Stein, *Selbstbildnis in Briefen I (1916–1933)*, ed. Maria Amata Neyer and Hanna Gerl-Falkovitz, Edith Stein Gesamtausgabe 2 (Freiburg im Breisgau: Herder, 2000), n. 3, Brief 37:1922.

[28] Waltraud Herbstrith, *Edith Stein: The Untold Story of the Philosopher and Mystic Who Lost Her Life in the Death Camps of Auschwitz*, trans. Bernard Bonowitz, 2nd ed. (San Francisco: Ignatius Press, 1992), 73.

Catholic."[29] Edith's niece Susanne Batzdorff disputes this account by arguing that such histrionics were not in Edith's character. Batzdorff confirms that there were silent tears when the decision to enter Carmel had been announced years later.[30]

Edith's spiritual director encouraged her to delay entering Carmel for positive reasons also. While she had been pursuing a secular career as a philosopher, and now felt the call to lead the religious life of a cloistered nun, Canon Schwind recommended a middle path. He directed her to a teaching position at the nearby St. Magdalena's School, run by the Dominican sisters.[31] Edith would work and live with the sisters from 1923 to 1931, teaching German in both the teachers college and the girls school. The position allowed her to live a relatively secluded life, residing on campus near the convent, while engaging in the apostolic work of teaching. During this time, she gained the love and admiration of her students, and a reputation of holiness and intense devotion to prayer ("her" place for kneeling in the chapel at the convent is remembered to this day).

Accounts from her students at this time reveal how deep an impression Stein made on them, particularly how she was energetic and zealous in both her teaching and her prayer:

> We were seventeen years old, and the Fraulein Doktor taught us German. She really gave us everything. We were still very young, but none of us has forgotten the magic of her personality. We saw her every day at Mass up front in the chapel on her kneeler, and we began to get an inkling of what it means to bring faith and conduct into perfect harmony. To us at that critical age she provided an example simply by her bearing. I would not be able to repeat a single thing she said, not so much because it has not stayed in my memory as because she was a still and silent person who led us only by what she **was**.[32]

[29] Posselt, *Edith Stein*, 294, 348.
[30] Batzdorff, *Aunt Edith*, 83–84.
[31] Posselt, *Edith Stein*, 296.
[32] Ibid., 69.

The middle path between active and contemplative life, imitating the "mixed life" of the Dominican sisters, helped Edith flourish. Her lifelong search for truth had delivered her to a new way of being that was animated by interiority. In a letter from 1928, Stein reflects on her discovery of the interaction between interiority and apostolic work:

> Immediately before, and for a good while after my conversion, I was of the opinion that to lead a religious life meant one had to give up all that was secular and to live totally immersed in thoughts of the Divine. But gradually I realized that something else is asked of us in this world and that, even in the contemplative life, one may not sever the connection with the world. I even believe that the deeper one is drawn into God, the more one must "go out of oneself"; that is, one must go to the world in order to carry the divine life into it.[33]

In addition to her teaching work, her philosophical pursuits began anew when she met a Jesuit priest, Erich Przywara (1889–1972). Przywara and Stein were about the same age, both were Silesian, and both were intellectuals. The two began an academic and spiritual friendship that would last until the martyr's death. Stein had set her philosophical work aside in order to focus on her teaching and prayer, but Przywara introduced her to the intellectual dimension of Catholicism. At Przywara's prompting, Stein took up several philosophical tasks, including translations of Thomas Aquinas and John Henry Newman. Her philosophical pursuits would continue through the rest of her life, thanks to her Carmelite superiors who later assigned her to such work.

At the suggestion of Fr. Przywara, Edith traveled to the Benedictine Abbey of Beuron in 1928 to celebrate the Holy Week liturgies at the place where the liturgical movement was flowering.[34] She visited again and met with the young Abbot Raphael Walzer (1888–1966), a near contemporary of Stein who would become a spiritual confidant and director. Walzer writes of Edith:

[33] Stein, *Self-Portrait in Letters*, Letter 45.
[34] Posselt, *Edith Stein*, 80.

I have seldom met a soul that united so many excellent qualities, and she was simplicity and naturalness personified. She was completely a woman, gentle and even maternal, without ever wanting to "mother" anyone. Gifted with mystical graces, in the true sense of the word, she never gave any sign of affectation or a sense of superiority. She was simple with simple people, learned with the learned yet without presumption, an inquirer with inquirers, and I would almost like to add, a sinner with sinners.[35]

Walzer also attests to Stein's remarkable intensity in prayer, remembering that during one Good Friday she spent the entire day "from early morning until late at night in the abbey church."[36]

Perhaps without realizing it herself, Stein was becoming something of a spiritual director or guide to her students and the Dominican sisters in Speyer. It is remarkable that her predilection for silence, vigils, and speaking readily about God did not alienate her from those around her. Despite her quiet demeanor, she attracted the attention of her pupils and colleagues, until eventually she was invited to deliver various lectures around Europe. After several years of teaching at Speyer, she was offered a lectureship at the German Institute for Scientific Pedagogy in Münster. Through her experience of teaching, and the study of philosophy, Stein developed an anthropology that oriented teachers to the significance of their students as human persons.

The opportunities for entering Carmel may have seemed more remote, since Edith was entering her forties, but circumstances in Germany eventually made it possible. In January 1933 Adolf Hitler came to power in Germany, and soon a series of anti-Jewish laws were passed. Stein was not allowed to return to her lectureship in the fall that year. She traveled to Beuron for Holy Week that year, and on her way stopped to pray at the Carmel in Cologne, on the first Friday of April. During the Holy Hour, Stein experienced this movement in prayer: "I told our Lord that I knew it was His cross that was now being placed upon the Jewish people; that most of

---

[35] Jakobus Kaffanke, ed., *Wie der Vorhof des Himmels: Edith Stein und Beuron* (Beuron: Beuroner Kunstverlag, 2009), 227.

[36] Ibid., 229.

them did not understand this, but that those who did would have to take it up willingly in the name of all. I would do that. At the end of the service, I was certain that I had been heard. But what this carrying of the cross was to consist in, that I did not yet know."[37] Around this same time Stein's desire for entering Carmel reasserted itself, and she consulted her spiritual director, Abbot Raphael Walzer at Beuron. Walzer had even as recently as the previous year refused to bless Edith's request to enter Carmel. She writes: "Before I began my job in Münster and after the first semester I had urgently pleaded for permission to enter the Order. It was denied me with reference to my mother and because of the effectiveness that my work had had in Catholic circles in recent years."[38] Since Stein could no longer lecture in Münster, Abbot Raphael gave his blessing, which Stein received in May 1933. She entered the Carmelite monastery in Cologne in October 1933. After the long wait of a dozen years, her wish had come to fulfillment.

Teresa Benedicta had not been able to wait until either her mother's reconciliation with the Carmelite vocation or her passing from this life, so as to avoid inflicting such a confusing pain on her. Two years after entering the Carmelite monastery, however, she received the first letter from her mother. A year later Auguste Stein passed away, and Edith could not attend the funeral. Rosa Stein (1883–1942), Edith's older sister, had also been seeking baptism but decided to wait until her mother's death. Rosa was baptized on Christmas Eve 1936, and Edith was able to attend due to a providential circumstance.[39]

Teresa Benedicta's first years in Carmel followed the usual plan of postulancy, investiture, first profession, and final profession. During these happy years she continued her spiritual correspondence, and her superiors directed her to resume a degree of philosophical work. On November 8, 1938, anti-Jewish violence erupted

[37] Posselt, *Edith Stein*, 116.

[38] Ibid., 118.

[39] Ibid., 169. Teresa Benedicta had tripped down some stairs in the dark and broke her left foot and left wrist on December 14; she was discharged from the hospital on December 24, and she was able to make the detour to a parish in Hohenlind to witness Rosa's baptism.

in Germany during *Kristallnacht*. Fearing for the safety of her sisters, Teresa Benedicta was transferred to a Carmelite community in Echt, Holland. She crossed the border around midnight on December 31, 1938. She stayed at Echt and awaited the arrival of her sister Rosa. In this Carmelite community, while Rosa assisted the cloistered sisters in their daily business with the outside world, Teresa Benedicta began to write a biography and spiritual treatise on John of the Cross. The Carmelite superiors requested her to prepare the manuscript for the 400th anniversary of John's birth. The mostly completed manuscript for *Science of the Cross* was found on her desk after her arrest and deportation.

On Sunday, July 26, 1942, the Catholic bishops in the Netherlands issued a pastoral letter to be read in all parishes, denouncing the racist and anti-Semitic policies of the occupying Nazi forces. The following Sunday, Teresa Benedicta and Rosa were deported to the Amersfoort prison camp, along with more than one hundred other Catholic Jews in the Netherlands. The group was transferred to Westerbork, and then most of them, Teresa Benedicta and Rosa included, were put on a train to the east. The Red Cross, after the war, determined that the train carrying the two sisters arrived at Auschwitz-Birkenau on Sunday, August 9, 1942, one week after their arrest. That same day they were gassed and cremated without being processed for the labor camp at Auschwitz. St. Pope John Paul II beatified Teresa Benedicta in 1981 in Cologne, canonized her in 1998 in Rome, and named her one of three women patrons of Europe in 1999.

Letters from a Saint

St. Teresa Benedicta carried on a substantial correspondence before and after her conversion to Catholicism. As a philosopher she shared ideas with colleagues, reviewed and commented on drafts of academic works, and directed others to helpful resources in their work. As a Christian, she encouraged her correspondents in their spiritual life, described practical ways of ordering one's life toward prayer and ministry, and in some moments revealed a rich interior life of prayer. Her letters to students, friends, and religious sisters and priests contain bright words of encouragement, naming blessings in their lives that they may have not recognized. There are elements of vocational discernment and advice on preparing for baptism as an adult. She also wrote gently and directly to point out when she sensed that someone was going in the wrong direction or was holding something back in their spiritual life. Reading her letters to spiritual friends is like receiving spiritual direction from a saint who knows what she is doing.

The following excerpts come from Stein's correspondence and her spiritual and theological writings. The texts were written during the period after Stein's baptism, both before and after she entered Carmel. Out of the dozens of letters she wrote of spiritual direction and encouragement, I have selected correspondence from Stein to several women from her years in Speyer. Stein's approach with each one is personalized, responding to unique circumstances and questions. The four women all were in their twenties and thirties, at least ten years younger than Stein, and they were students of hers at St. Magdalena's School. The archival record is one-sided, since most of the letters that Stein received have been lost. It is impossible to know beyond these fragments of spiritual direction how much more deeply these spiritual relationships developed face-to-face. It is presumed that the written advice corresponds well to the spoken conversations in tone and substance. With one of the women, Sr. Callista Kopf, OP (1902–1970), Stein carried on spiritual correspondence for eleven years. I will focus on the spiritual direction in this relationship and supplement it with similar examples from other correspondents.

Sr. Callista was a Dominican sister at Speyer. The editors of Stein's correspondence note that Stein helped prepare Sr. Callista for her *Abitur*, the qualifying exit exam at the end of secondary education, and that she was studying in Munich at the time of the first letter.[40] Their correspondence proceeded from October 1927 to October 1938, and so continued after Stein left Speyer. Kopf

---

[40] Stein, *Selbstbildnis in Briefen I (1916-1933)*, n. 1, Brief 59.

eventually taught German and so was a colleague of Stein's in the school. Some of their correspondence deals with practical advice for managing the balance of work and prayer, and a sense of warm friendship permeates all of the letters. Here are excerpts from four letters that show a variety of Stein's approaches to spiritual direction.

The first letter is addressed October 12, 1927, shortly after Canon Schwind had passed away. Sr. Callista is studying German and history in Munich, and Stein writes to her from Speyer. After some pleasantries, Edith encourages Callista not to worry about one of her confreres, Sr. Agnella Stadtmüller (1898–1965). It is not clear what "cross" Sr. Agnella carried, but one can surmise that Callista had expressed sympathy for her. Stein writes:

> But let me tell you something encouraging now that the new semester is beginning. Sr. Agnella . . . visited me several times even after the Newman manuscript was completed. I believe we need not really worry about her so much. She bears a cross like everyone else, but it has borne fruit for her, and she knows that and so would not wish to give it up. We too, dear Sister, have to learn to see that others have a cross to carry and to realize we cannot take it from them. It is harder than carrying one's own, but it cannot be avoided.[41]

After her decisive encounter with Teresa of Avila's *Life*, it is likely that Stein began a serious study of Carmelite literature, especially works by Teresa and John of the Cross. The advice that Stein offers here seems to stem from at least two sources: Stein's encounter with her friend Adolf Reinach's widow, who found courage in the cross of Christ, and the love of the cross expressed in John of the Cross's writings. Edith witnessed how a cross, carried well, bore fruit for Anna Reinach, who found meaning rather than despair by recognizing the cross in her husband's early death.

Stein continues her advice to Callista, noting that the young sister also has a cross to bear, which she will soon encounter in

[41] Stein, *Self-Portrait in Letters*, Letter 44.

attempting to combine her religious life with her advanced studies:

> I believe you can be of the greatest help to others when you trouble yourself least about how you are to accomplish that, and remain, instead, as unconcerned and cheerful as possible. And when you yourself get to have the difficulties of a religious who is also a student, then tell yourself that this is the very way you are to serve. I expect great benefits for the entire house from Sisters who are pursuing studies: not merely for the schools (obviously, for them they are a necessity) but also for the religious life. Even though you may think, at this moment, that you do not know what I mean by that, you will surely know it after a few semesters.[42]

As a spiritual guide, Stein foresees a further step in Sr. Callista's spiritual development and encourages her toward this growth. In the writings of John of the Cross, Stein discovered the spiritual logic or the "science of the cross" that reveals the connection between cross and resurrection, suffering and glory. Broadly speaking, in John's spiritual schema, the "dark nights" of the senses and the soul are a kind of crucifixion that serve to free one from attachments to anything except God. The result of detachment from all that is not God is attachment or union with God himself. While it is painful to watch another person suffer some deprivation and pain, the outside observer is not privy to the potential transformation of suffering into union with God. Stein encourages Callista to trust that Agnella is finding spiritual fruit from bearing her cross, and so she should be allowed to bear it without interference. With time, Stein predicts that Callista will find the same consolation from bearing her own cross.

To a younger student, Anneliese Lichtenberger (1912–1935), Stein addresses a similar sentiment about the science of the cross in 1932. Here, the redemptive dimension of the cross comes to light. She writes: "There is a vocation to suffer with Christ and thereby to cooperate with him in his work of salvation. When we are

---

[42] Ibid., Letter 44.

united with the Lord, we are members of the mystical body of Christ: Christ lives on in his members and continues to suffer in them. And the suffering borne in union with the Lord is his suffering, incorporated in the great work of salvation and fruitful therein."[43] Again in 1933, Stein joins suffering and union with God in the science of the cross: "For now, I want to wish you very much patience in your suffering, and the ultimate consolation that I have often had to point out to you: that the way of suffering is the surest road to union with the Lord."[44] Stein's awareness of the science of the cross already by 1933 helps explain why she requested her name in Carmel to be Sr. Teresa Benedicta of the Cross. The name bears a double meaning. The apparent meaning is that Stein wished to be known by the same moniker of St. John "of the Cross," while also honoring her devotion to St. Teresa of Avila and St. Benedict of Nursia.[45] The second meaning appears in the Latin form of the name "Teresia Benedicta a Cruce," "Teresa *blessed by the Cross*." Stein describes her choice to Mother Petra Brüning, OSU (1879–1955), in 1938:

> I must tell you that I already brought my religious name with me into the house as a postulant. I received it exactly as I requested it. By the cross I understood the destiny of God's people which, even at that time, began to announce itself. I thought that those who recognized it as the cross of Christ had to take it upon themselves in the name of all. Certainly, today I know more of what it means to be wedded to the Lord in the sign of the Cross. Of course, one can never comprehend it, for it is a mystery.[46]

Less than a year before her death, while residing at the Carmel in Echt, Stein was awaiting an opportunity to move to the Carmel of Le Pâquier in Switzerland. She wrote a letter to the superior at

---

[43] Ibid., Letter 129.

[44] Ibid., Letter 148.

[45] Stein made many trips to the Abbey of Beuron, as well as the Benedictine community of nuns in Freiburg, Saint Lioba Monastery. She kept a holy card of St. Benedict on her door in Carmel as a nameplate.

[46] Ibid., Letter 287.

Echt, Mother Ambrosia Antonia Engelmann, OCD (1875–1972), expressing her hope and resignation at whatever may happen:

> Once Y.R. has read the letter from [Fr. Hirschmann, SJ] you will know his opinion. Now I would like to do nothing more at all about the matter of my stability. I put it in Your Reverence's hands and leave it to Your Reverence whether to call on the Sisters, Pater Provincial, or our Father Bishop for a decision. I am satisfied with everything. A *scientia crucis* [science of the cross] can be gained only when one comes to feel the Cross radically. I have been convinced of that from the first moment and have said, from my heart: *Ave, Crux, spes unica!* [Hail, Cross, our only hope!][47]

The logic of the connection between cross and resurrection, or cross and union with God, might need to be experienced in order to be believed. The difference between mere suffering and suffering that deepens one's spiritual life perhaps depends on finding a degree of interiority. If Stein learned the "science of the cross" from John of the Cross, she learned the "science of the soul" and how to navigate its interior depths from Teresa of Avila. As an appendix to her longest philosophical treatise, *Finite and Eternal Being*, written while she was in the Carmel in Cologne, Stein summarizes Teresa's metaphor of the soul as an "interior castle."[48] Broadly speaking, Teresa's spiritual teaching on interiority is that God dwells in the inmost depth of the soul. Throughout life God calls each person to enter more deeply into his or her soul and so to come closer to perfect union with God.

Stein's practice of phenomenology required a parallel persistence in introspection and interiority, in order to carefully observe and describe the phenomena that appear to consciousness. The two saints agree on the grades of interiority, but Stein adds a philosophical interpretation. In addition to its vocation to interior union

---

[47] Ibid., Letter 330.

[48] Edith Stein, *Endliches und ewiges Sein: Versuch eines Aufstiegs zum Sinn des Seins; Anhang: Martin Heideggers Existenzphilosophie, Die Seelenburg*, ed. Andreas Uwe Müller, Edith Stein Gesamtausgabe 11–12 (Freiburg im Breisgau: Herder, 2006), 501–25.

with God, phenomenology reaches out to the objects of the world. Stein adds that the soul, as an intellectual spirit, also "has the task of taking in the entire created world in knowledge and love, of understanding its own calling in the world, and of acting in keeping with this calling."[49] Both tasks require a practice of deepening interior awareness. Stein advises Sr. Callista about a practical way to integrate contemplative interiority with a life of study and ministry:

> The only essential is that one finds, first of all, a quiet corner in which one can communicate with God as though there were nothing else, and that must be done daily. It seems to me the best time is in the early morning hours before we begin our daily work; furthermore, [it is also essential] that one accepts one's particular mission there, preferably for each day, and does not make one's own choice. Finally, one is to consider oneself totally as an instrument, especially with regard to the abilities one uses to perform one's special tasks, in our case, e.g., intellectual ones. We are to see them as something used, not by us, but by God in us.[50]

The advice that Stein offers likely reflects her own spiritual practice. The key points of this passage are that prayer requires a daily commitment and that this time be totally dedicated to communicating with God. The first point recalls Teresa's image of prayer as watering a garden.[51] The beginnings of the spiritual life require a great effort, as when one must gather water from a well. As spiritual life deepens, water comes more easily, as through a water wheel, an aqueduct, and eventually effortlessly as rain. The daily commitment to prayer comes at a time when Stein's friend is apparently struggling to maintain the spiritual life she once enjoyed.

---

[49] Edith Stein, *Finite and Eternal Being: An Attempt at an Ascent to the Meaning of Being*, ed. Andreas Uwe Müller, trans. Walter Redmond, The Collected Works of Edith Stein (Washington, DC: ICS Publications, forthcoming), 520.

[50] Stein, *Self-Portrait in Letters*, Letter 45.

[51] Teresa of Avila, *The Collected Works of St. Teresa of Avila*, trans. Kieran Kavanaugh and Otilio Rodríguez (Washington, DC: ICS Publications, 1987), Book of Her Life, chap. 11.

Stein's advice points her to the foundational practices that will lead her again deeper into prayer. The second point, of total dedication to God in prayer, recalls the goal of perfect union with God, as described by both Teresa and John. Continuously redirecting the errant will toward God with renewed dedication foreshadows the total union of wills to which prayer is ordered.

Sr. Callista appears to have requested advice for a related challenge in the spiritual life a few years later, when in 1930 she was studying at Würzburg. Stein offers a word of encouragement to a graduate student who feels swamped by work and who does not know how to accomplish all that is being asked of her. The advice offered here is practical, but bears a sense of detachment and trust in Divine Providence:

> I will answer your questions briefly. I do not use extraordinary means to prolong my workday. I do as much as I can. The ability to accomplish increases noticeably in proportion to the number of things that must be done. When there's nothing urgent at hand, it ceases much sooner. Heaven is expert at economy. Therefore, whatever comes your way after nine o'clock is evidently no longer essential. That, in practice, things do not proceed smoothly according to reason is due to our not being pure spirits. There's no sense in rebelling against that.[52]

After encouraging a directee toward a high ideal of spiritual practice, a director often helps imagine realistic expectations for progress. Simply knowing about and even earnestly desiring a deep union with God, to dwell continuously in the inner mansions of the soul, does not produce a swift transformation in holiness. The duties and demands of life, and the general state of being an embodied creature, make the spiritual life a series of negotiations between interior and exterior, soul and body. Stein encourages Sr. Callista to do the work she can do within a set period, and then

---

[52] Stein, *Self-Portrait in Letters*, Letter 69.

to let the rest go. The prayer of the Swiss saint "Bruder Klaus" is appended, as an aid in trust and detachment.[53]

Stein also offers corrections to some of those with whom she corresponded, urging them to put more effort into their spiritual life. One helpful correction was offered to Erna Herrmann (1902–1977) who was also Stein's student at Speyer. Erna sometimes required gentle prodding. She was preparing for baptism, which she received in 1931 at the same bishop's house chapel in Speyer where Edith was confirmed.[54] Although Edith was not her sponsor, she helped prepare Erna for baptism, which both women received around the age of thirty. As the date of baptism came closer, Edith answered practical questions about the rite, described her own experience, and encouraged Erna to prepare for the momentous occasion: "It is in the nature of such an event that before the decisive step is taken, you see before you once more all you will be renouncing and risking. That is how it ought to be: that, without any kind of human assurance, you place yourself totally in God's hands, then all the deeper and more beautiful will be the security attained. My wish for your Baptismal Day and for all of your future life is that you may find the fullness of God's peace."[55]

The peace that Edith wishes for Erna echoes the peace she received upon her initiation into the Church. Stein describes the peace that is found in "carrying out their daily duties faithfully," a service which is "perhaps a silent, life-long martyrdom that no one suspects and that is at the same time a source of deep peace and hearty joyousness and a fountain of grace that bubbles over everything."[56] When such peace is not found, it may be an

---

[53] Ibid., Letter 69. "'O Lord God, will to give me / All that leads me to you. / O Lord God, take away from me / All that diverts me from you. / O Lord God, take me, also, from myself / And give me completely to yourself.' These are three graces; the last is the greatest and includes the others; but, take note: one must pray for it. . . ."

[54] Stein, *Selbstbildnis in Briefen I (1916-1933)*, n. 2, Brief 153.

[55] Stein, *Self-Portrait in Letters*, Letter 105.

[56] Edith Stein, *The Hidden Life: Hagiographic Essays, Meditations, Spiritual Texts*, ed. Lucy Gelber and Michael Linssen, trans. Waltraut Stein, The Collected Works of Edith Stein, vol. 4 (Washington, DC: ICS Publications, 1992), 6.

opportunity for a spiritual director to offer a "course correction" to the person's spiritual life. Erna had received such a correction in 1930. It seems that Edith had been stern with Erna in their face-to-face conversations, and thus explained and repeated her instructions. Stein writes that she wishes she could give Erna

> the true childlike spirit that opens the door to the approaching Savior, that can say from the heart—not theoretically but practically in each and every case—"Lord, not mine, but thy will be done." I am telling you this because I would like to help you attain the one thing necessary. In the past months I have often been concerned because, repeatedly, I had the impression that there is still something lacking on this most important point, that an obstinate self-will is present, a tenacious clinging to desires once conceived.[57]

In this passage, Stein expresses her desire for Erna's good, her spiritual flourishing. This wish is expressed through a judgment, spoken tentatively, that Erna is holding herself back from the Lord. Voicing concern in such a direct way is a perilous proposition for spiritual directors, because of the power differential between director and directee. Stein's boldness is all the more remarkable because Erna is not yet baptized and perhaps has not yet decided to request the sacrament. Edith's words have the potential to drive her away, not merely from this spiritual relationship, but from the Church. In the next lines Stein softens, or rather explains, the loving concern behind her stern words:

> And if I have seemed to you, perhaps, hard and relentless because I would not give in to your wishes, then believe me, that was not due to coldness or a lack of love, but because of a firm conviction that I should harm you by acting otherwise. I am only a tool of the Lord. I would like to lead to him anyone who comes to me. And when I notice that this is not the case, but that the interest is invested in my person, then I cannot

---

[57] Stein, *Self-Portrait in Letters*, Letter 76.

serve as a tool and must beg the Lord to help in other ways. After all, he is never dependent on only one individual.[58]

Stein confirms the deep faith she has in Divine Providence, recognizing that her own role in her friends' spiritual lives is not the conductor, but merely one of the instruments of God. This is a lesson that Edith learned throughout her own conversion story, which was filled with providential encounters that brought her to the Lord over a long period of searching. All the while that Stein was searching for the truth, the Truth was drawing her to himself.

Conclusion

I draw three preliminary conclusions based on the example of Stein's life and spiritual direction through correspondence. First, Stein's life gives testimony to the phenomenon that much spiritual direction occurs under another label, between friends and acquaintances. Stein was remarkably perceptive, which contributed to her philosophical abilities and also made her apt to develop a deeply interior spiritual life. Her autobiography and letters reveal a woman well practiced in observation and introspection, noticing subtlety and meaning in small events and short conversations. She realized that God was leading her through the events of her life toward a more and more perfect union with himself. This awareness of Divine Providence acting through circumstantial events and unaware agents seems to have compelled her to cooperate with God's plans by speaking about him to her friends. Even without the title or explicit mandate of being a "spiritual director," all who love God are called to help bring others deeper into divine life. Spiritual direction goes by different names and via many media: on the phone, in emails, letters, and brief conversations. It can take the form of a single interaction that nevertheless proves decisive in a person's life. In this respect, occasional and even "accidental" spiritual direction has much in common with the anonymous celebration of the sacrament of reconciliation. In the

[58] Ibid., Letter 76.

brief words that are shared between penitent and confessor, a new depth and direction in life may be found.

The second conclusion is that holy persons attract the attention of those seeking holiness. The testimony of her students at Speyer bears witness to the deep impression Stein made on them, as much by her way of life as by her words. The heroic holiness of Stein's life and death challenge spiritual directors not only to practice what they teach, but to push forward in their own spiritual lives with unrelenting persistence and good zeal. Such intensity of spiritual life will surely attract more directees, but also supply the wisdom and energy required to respond positively to these calls for help. Those who seek spiritual direction expect that their directors live deeply spiritual lives, or at least have progressed at some length on that path. Directors may feel themselves to be flailing about in their own spiritual lives and may even believe that their directees are more advanced in prayer, discipline, and virtue. The directees, however, hope and expect that their directors speak from a place of experience and insight. Spiritual direction is, therefore, not a self-chosen profession, but a vocation that must also be confirmed by the people of God before it can bear fruit.

The third conclusion concerns the logic of prayer and the cross—that the goal of spiritual direction is a fuller participation in the paschal mystery of the passion, death, and resurrection of Jesus Christ. By a mysterious guidance, Edith Stein was attracted to the cross of Christ once she saw its paradoxical logic at work in Anna Reinach. Spiritual directors can be inspired by Stein's life and teaching to take up their own crosses, and by word and deed to encourage others to walk along the way of the cross with faith in God's love. Wise directors know when to encourage a person to follow through with an intention of personal sacrifice, and how to accept unavoidable suffering in such a way that draws the person closer to Christ. This "tough love" is borne of a well-lived and hard-earned faith in the power of the cross. Such faith is similarly borne of an experience of the paschal mystery unfolding in one's life. Teresa Benedicta encountered the cross of Christ and was converted to Christianity through this mystery.

These three conclusions lead to a fourth, which is the secret engine of this chapter and of St. Teresa Benedicta's spirituality: God is the true and only "spiritual director," who providentially calls and guides his children to union with triune love. Put another way, spiritual direction is one more element of Divine Providence and the economy of grace that God unfolds throughout salvation history. In Stein's words: "Things were in God's plan which I had not planned at all. I am coming to the living faith and conviction that—from God's point of view—there is no chance and that the whole of my life, down to every detail, has been mapped out in God's divine providence and makes complete and perfect sense in God's all-seeing eyes."[59]

Teresa Benedicta's faith in Divine Providence is borne from reflecting on her experience. Throughout her life, seen in hindsight, God had been calling her to himself, into his church, into Carmel, and into eternal life through a consciously self-sacrificial death like Christ's. Within and beyond the formal relationships of spiritual direction, Stein saw God guiding her through apparently accidental encounters with strangers, friends, hymns, and books. Stein recognized the immense value of a small word of encouragement, a confident affirmation of God's love, and a clarion call to the cross. Perhaps this is why she lent herself to such forms of occasional and accidental spiritual guidance; she was one of many instruments in God's hands, leading his children home. Spiritual directors never work alone, nor do they do the lion's share of work, in shepherding souls. Spiritual directors, like Stein herself, are mere instruments of Divine Providence.

[59] Stein, *Finite and Eternal Being*, 113.

CHAPTER SEVEN

A Spiritual Master at Montmartre: Bouyer, Marion, and the Divine Event of Love

Keith Lemna

The appearance of *The Paschal Mystery* by the French Oratorian priest Louis Bouyer (1913–2004) in 1945 established the young theologian as one of the biggest names in his field.[1] This book is one of the writings that helped the Roman Catholic Church in the middle of the twentieth century to rediscover God first and foremost under the figure of living love, not of abstract truth or of judgment, and was instrumental in introducing the very expression "paschal mystery" into the common parlance of the Church. Bouyer went on to write many books, essays, and articles. He was much esteemed by many in his day, including Pope Paul VI, who appointed him to the first International Theological Commission and recommended, in 1976, the Oratorian to the Roman clergy as one of three theologians they should read in order to expand their doctrinal horizons and improve their teaching and preaching.[2]

---

[1] Louis Bouyer, *The Paschal Mystery: Meditations on the Last Three Days of Holy Week*, trans. Sister Mary Benoit (Washington, DC: Regnery, 1950).

[2] Bertrand Lesoing, *Vers la plénitude du Christ: Louis Bouyer et l'oecuménisme* (Paris: Les Éditions du Cerf, 2017), 245, n. 4. The other two theologians were Henri de Lubac (1896–1991) and Charles Journet (1891–1975).

The French Oratorian is a singular figure. He did not belong to any established school of thought. He is certainly not a mouthpiece for any of the varieties of Thomism on offer in the twentieth century and even less so a follower of Franciscan traditions. Yet he is also not classifiable, as he is sometimes said to be, as a strict proponent of the "*ressourcement* theology" so influential in the Church in the middle of the century that featured a renewed discovery of the church fathers as ultimate guides for understanding the mystery of faith. It is truer to speak of Bouyer, as his friend and colleague Hans Urs von Balthasar (1905–1988) once did, as an eminent representative of a "school" of theologians (including Balthasar himself) who communicate in their work a profound sense of being overwhelmed by the love of God in the way the beloved is by a lover. Balthasar referred to this school as a "school of love" that emphasizes God's self-revelation in the cross of Christ.[3]

This loosely constituted school continues to impact the Church today, especially in and through the work of some eminent French theologians and philosophers whom both Balthasar and the Oratorian influenced as spiritual and theological mentors at a decisive period in their formation. I refer to certain figures who were members of a community of Catholic scholars then at the beginning of their careers and who met at Sacré-Coeur Basilica in Montmartre in Paris in the late 1960s and early 1970s. These young scholars were conscripted by the rector of the basilica at the time, Monsignor Maxime Charles (1908–1993), to carry out the publication of the student journal *Résurrection* and got their start in publishing through this work.[4] These students included such figures of note as Jean Duchesne (b. 1944), Jean-Robert Armogathe (b. 1947), Rémi Brague (b. 1947), Jean-Luc Marion (b. 1946), and, later, Jean-Yves Lacoste (b. 1953). They met Bouyer through this publishing venture and became well acquainted with his work. I want to suggest

---

[3] Hans Urs von Balthasar, "Current Trends in Catholic Theology and the Responsibility of the Christian," in *Communio* 5 (Spring 1978): 77–85, at 80.

[4] Cf. Jean-Yves Lacoste, "Travail théologique et urgences de l'évangélisation: L'exemple de Maxime Charles," in *Résurrection* no. 120–21 (July–October 2007), accessed July 3, 2019, https://www.revue-resurrection.org/Travail-theologique-et-urgences-de.

in this chapter some ways in which Bouyer's influence as a spiritual director may be evidenced in the work of this family of thought, particularly in that of Marion, who is the most internationally famous figure from the above list. On this basis I want to extract some important insights, especially relevant to those engaged in spiritual direction in our time, from the theology and spirituality shared by Bouyer and Marion, especially with respect to the eschatological standpoint of Christian faith that moves the Christian disciple to recognize himself or herself as the one who is first and foremost a receiver of the divine event of love.

A Theologically Informed Spiritual Direction

In the intellectual autobiography *The Rigor of Things*, the text of his that will be the primary focus for expounding his thought in this chapter, Marion describes his time at Montmartre and the decisive role it played in his spiritual and intellectual development.[5] While a student doing preparatory classes for advanced study in the humanities, Marion was first brought to Montmartre by Duchesne in order to join in silent prayer before the Blessed Sacrament, and he followed the practice of eucharistic adoration there before becoming a student of philosophy at the École Normale Supérieure (ENS). Over time, Marion got to know Monsignor Charles, the rector at Sacré-Coeur, who appointed Duchesne and Marion as consecutive editors of the aforementioned *Résurrection*. Marion and his compatriots working on the journal were brilliant young students, but they did not have any formal training in theology, even though theology was the primary subject matter of the journal. Charles wanted it this way. He wanted the journal to be run by extremely bright students for whom theology was an avocation, not by professional theologians. Marion writes that this made the production of the journal "dreadful and crushing work."[6] With the help of Charles, these student-editors sought

---

[5] Jean-Luc Marion, *The Rigor of Things*, trans. Christina M. Gschwandtner (New York: Fordham University Press, 2017), 21.

[6] Ibid.

out the counsel of eminent theologians, and this is how Marion first got to know Fr. Bouyer, Cardinal Jean Daniélou (1905–1974), Cardinal Henri de Lubac (1896–1991), Marie-Joseph Le Guillou (1920–1990), and Christoph von Schönborn (b. 1945), named the archbishop of Vienna in 1995. They also later got to know Balthasar through this work. Marion notes that these theologians became for him and his friends "tutors, in the Oxonien sense of the word."[7] From 1968 to 1973, Marion and company "stuffed" themselves "with theology," which included the many writings of the great contemporary theologians the students got to know personally.[8] This training has, in the long run, deeply impacted continental philosophy and theology precisely through Marion's decisive influence. The effect has been to bring theology and philosophy together in a way that had been unknown to Western thought since the patristic era.[9]

Marion reports in *The Rigor of Things* that the students saw Louis Bouyer quite frequently at the Oratorian residence in Paris, the Villa Montmorency, and at Lucerne Abbey in Normandy. These encounters were often joyous affairs, involving no small amount of feasting and drinking. It would be too much to say that Bouyer is the most important theological influence on Marion. That title clearly belongs to Balthasar, whom Marion considers to be the greatest theologian of the modern age.[10] Yet the French philosopher and theologian has publicly presented on Bouyer's theology on two occasions, and he has no small esteem for the Oratorian's thought, which, he says, possesses "a breadth, a space, and a breath that few have had since the Patristic Age."[11] He recognizes Bouyer

---

[7] Ibid., 17.

[8] Ibid.

[9] Cf. Dominque Janicaud and Jean-Francois Courtine, *Phenomenology and the "Theological Turn": The French Debate* (New York: Fordham University Press: 2001).

[10] Ibid., 25.

[11] See Jean-Luc Marion, "Cinq remarques sur l'originalité de l'œuvre de Louis Bouyer," presentation at session of *Groupe de Recherche sur l'Œuvre de Louis Bouyer* (November 9, 2016), accessed July 3, 2019, https://media.collegedesbernardins.fr/content/pdf/formation/etudier-louis-bouyer/2016-11-09-6-intervention-du-pr-j-l-marion.pdf.

as a man of serious spiritual penetration and discernment. The biggest overall *personal* influence on Marion may well have been Cardinal Jean-Marie Lustiger (1926–2007), but Bouyer was Lustiger's own teacher. Both men of the church, on Marion's view, seemed to possess the power to read souls, although this power was particularly evident in Lustiger: "[Lustiger] had this penetrating stare, which said: 'Here is my diagnosis.' I felt it almost physically. Certainly, this kind of charisma is found in other spiritual directors (in Charles or Bouyer, for example), but in him it was particularly evident."[12]

Duchesne, one of Marion's lifelong confidants, has explained to me what he thinks Marion means in this passage: "What Jean-Luc meant by 'spiritual directors' was guidance for intellectual discernment: assessing the relevance of ideas as keys for the understanding of the history of the world and of thought as not autonomous, but parts of the History of creation, Fall and Redemption."[13] The context of Marion's passage indicates that he may have had a rather more personal significance than this in mind, but it is a provocative observation nonetheless, and one that we shall return to at the end of this chapter. It indicates that spiritual direction involves help in seeing the world and history in light of the Christian mystery. In this understanding, theology should play a crucial factor in spiritual discernment, particularly a theology that remains closely wedded to what the church fathers referred to as *oikonomia*, or the economy of creation and salvation. The church fathers distinguished theology, or *theologia*, from *oikonomia*, the former having to do with the inner life of God or the face of Christ turned toward the Father, and the latter having to do with the face of Christ turned toward creation and with Christ's action in the world for its salvation. Bouyer's corpus of writings is especially pertinent in this regard. He never separated *theologia* from *oikonomia*. He wrote widely on spirituality, but this writing was always deeply informed by theology rooted in profound reflection on the *oikonomia*.

[12] Marion, *The Rigor of Things*, 180.
[13] Personal e-mail, Friday, May 25, 2018.

As a real-life spiritual director, Bouyer was known to be unobtrusive and decidedly lacking in tragedy in his take on the present moment. He preached the mercy and patience of God and recommended frequent personal reading of the Bible. Jean Duchesne reports that in Bouyer's later years, after suffering from Alzheimer's disease and being consigned to the care of the Little Sisters of the Poor in Paris, the simplicity of Bouyer's own spiritual life was at last revealed in full to his friends who came to visit and to care for him. He could no longer read or write, but he would frequently recite the rosary and, lying in a final state of impotence on his bed, repeat over and over the "Jesus Prayer."[14]

Trinitarian Mysticism and the Eschatological Standpoint

There are three consistent themes in Bouyer's writings that are especially pertinent to his influence on those for whom he was a mentor at Montmartre. The first is a theology of the existence of the world in the triune God, an understanding that is at the heart of his work from the time of his first published writings. His book *Women Mystics* sums up his own trinitarian theology in broad strokes through select exposition of the writings of others.[15] In this little book, he explores what he takes to be a consistent tradition of spiritual and mystical theology that runs from the writings of the thirteenth-century mystic and poet Hadewijch of Antwerp to St. Teresa Benedicta of the Cross (Edith Stein) in the twentieth century. The book appears on the surface to be a brief (and inadequate) general historical survey of the tradition of modern women mystics in the Western Church, but it has a more precise significance as an exposition of what Bouyer considers the profoundest trajectory of trinitarian understanding in modern theology and spirituality, which draws together and develops the best insights of the patristic tradition, both East and West.

[14] Ibid.
[15] Louis Bouyer, *Women Mystics*, trans. Anne Englund Nash (San Francisco: Ignatius Press, 1993), 13–50.

The first two chapters of this book are on Hadewijch as well as her greatest immediate successors and synthesize the most important points. Bouyer argues that Hadewijch—by virtue of her own visionary, spiritual, and intellectual gifts, as well as through the influence of the twelfth-century Cistercian theologian William of Saint Thierry—was able to articulate a mystical way of seeing the relation of the human person to the triune Creator that was of decisive, if only implicit, importance for some of the most significant spiritual writers in the subsequent Western tradition. Seminal themes in the later medieval and modern mystical traditions of theology are found in her writings in a form that indicates the influence of her thought, themes such as divine exemplarism, the mystical marriage of the creature with the Creator, and divinization or deification as the ultimate fruit of the incarnation. Each of these themes in fact gives shape to the whole of Bouyer's own writings.[16]

In line with William of Saint Thierry, Hadewijch's texts center on the love of God, who has loved each and every one of us from all eternity in his Son, calling forth in us a response of self-surrendering love in participative imitation of the eternal triune life. According to Bouyer, this vision of love calling to love—of God's love adopting us "to live in the mutual, constant, total, infinite renunciation of self that characterizes the three Divine Persons"—is the foundation for Hadewijch's "exemplarism," an expression not used by her but that captures well her view that we are always known and loved in God or, more precisely, in the Father's projection of his own life in his eternal Son.[17] Bouyer explains that "even before we existed concretely in our free individuality, we were all, in the living thought of the Father in his Son, eternally conceived and loved with him."[18] In this mystical view, each human person and all human persons together are "predestined" in the Son to return

---

[16] Bouyer, *Women Mystics*, 13–50. Cf. Guillaume Bruté de Rémur, *La théologie trinitaire de Louis Bouyer* (Rome: Editrice Pontificia Università Gregoriana), 201–338. Rémur synthesizes Bouyer's trinitarian theology in these pages, at various points covering all the themes listed here.

[17] Ibid., 25.

[18] Ibid., 27.

by their free consent in grace the love with which they have been loved by God eternally in the Holy Spirit, who is the fruit of the divine love. We exist ideally and eternally in the divine Word and are called in the concrete actuality of our historical existence to be raised by the incarnate Word and drawn, as Hadewijch herself says, "by his divine power and his human justice to our first dignity, giving us the freedom in which we had been created and loved by God, confirming his call and our election such as he had foreseen from all eternity for our good."[19] According to Bouyer, these words from Hadewijch mean that "the incarnate Word, as he includes us in himself ideally from all eternity, allows us through and in his Incarnation to become in ourselves, in time, what we were eternally in his divinity."[20] Everything is in the Son from the beginning as it will be forever.[21]

Our end is, in some sense, in our beginning in the Son, but this should not be taken with respect to some static and immobile construal of divine ideas. God's eternal knowledge and love for his creatures includes their individuality and the whole of their development. Bouyer holds that our individual vocation and destiny is in view of God himself and the work of redemption that he accomplishes in his Son. Moreover, it is inseparable from the act of creation. Creation includes the destiny of each individual person and all persons taken together, centered on the incarnation and redemptive mission of Christ. This trinitarian account of divine exemplarism consecrates the real historical actualization of finite freedoms. Bouyer stresses, in line with the tradition of women mystics that he takes to go back to Hadewijch, that the "idea" of each person in God has to do with the incarnate spiritual achievement in freedom of that person as a singular and unrepeatable being in history. The mystical vision of creation in God, in the Word, in the Christian tradition is connected to a profound understanding of the goodness that attaches to development in the time of creation. God's own existence is a movement, but

---

[19] Ibid., 29.
[20] Ibid., 30.
[21] Ibid.

uniquely, without change. It is a *regiratio*, as Blessed John Ruusbroec puts it, or a *bullitio*, as Meister Eckhart says.[22] These expressions refer to the divine life as an emanation and return, an eternal coming forth of divine life from the Father through the Son to the Holy Spirit and returning to the Father in a circling, or *perichoresis*. This trinitarian emanation of the persons is the exemplary model for what Eckhart refers to as the *ebullitio*, or expression of divine causality in creation.[23]

Christian spiritual life in this tradition is ordered by a vision of the whole creation eternally existing in the trinitarian communion of persons. Creation and redemption are thought of as a unity (without confusing them), a point that was often de-emphasized in Catholic manuals of theology that formed the basis for theological training in seminaries until the Second Vatican Council. From as early as the 1930s, the French Oratorian highlighted this unity between creation and redemption, and he urged theologians to order their systematic theological expositions in accordance with the mystical and trinitarian basis of Christian experience taken in its totality.

Anticipating far in advance Pope Francis's encyclical *Lumen Fidei*, Bouyer emphasizes throughout his work that the act of belief brings about a new way of seeing, indeed a properly Christian "gnosis": In this life, as faith is moved by the Father toward charity, the Christian mystic is given a vision of the Trinity, albeit in chiaroscuro.[24] Through the gift of an elevating interior light, Christian believers come to know all things in Christ as we have been known by him eternally, and we are given the power to love God, self, and others with the very love of the Holy Spirit by which we

[22] Cf. Rik Van Nieuwenhove, Jan Van Ruusbroec, *Mystical Theologian of the Trinity* (South Bend, IN: University of Notre Dame Press, 2003), 77–99. See also, Louis Bouyer, *The Invisible Father*, trans. Hugh Gilbert (Petersham, MA: Saint Bede's Publications, 1999), 268–71.

[23] Cf. Bouyer, *Women Mystics*, 62–65.

[24] See Pope Francis *Lumen Fidei* (May 24, 2015), available at http://w2.vatican.va/content/francesco/en/encyclicals/documents/papa-francesco_20130629_enciclica-lumen-fidei.html, sections 26–31. See Louis Bouyer, *The Meaning of the Monastic Life*, trans. Kathleen Pond (New York: P.J. Kennedy and Sons, 1955), 201–9.

have been eternally loved. We are given the gift to know and love God, ourselves, and others with God's own knowledge and love. We see the world with God's own eyes and love our neighbor with God's own love. The knowledge and love that elevates faithful Christian souls to a condition of "connaturality" with God is the fruit of the presence and activity within us of the trinitarian persons in accordance with their eternal mutual exchanges of interpersonal life and love.

Christian mysticism, in this view, is not primarily a matter of exaltations, visions, and ecstasies, although these may certainly be present in some particular cases. Rather, it is the fruit of God's communication of his own triune mystery to us, in connection with the incarnation of the eternal Son. Christian mysticism is a matter of filial adoption in the Son, a unification of each human person freely brought into union with the Creator through the perfection of God's plan (his "idea" or "logos") for each free individual in communion with the whole church. On Bouyer's understanding, the vocation of mysticism is not something that is given to only a select few elevated Christians to attain; it is the vocation of all. Indeed, salvation, which God wills for each and every human being, is mystical deification. This understanding must not be taken in the sense of escape from the world. Bouyer insists that we can only know and love God with the very knowledge and love of God communicated to us by the Son in the Holy Spirit if we love our neighbor as ourselves. Mystical vision is deceitful if it does not flower in the love of neighbor.[25]

Sacraments, liturgy, prayer, and charity all have a mystical quality. They are the privileged means by which God communicates his eternal mystery to us in and through the church, which is the very Body of Christ and temple of the Spirit. Christian mysticism is the fruit of the extraordinary mystical grace that God efficaciously gives to all those who freely give themselves over by the power of the Holy Spirit to the Father in Christ and allow themselves to be led wherever he wills to lead them.

[25] Cf. Louis Bouyer, *Introduction to the Spiritual Life*, trans. Mary Perkins Ryan (Notre Dame, IN: Christian Classics, 2013), 351–83.

This brings us to the second point that I wish to consider. For Bouyer, the spiritual life is one of pilgrimage, of a journey that never finds its conclusion in this world as it is now. The Oratorian stressed the non-negotiable need for asceticism in the Christian spiritual path, and this is for him inextricable from the view that Christian disciples, no less than Christ himself, have no place to lay their heads in this world. As Pope Francis recently put it, Christian disciples are "itinerant."[26] How is that we are able to follow the Lord wherever he leads us and thereby receive his gifts in the Holy Spirit? The spiritual life of the Christian requires conversion, or *metanoia*, and this means that mysticism cannot be juxtaposed to asceticism, as is sometimes done. This is to say that Christian mysticism requires a new way of relating to the world. The world is fundamentally good, a gift of the perfectly good Creator, reflecting God's eternal goodness and wisdom. But sin has made us relate to the world in egoistic ways, driven by pride, greed, and lust. In this condition, we cannot love God, the world, our neighbors, or our very selves in the way we should without a turning away from what is and has been in our lives. Mystical love is not available to us without asceticism. A new "exercise" (this is the meaning of the Greek *askêsis*) of human freedom is required.

Bouyer's work is balanced in this regard. He is averse to both Jansenist rigorism and laxist forms of spirituality, both of which may lead us to believe that the gifts of grace do not really transform us interiorly and thereby enable us to relate to the world through the power of transformed freedom. The mystery at the heart of Christian mysticism is the mystery of the cross, the center of divine wisdom, and all Christians are called to follow the way of the cross.[27] However, this is only in light of the resurrection. Bouyer saw the "paschal mystery" as a unity of divine action at work in us through the Eucharist. God does not glory in our suffer-

---

[26] Pope Francis, Angelus Address, July 1, 2019, accessed July 3, 2019, https://www.nwcatholic.org/news/international-news/disciples-seek-gods-glory-not-their-own-pope-says-at-angelus.html. Pope Francis emphasizes this point in the context of a need for immediate evangelization that cannot delay.

[27] Cf. 1 Cor. 2:1-19. Bouyer links Pauline mystery and wisdom together in this way.

ing and frustration. These are not the ends of the ascetical path, and what counts in the *metanoia* is the intended aim: perfection of communion with God through filial adoption. Self-giving and renunciation are non-negotiable requirements of Christian life. There is corruption in the world and in the heart of the human being. Our heart must be liberated from its propensity to move us to grasp the world in an egoistic fashion or to be fascinated by goods that are easily accessible and received. The end or aim of asceticism is to receive the gifts of the world precisely as gifts of the transcendent giver.

The Christian East sees the monk as a point of reference for human perfection, and this is Bouyer's view.[28] After the fourth century, in the wake of the establishment of the peace of the Church with the Roman Empire, the white martyrdom of the monk carried into a new context the example of a life given fully over to God of the red martyrs in early Christianity who gave testimony to the faith by shedding their blood in periods of imperial persecution of the Church. The spiritual counsels of poverty, chastity, and obedience—necessary vows for monks, as for all those who enter into religious life—are, in Bouyer's view, meant for all Christians. These counsels are derived from the precepts of the Sermon on the Mount and are meant for all who would assume the mantle of discipleship to Christ. The vowed religious, the "monk," differs from Christians in other states of life only in that he or she is able to live these counsels with a greater literal consistency. Other Christians can live the vows only for specific periods of time.

In living the counsels, a new relationship to the world is established in the experience of the Christian mystic, who comes to see that the world as it is in its corrupt state is not our true home. The Church is a pilgrim Church, and all Christians are "pilgrims" and

[28] See John Paul II, *Orientale Lumen* (May 2, 1995). Available at https://w2.vatican.va/content/john-paul-ii/en/apost_letters/1995/documents/hf_jp-ii_apl_19950502_orientale-lumen.html, sec. 9. John Paul II says: "Moreover, in the East, monasticism was not seen merely as a separate condition, proper to a precise category of Christians, but rather as a reference point for all the baptized, according to the gifts offered to each by the Lord; it was presented as a symbolic synthesis of Christianity."

"travelers."[29] Even the Benedictine monk, vowed to a rule, is a disciple in exile. Bouyer explains: "Hence, even if the monk is in fact fixed by the vow of stability in a monastery chosen once for all (as in the Benedictine Rule), his is to be a nomadic existence, and one of eagerness for the desert—which makes it almost the exact opposite of such a life as found in a world that tends with all its weight toward settling down, becoming established."[30] The French Oratorian understood the monk to embody in exemplary fashion the meaning of human vocation in relationship to the triune God who called Abraham out of Cana and sent his people into exile from Egypt into the desert or into Babylonian captivity and away from Jerusalem. Jesus Christ's own mission was an itinerant one, foreshadowed by John the Baptist and consummated in his free acceptance of the cross. The Jewish mystical theme of the *Shekinah Yahweh*, which refers to the light of God that the people of God followed in their journey through the desert in the exodus from Egypt, is exemplified on a surpassing level in the relationship of Christ to the people of God: Christ is the new and more tangible *Shekinah Yahweh*.[31] To be a disciple of Christ is to follow him wherever he leads, even if we do not know the specifics of the destination that he has in mind for us.

For Bouyer, this understanding of Christian mystical vocation should shape our overall theological comprehension of God's relationship to the world. God reveals himself and gives himself to his people by means of the "event," a term referring to the in-breaking of God into our self-enclosed world, which is too often dominated by human egoism.[32] Mysticism should have, on this understanding, an eschatological and apocalyptic orientation. This is well summed up in Bouyer's description of the eschatological meaning of Sacred Scripture: "The total interpretation of Scripture . . . should always lead us to the eschatological perspective of the 'Jerusalem from on high which is our mother,' according to the

[29] Bouyer, *Introduction to the Spiritual Life*, 320.
[30] Ibid., 244.
[31] Cf. Bouyer, *The Invisible Father*, 140–42.
[32] Ibid., 302.

phrase of St. Paul (Gal. 4:26), of that 'Bride of the Lamb, coming down from heaven like a wife adorned for her husband,' according to the final vision of the Apocalypse (Rv. 21:2). Thus it is revealed that the mystery is not only Christ and Christ in us, but the 'hope of glory.' "[33]

Eucharistic Event

Jean-Luc Marion describes and assesses well the third aspect that I wish to focus on in Bouyer's thought as a point of connection between these two eminent figures—namely, its eucharistic and liturgical centering. From his student days in Paris, Marion absorbed Bouyer's writings, and he has in recent years explicated the central insights that govern their organization.[34] Bouyer wrote several books on liturgy. The great majority of his books were not directly on this subject, but in all his works the liturgical ordering of his thought is palpable. Marion explains that Bouyer is unique among the great theologians in the twentieth century in that he makes liturgy and spiritual practice the norm for theology. Bouyer, Marion explains, does not lead us by way of theory into the domain of practice. On the contrary, the "theory" in Bouyer's theology always results from a practice that is above all liturgical.[35] Theology is, on this understanding, eminently practical. Spiritual direction is tied to theological understanding, because theology expounds and explicates a fact and an act in order to permit the faithful to receive the "creative event" of God by which the divine Word forms his people. Theology, in the Bouyerian optic, should be always "spiritual," because it concerns the repetition by the faithful of the very action of Christ. It should be liturgical because liturgy is the very life that the Bible reflects in its passages.

---

[33] Bouyer, *Introduction to the Spiritual Life*, 57.

[34] Jean-Luc Marion, "Introduction," in *La théologie de Louis Bouyer: Du mystère à la sagesse*, ed. Bertrand Lesoing, Marie-Hélène Grintchenko, and Patrick Prétot (Paris: Parole et Silence, 2016); Marion, "Cinq remarques sur l'originalité de l'œuvre de Louis Bouyer."

[35] Marion, "Cinq remarques sur l'originalité de l'œuvre de Louis Bouyer," running text.

On this understanding, liturgy is the origin, heart, and accomplishment of all theology. It alone delivers to us here and now the performance and action of Christ. "Where," Marion asks, "do we have access to Christ?" "The Church alone," he explains, "provides this access." But it is the "real Church" that does so, that is to say, the Church in its concrete embodiment in history, centered on the liturgical action of the Eucharist.[36] The Church is the norm of Christian experience and action, but the Church as "seen, experienced, and practiced in its essence [which] is not first of all dogma, Scripture, the Magisterium, or the *sensus fidelium*." The Church is "that from which all these instances come: the liturgical act, where Christ accomplishes, here and now as well as once and for all, the salvation of human beings for the glory of the Father in the unity of the Spirit."[37] Eucharist and liturgy are not, then, possible objects of study on the same footing as other possible objects. Theology, when true to the mystery of revelation, is fundamentally a theology of the Eucharist.

A eucharistic logic penetrates the whole of Bouyer's thought, whether he is discussing the Trinity, Christ, Mary, the Church, eschatology, anthropology, spirituality, or contested issues in fundamental theology. There is little doubt that Bouyer exercised an enormous influence on Marion's own work in this regard. Remarkably, the contemporary French philosopher's very speculative philosophy exudes a profoundly liturgical and eucharistic sensibility, and among all the influences, great and small, on his thought Bouyer is the most consistently, systematically, and overtly liturgical thinker among them, as Marion's exegesis of the Oratorian makes clear.

It is precisely in a liturgical context that Marion's understanding of God's relationship to the world and the human person was decisively shaped. His vision of the world is imbued with a contemplative perspective formed in him by eucharistic adoration and by a deep reading of the eucharistic theology of the tradition of thought, beginning with Scripture and the church fathers, that

---

[36] Ibid.
[37] Ibid.

Bouyer's writings were instrumental in helping the Church to recover. Through the practice of eucharistic adoration at Montmartre, Marion learned to understand Christian spiritual life as a dialogue in which one discovers the word of God speaking through the presence in the consecrated host to which one's contemplation is directed. This led him to discover the existence of the world in God: "[Eucharistic adoration] gives you the conviction that God is not found elsewhere, in some other world. And even, in a sense, that you are the one who remains elsewhere, far from the stage where all takes place, but that God himself is already there where you cannot manage to go. . . . The spiritual life becomes the objective space where everything else takes place and not a part, a margin, or a limit experience of the world."[38]

Eucharistic adoration, according to this understanding, communicates the sort of mystical trinitarianism that I described in the first point above. All of human life and experience is discovered in its spiritual ground through adoring contemplation of Christ present in the Blessed Sacrament. Creation, we come to see, is in God, and the trinitarian basis of all reality becomes apparent:

> There is nothing exterior, absolutely nothing that is not found already and above all given a norm by God, including the questions of his being and his potential existence. . . . For the world is not created *outside* of God but inevitably *within* the Word—for where would you want it to be? The world is found *within* the Trinity, more exactly *within* the Principle, the Word, the Son. . . . Everything takes place within the interior of God, and the world remains a subsidiary of the Word. The idea that there is anything outside of God has no meaning at all.[39]

Marion asserts that the depths of our finitude cannot separate us from God, because all distance between God and creation is prefigured and surpassed in an intra-divine *kenosis* or self-emptying and communion in the Holy Spirit: "God himself, at least if one

---

[38] Marion, *The Rigor of Things*, 27.
[39] Ibid., 28.

recognizes his Trinitarian dimensions—the distance between the Father and the Son, which is crossed and unified by the Spirit—in advance surpasses and definitively recapitulates any death, any kenosis, any exteriority, any negativity, and any depth of finitude that we could ever experience or even less one that we could imagine in our entire heart and in our worst chaos."[40] In Bouyer's understanding, God makes room for the other within himself eternally, in the shared relationships of the divine persons, by a kind of contraction.[41] He explicates the nature of the divine communion as fundamentally a sharing and receiving of life between Father, Son, and Spirit that constitutes an eternal thanksgiving: "The whole divine life is nothing other than love given eternally, or rather giving itself, but this love lives only in the interchange by which everything flows from the Father through the Son so completely that everything also returns to him, recapitulates itself in him in the Spirit."[42] The inner life of the Trinity is eternal thanksgiving, that is, eternal Eucharist (the term *Eucharist* originally meant "thanksgiving"). This view of God's eternal nature is deeply concordant with significant accents in the trinitarian understanding of both Balthasar and Marion and encapsulates a fundamental spiritual as well as theological position common to the "school of love" of which Balthasar spoke.

If the spiritual life should uncover for disciples of Christ the presence of all things in God, it should no less make us aware that we remain "elsewhere" in this life. We have seen that Bouyer argued for the importance of the ascetical dimension of Christian existence. Christian disciples are itinerant figures who, like Christ himself, have no place to rest their heads. The Christian life requires an eschatological standpoint, following God wherever he leads us, always a step behind. God is present everywhere, as all things are present in the divine communion of persons, but the pilgrim Church, with all of its members united in their individual destinies, is not yet present where it wants to go and where it

---

[40] Ibid., 107–8.
[41] Bouyer, *The Invisible Father*, 306.
[42] Ibid., 232.

cannot go on its own. Marion attempts in his work to transpose this eschatological and eucharistic sense of human emplacement in the world into a universal philosophical understanding. *All* human beings are pilgrims, itinerants. *All* human beings are fundamentally constituted by realities that they can only receive and cannot make themselves masters over. This understanding underlies his well-known doctrine of "saturated phenomena."[43] The human person is *l'adonné*, the "given self," and the world often gives itself to us in a way that confounds our a priori concepts. Experiences of beauty and love are paradigmatic in this regard. The "event" or, more precisely, "eventness" is the governing logic of these experiences or saturated phenomena that overwhelm the settled categories of thought that govern our way of organizing the realities given to us in intuition or perception.

The event overturns the conditions of possibility that we set for the world and divine action in it. The event brings "the impossible" into our midst, which is to say that it is not foreseeable as possible or thinkable until it actually appears. One can point to truly momentous historical occurrences as examples of events, such as the start of the Great War in 1914 or the fall of the Berlin Wall in 1989. God also works in and through the event, both with regard to salvation history and with regard to his guidance of those who would follow the path in which he seeks to lead them.[44] All things are possible with God, but we cannot really know this unless we embrace a rationality open to God's communication of grace to us through the modality of the "impossible."

A Spirituality of the Event in an Age of Crisis

Both Bouyer and Marion promote an understanding of the spiritual life that is a fitting resource to address a widespread sense

---

[43] Cf. Marion, *The Rigor of Things*, 86–94. See Jean-Luc Marion, *Being Given: Toward a Phenomenology of Givenness*, trans. Jeffrey L. Kosky (Stanford, CA: Stanford University Press, 2002). This latter text is Marion's seminal work on givenness and the gift.

[44] Marion, *Givenness and Revelation*, trans. Stephen E. Lewis (Oxford: Oxford University Press, 2016), 48–50.

of crisis that permeates contemporary culture, and this is perhaps an especially important consequence of the "Montmartrian school of love," inasmuch as this crisis impacts those seeking spiritual direction. This crisis has to do, both theologians hold, with the breakdown of the certainties of calculative reason to which many Christians themselves have been wedded as the basis of their hope for the future of humanity and of the world. Bouyer in fact argued that the construction of the distinctively modern technological culture, which seeks control over the world through calculative reason, came into being through the designs of a degraded Christian consciousness and will to power connected to the arising of bourgeois civilization in the late medieval and early modern period. Wealth creation, connected to an inordinate desire to attain comfort and security, became the primary activity of European civilization, because Christians themselves had lost the properly eschatological standpoint that should be a hallmark of the spiritual life. This led to a cramped epistemology that overprivileged the status of quantitative analysis through which humanity hoped to become master over the processes of nature. Monks and mendicants themselves fell into the proto-consumerist trap that arose already toward the end of the thirteenth century. Indeed, they led the way for others in the formation of a new civilization centered on wealth creation that nevertheless tried, for a time, to maintain the overt appearance of Christian conviction. Bouyer writes: "Infiltrating and consolidating itself everywhere under the outward appearances of Christianity (appearances which would last a few centuries), this new civilization was progressively to inactivate all specifically Christian characteristics, simply by substituting the worship of Mammon for that of Christ, while maintaining Christian forms."[45]

It is clear that Bouyer intends the eschatological focus of his thought to be a reminder of the true orientation of Christian discipleship. One cannot become settled into this world, seeking comfort and security, or the power that wealth creation provides,

[45] Louis Bouyer, *Cosmos: The World and the Glory of God*, trans. Pierre de Fontnouvelle (Petersham, MA: Saint Bede's Publications, 1988), 122.

above all else if one is to be a follower of the incarnate Lord of history. The spiritual practice he promoted in his writings and in his personal counsel centers all things on the immeasurable bounty of divine love that calls us out of the settled patterns of being into which we easily become accustomed.

Marion's phenomenology of the event clarifies and renders more precise the underlying problem of the epistemic privileging of calculative reason and why we have entered a period of secular, apocalyptic foreboding. The triumph of calculative reason in the modern age, he explains, came about in no small part because of the objectification of the world that was achieved through figures such as Galileo and Descartes.[46] Triumphant calculative reason corresponds to the bourgeois mentality that turns all questions of meaning and the good into questions of "value" determinable by the human will. Marion argues that the modern scientific, political, and economic projects that gave us the world as we know it today are based not on an attempt to know things such as they really are; rather, they replace things with the construction of objects upon which we place an evaluation through our constructive desires. Yet reality has, in the form of the environmental crisis, lately insisted on intervening in our lives and disrupting our settled patterns of thought and behavior. We are learning that we do not ultimately live in a world of objects but of really existing things. The French philosopher explains that "we produce lots of them [objects] and they cover the whole Earth with a mantle that very quickly thickens and even already spills out into space—but in the end we live toward things such as they are (if there are any left), and our access to these things disappears."[47] He distinguishes things from objects and points out that the latter cannot be fully integrated into the former.

Marion provides the example of the development of the modern economy. We moved in the modern period, he explains, from an economy based on wealth creation linked to natural resources to an economy based entirely on wealth creation for its own sake,

---

[46] Marion, *The Rigor of Things*, 168.
[47] Ibid., 168.

made possible by the construction of the objective, idealized cultural sphere of credit. The credit economy is economy as object. Objectified in this way, economy no longer maintains living contact with real things, with the earth and ground rent, for example. Environmental crisis has forced us to seek renewed contact with reality specifically through the dilemma of the "excess of pollution," which has caused us to realize anew that nature is not an object, that our excessive, "objective" waste cannot be absorbed into the "spatial reserves of nature."[48] The leftover of the object cannot be brought back into the thing itself (nature). Reality is not the same thing as objectivity, and human valuation by means of the will to power, which operates with absolute effectiveness only in the domain of the object, does not get us to the thing in itself.

The newly recognized discrepancy between the objects of modern human culture and things in themselves has led to the widespread sense of crisis and foreboding. Reality obeys the logic of the event, while the object of valuation obeys the logic of the human will to power with its privileging of technological calculation. The irreducible excess of the thing in itself to object status confounds calculative rationality. Our sense of crisis and foreboding stems directly from our habitual neglectfulness of eventness, which is tantamount to a habituation away from reality as it gives itself to us from the excess of its givenness.[49] The event has become inordinately frightening to us. The security of the age of the object has been replaced by a sense of crisis with regard to the capacity of human reason to know reality. Human understanding requires, in contact with the event, a new openness to the logic of surpassing givenness. Marion speaks of phenomenology, the philosophical approach he embraces, as capable of receiving the event in a non-nihilistic way: "It obviously does not foresee the event, but is able to make it out when it arrives, to face up to it and receive it, in short to see it, to *go see* it."[50]

[48] Ibid., 168–69.
[49] Ibid., 170.
[50] Ibid., 171.

It is not only phenomenology that has led Marion to counsel a new openness to the event. His spiritual training and study of theology has given him an eschatological perspective that has habituated him to think of God's giving of himself to us as an event of divine action. He has come to correlate his phenomenological rendering of events within the world to the manner of givenness by which God gives himself to us in divine revelation.[51]

One important upshot of this turn to eventness, in my view, is that it establishes a new condition for recovering a more monastic style of spirituality in an age when Christians are as perplexed as anyone about where the world is running as well as about their place within it. It teaches us to receive God in the figure of a lover who overwhelms us through surpassing presence, calling forth a new way of life, a full recognition of one's pilgrim status on earth. The detachment that Bouyer counsels as a necessary part of every Christian's spiritual development has a philosophical justification in Marion's philosophy of *l'adonné* and the event. Bouyer's understanding of detachment is a call to openness to the "creative event," a conditioning of the believer to receive the world as it runs according to its transcendent "thing-ness," beyond the objectivity of calculative reason that tempts Christians themselves to turn away from the living presence of God in the world. This is all deeply congruent with an essential thrust of Pope Francis's teaching, with respect to his view that every Christian disciple is an itinerant. The God of Christian faith is, in his words, a "God of surprises." The "preferential option for the poor" is, in part, a call to recognize the importance of voluntary poverty for Christian believers and a deep critique of modern objectification, such as one finds in his striking analysis of technocratic civilization in *Laudato Si'*. It is perhaps no surprise that the Argentinian "theology of the people," so influential to Pope Francis, is steeped in French phenomenology as well as the writings of French Catholic theologians who exist in a familial sympathy with the Montmartrian school.

---

[51] See Jean-Luc Marion, *The Erotic Reduction*, trans. Stephen E. Lewis (Chicago: University of Chicago Press, 2007). It is in this book that Marion first makes this connection explicit.

Conclusion

We recall that Jean Duchesne observes that spiritual directors provide "guidance for intellectual discernment: assessing the relevance of ideas as keys for the understanding of the history of the world and of thought as not autonomous, but parts of the History of creation, Fall and Redemption." Spiritual directors cannot provide this counsel unless they are themselves theologically informed, moved by intimate, personal assimilation of the divine Word revealed in the *oikonomia*. They require familiarity not only with practical guidelines or spiritual and psychological methodologies in order to effectively carry out their task, but also with the integrated theological view of reality found in the church fathers and the great mystical writers. The tradition of spiritual wisdom that Bouyer helped to bring to the fore and in which Marion was formed is theologically rigorous and marked by profound scriptural as well as liturgical understanding. Theological reflection, rooted in Scripture and liturgy, is part and parcel of the spiritual life, and it is capable of being developed over time not only by professionals but by all who are open to the direction of the Holy Spirit in their lives. Initiates aspire to see their individual lives in connection with the plan that God has for them in his eternal wisdom. This plan is centered on the mystery of Christ made present in the Eucharist and narrated in the biblical word. Spirituality is meaningless if practiced in abstraction from both the *oikonomia* through which the divine plan is revealed to us and the *theologia* in which the divine plan is related to the eternal mystery of God. The Montmartrian school of thought renders problematic the very idea that there should be a separation between spiritual theology and dogmatic theology as taught in academic settings. Spirituality is not a-theological, and the great spiritual masters of the tradition transmit to us not only psychologies of belief, descriptions of states of soul, or methods of prayer, but veritable theological doctrine concordant with the underlying meaning of Scripture.

Christian discipleship requires education into the trinitarian basis of reality. We have to learn to see our very lives, and all things, in the Trinity. Education into this way of seeing cannot be a-theological, and it should carry with it a properly eschatological understanding of the horizon of faith, a profound sense of the gap that exists between who we are and who God wants us to become. Christians have to learn to read the events of grace in their lives in connection with all that God has done for his people in history and with an openness that enables them to see that God is calling us forward, out of what is only our seeming homeland, which tempts us to settle into it all too comfortably and complacently. The love of God calls us out of ourselves. It unsettles us. It also directs us to our real and enduring homeland, the heavenly Jerusalem that God has promised to bring fully to earth. The kingdom of God is already present in our midst in the eucharistic body of Christ, but Christ's body has not yet been filled in and all things are not yet subjected to him. The school of Montmartre teaches us that spiritual training requires becoming familiar with the ways of God's surpassing love given to us in the form of the event. It requires familiarity with the story of salvation that describes God's communion with his pilgrim people. Spiritual directors should encourage their flocks to read Scripture frequently and with due attention to its most encompassing, eschatological meaning. This deeper reading of Scripture requires that the director has access to and is able to communicate the riches of the Church's tradition of mystical theology that invites us to envision our lives as integrally related to the grand narrative at the very heart of the faith. We are pilgrims with a higher purpose that is inscribed in the heart of the eternal Word and communicated in the *oikonomia* of creation and redemption. All our lives are enfolded and unfold therein.

CHAPTER EIGHT

The Lens of Discernment: St. Ignatius of Loyola's First and Second Rules in *On the Waterfront* (1954) and *Diary of a Country Priest* (1951)

Fr. Guerric DeBona, OSB

When St. Ignatius of Loyola wrote the *Spiritual Exercises* (1522–24), he had no idea that his revolutionary process of discernment would open up an enormous window for enlarging our understanding of spiritual direction for centuries to come. Like many Christian humanists of the sixteenth century, Ignatius prioritized the *imago Dei*, underlining that the glory of God is reflected in a spirit-filled person, fully alive. He understood the Holy Spirit to be close at hand, waiting to be discovered in interior prayer. We know from Ignatius's autobiography and other writings[1] that, with the grace of deepening discernment, he came to recognize the movement of the Spirit within himself, from consolation to desolation to conversion, a process that yielded a greater awareness of God's will, a more intense friendship with Christ, and "spiritual freedom."[2] With his *Spiritual Exercises*, he developed a

---

[1] See *San Ignacio de Loyola: Obras*, ed. Manuel Ruiz Jurado, SJ (Madrid: *Biblioteca de Autores Cristianos*, 2013).

[2] For an intelligent discussion of discernment, see George A. Aschenbrenner, SJ, *Stretched for Greater Glory: What to Expect from the Spiritual Exercises* (Chicago: Loyola

method for guiding others along this same journey, employing specific meditations on a series of episodes in the gospels. Initially practiced by Jesuits and other clergy and religious, Ignatius's ingenious model has steadily grown in popularity, especially after the Second Vatican Council, attracting men and women of all faith traditions into an ongoing process of spiritual direction.[3]

I am interested in how discernment in spiritual direction unfolds in a variety of circumstances and conditions, and particularly in the role that Ignatius's so-called Rules for the Discernment of Spirits play in the process.[4] Engaging the progress of discernment is most helpfully described by Fr. Timothy Gallagher as a threefold paradigm of *awareness, understanding,* and *action,* in which one accepts what is of God and rejects what is not.[5] But what does this Ignatian discernment look like in real life? This question prompted the genesis of this chapter on spiritual direction and its place in film culture because, in a certain sense, the *Exercises* are a practical handbook in search of case studies. Where can we find these records of discernment? In my estimation, cinematic narratives, which shape our lives in so many ways, also provide us with a road map of how we intuit the work of the Spirit in everyday life.

I do not think it a stretch to establish a connection between secular narratives and discerning the movement of the Spirit. Read one way, any character development or plot progression in Western narrative tends to be determined by making sense of the self in a process of awareness, understanding (or not) its directional fate, and then acting or choosing amid conflicts (between good and evil) with the world around it. This process might also be likened to what Aristotle called *anagnorisis* or "recognition" in the

---

Press, 2004); Timothy M. Gallagher, OMV, *The Discernment of Spirits: An Ignatian Guide for Everyday Living* (New York: Crossroad, 2005); Herbert F. Smith, SJ, "Discernment of Spirits," repr. in *Notes on the Spiritual Exercises of Ignatius Loyola: The Best of the Review, 1,* ed. David L. Fleming, SJ (St. Louis, MO: Review for Religious, 1983), 226–48.

[3] For an expansive overview of the *Spiritual Exercises,* especially regarding their background and method, see Fleming, *Notes on the Spiritual Exercises,* 19–84.

[4] See Timothy M. Gallagher, OMV, *Setting the Captives Free: Personal Reflections on Ignatian Discernment of Spirits* (New York: Crossroad, 2018).

[5] Gallagher, *The Discernment of Spirits,* 17ff.

discussion of *peripeteia* (a sudden change in fortune) in the *Poetics*.[6] In Aristotle's paradigmatic analysis, a character moves from ignorance to knowledge, especially in connection with a new revelation in the dramatic unfolding of the plot. I raise this connection between the dramatic circumstances in narration and the process of discernment in life to establish an important link between how we understand and represent our lives on the one hand, and the work of the Spirit on the other. Ignatius was not imagining extraordinary or paranormal occurrences: The movement of the Spirit happens in everyday circumstances—the plots of our lives, if you will—and is discernible within the human heart as manifestations of these changes.[7] In a certain sense, Western narratives offer exemplary windows into the dynamics of discernment because they invite us into the lives of characters and events amid a detectable axis of change and potential transformation, a momentum of enlightenment that echoes the movement of the Spirit.

For the remainder of this chapter, I will discuss the interface between Ignatian discernment and film narrative. I believe that the first two of Ignatius's "rules" are most helpful in establishing an understanding of a character's struggle or "recognition" because they both identify a specific area of palpable awareness, understanding, and action inside dramatic circumstances. Where the first rule helps us discern through the Good Spirit's intervention by the pricking of our conscience, the second rule (acting in a contrary motion) finds a faithful person embattled with an enemy of the soul, but which the Good Spirit actively thwarts.[8]

---

[6] Aristotle, *Poetics*, ed. and trans. Michelle Zerba and David Gorman (New York: Norton Critical Editions, 2018), 27.

[7] In fact, the richness of the *Exercises* allows for the so-called Nineteenth Annotation retreat, which "does not separate a retreatant from concrete, ordinary life experiences; it plunges her further into them as she prays each day." See Mary Sullivan, R.C., and Dot Horstman, "The Nineteenth Annotation Retreat: The Retreat of the Future?" in Fleming, *Notes on the Spiritual Exercises*, 302ff.

[8] Ignatius lists the "Rules for the Discernment of Spirits" as an appendix to the *Spiritual Exercises*. Ignatius says the first and the second rule are more suitable for the first week in the four-week retreat sequence of the *Exercises*. See, for instance, George E. Ganss, SJ, *The Spiritual Exercises of Saint Ignatius Loyola: A Translation and Commentary* (Chicago: Loyola Press, 1992), 121–25, and Gallagher, *The Discernment of Spirits*, 27–46.

The films I have selected are *On the Waterfront* (Elia Kazan, 1954) and *The Diary of a Country Priest* (Robert Bresson, 1951), widely regarded as masterpieces of the mid-twentieth century. By illuminating the characteristics of these rules of discernment in these cinematic texts, we might gain some insight into the workings of the Spirit in the lives of those around us and begin to apply these observations to the spiritual direction setting. As an aside, I hope this interrogation, brief as it is, might encourage further discussion in those interested in Ignatian spirituality, as well as those pursuing the fascinating dialogue between religion and film culture.

The First Rule:
Terry Malloy, *On the Waterfront*, and the
Raising of Consciousness in the 1950s

When Ignatius describes the function of the fourteen Rules for Discernment in the appendix to the *Spiritual Exercises*, he says they are "to aid us toward perceiving and then understanding at least to some extent, the various motions which are caused in the soul: the good motions that they may be received and the bad that they may be rejected."[9] The first rule lays out one of the most dramatic and widely known encounters with the momentum of the Spirit, a divine activity evinced in both biblical and church history: "In the case of persons who are going from one mortal sin to another, the enemy ordinarily proposes to them apparent pleasures. He makes them imagine delight and pleasures of the senses, in order to hold them fast and plunge them deeper into their sins and vices. But with persons of this type the good spirit uses a contrary procedure. Through their good judgment on problems of morality he stings their consciences with remorse."[10] There are any number of famous examples that might emerge in our discussion of the first rule. In this regard, Gallagher cites St. Augustine and Thomas Merton as historical instances in which "the stinging and biting of their consciences" illustrate the way in which the Good Spirit

[9] Ganss, *Spiritual Exercises*, 121.
[10] Ibid.

has provoked their "apparent pleasures" by using a "contrary procedure."[11] In what follows, I hope to show how Elia Kazan's *On the Waterfront* can lead us into a further interrogation of the role of conscience—its "stinging and biting"—in the movement of the Spirit; it is the journey to freedom with a character's "good judgment on problems of morality" operating in the first rule.

The plot of *On the Waterfront* was inspired by a series of shocking, Pulitzer Prize–winning articles issued in a twenty-four-part series by Malcolm Johnson for the *New York Sun*, following a notorious murder in 1948 in New York and then produced as a screenplay by Budd Schulberg for Harry Cohn at Columbia Pictures and directed by Elia Kazan. Released in 1954, the film was practically as gritty and realistic as Johnson's articles in its depiction of underground corruption and practices of systemic evil on the city's waterfront. As the movie portrays it, the shipping on the New York docks is riddled with exploitation, bribery, and murder by the union boss Johnny Friendly (Lee J. Cobb) and his henchmen, among them "Gentleman" Charley Malloy (Rod Steiger), whose brother Terry (Marlon Brando), a washed-up prizefighter, does the mob's bidding for some fast cash and some easy positions working on the docks. A crisis occurs when Terry unknowingly lures a recalcitrant dock worker, Joey Doyle, to the roof of his high-rise apartment building, where Friendly's thugs hurl the young man to his death. Terry says he thought the mob was only going to "lean on" Joey a little bit and lives in a state of denial until he meets the local parish priest, Fr. Barry (Karl Malden), and Joey's sister Edie (Eva Marie Saint), with whom he has fallen in love. Together with Fr. Barry, Edie exposes Terry's blindness, and he begins to see the corruption of Friendly and his brother Charley, who is himself murdered for not silencing Terry. Fr. Barry is persistent, not only with provoking Terry's conscience, but with raising the moral intelligence of the longshoremen on the whole dock. Influenced by his emerging "biting" conscience, Terry decides to cooperate with the police investigators prosecuting Johnny

[11] Gallagher, *Setting the Captives Free*, 12–15.

Friendly, soon after which he is brutally beaten but makes his way as a new kind of union leader in solidarity with the remainder of the dock workers, who have cast Friendly and his mob aside to their fate with the law.

A good deal of what makes *On the Waterfront* a prime candidate for an examination of Ignatius's first rule is its director and the ensemble cast, many of whom had careers in consciousness raising in the theater.[12] Director Elia Kazan came of age acting in Group Theater of the 1930s and then directing hard-hitting Broadway smashes in the 1940s, most notably those by Arthur Miller (*All My Sons*, 1947) and Tennessee Williams (*A Street Car Named Desire*, 1947). Subsequently, he famously showcased the post–World War II "social problem" film as a genre for raising the country's temperature when it came to society's moral problems emerging after the war; these were films that confronted anti-Semitism (*Gentlemen's Agreement*, 1947), racism (*Pinky*, 1949), institutional corruption (*Boomerang*, 1947), and mob rioting (*Panic in the Streets*, 1950). Having founded the Actor's Studio in the late 1940s, Kazan brought the principles of what would be called "method acting" to both stage and screen. Much of the realistic, moody, and naturalistic characterization in *On the Waterfront* comes from Kazan's direction and the influence of Konstantin Stanislavski, whose Moscow Art Theatre had revolutionized nineteenth-century acting, making performances more emotionally available for a wider public and often referred to as "socialist realism."

It is well known that Brando's acting style brought a vulnerability and transparency to Terry's character, a style that was to influence generations of actors after him. Brando, who was trained by Stella Adler, one of the premier proponents of the method, was not alone in his depiction of the moody young man, deeply wounded by the past and society. Together with other contemporary performers

---

[12] For a fascinating account of the film as well as background material, see Kazan's autobiography *Elia Kazan: A Life* (New York: Alfred A. Knopf, 1988). A more recent personal account is his reflections in *Kazan on Directing* (New York: Random House, 2009), esp. 172–81. Also, Richard Schickel, *Elia Kazan: A Biography* (New York: Harper Perennial, 2005), esp. 282–90.

such as Montgomery Clift, Robert Mitchum, and James Dean, he tapped into an emerging postwar understanding of the afflicted and haunted male in American culture. Significantly, such self-revelations become particularly poignant in the discovery of a conscience, since the spectator senses the gradual unfolding of a moral instrument as something like an emotional striptease. In Brando's depiction of Terry, the revelation of the conscience that has been "bitten" begins to disclose the Good Spirit in action. Besides Brando, many of the cast members, including Malden, Saint, and Cobb, were also trained in the Method and some even worked with Kazan before on the stage and the screen. Other than the principals, the cast appears to smolder under the weight of the waterfront's venality waiting for liberation, which eventually comes at the prompting of Fr. Barry.

From the very first moments of the film, we note the tangibly dirty, naturalistic setting on location (shot in Hoboken, New Jersey, in very cold weather) and which more than hints at the moral troubles of filth and corruption. The opening sequence occurs at night and within moments Joey Doyle is thrown off the roof. The actors have heavy New York accents and suggest a local realism, as well as (lower) class signification. Along these lines, Brando struggles for an adult vocabulary (together with a number of his peers), while Edie Doyle (who attends a school run at a convent and is now back home on break) and Fr. Barry are less burdened by heavily accented, working-class traces. Terry is particularly associated with a kind of pre-moral sensibility, a naivete about the money-driven, ruthless world for which he acts as a kind of gofer and into which he has been entangled. Trapped in a role of what he will later himself famously identify as "bum" (when he could have been "somebody"), the ex-prizefighter's arrested development includes a moral price tag. Consider, for instance, the important associations that Terry has with adolescence. He keeps pigeons on the roof, together with a few other boys who are at least ten years his junior. Spending a good deal of his time with training pigeons, Terry was the founding member of the teenage group, the Golden Warriors. "I was their first Supreme Commander," he tells Edie. Yet Terry's shear physicality next to Jimmy (whom Terry calls "his shadow") and the young boy's companions underlines the age difference. Brando was in top physical shape during the shooting, working out with weights and aerobic exercises, and makes the "gang" association with young people almost pathetic. Terry seems frozen in his alliance with teenage boys who have themselves yet to reach maturity (their voices are only beginning to change and deepen like those of men). After meeting Edie on the roof with Terry, Jimmy wonders aloud, "I wonder how long she's going to hang around, huh, Terry?"

Terry's adolescent behaviors and stunted moral growth begins to hint powerfully at what Ignatius's first rule suggests as the "enemy proposing apparent pleasures." Indeed, Terry not only lacks a suitable vocabulary and maturity, but enjoys everything we know to be the appetitive associations with adolescence, including Terry's sensual practices of reading "girly magazines" instead of working, together with accepting bribery for a cushy place on the docks, even while his fellow longshoremen are supporting families and are working hard at their difficult jobs. Terry moves further into a perilous ethical situation and jeopardy when Charley asks Terry to spy on the church meeting between Fr. Barry, Edie, and the disgruntled union members, saying, "Johnny does you favors, kid. You got to do a little one for him once in a while." Terry's moral behavior goes hand in glove with his identity as the "kid," and his identity is wrapped up in being Charley's younger brother. In what is arguably the most famous scene in the film, in which Terry finally confronts Charley in the back of the car about his failed boxing career, the younger man says, "You was my brother, Charley, you should have looked out for me. Instead of making me take them dives for the short-end money." While he has settled for the kind of pleasures that permit him to go from one sin to another, escalating to cooperating with social sin and murder, Terry remains still something of a child awaiting an Augustinian moral conversion. But as we will soon see, the turning point of the film comes when Terry finds redirection with the intervention of the Good Spirit and accomplished through the mediation of Edie Doyle and Fr. Barry. What emerges is a new moral intelligence—a conversion—made possible by introducing what Lawrence Kohlberg might call a cognitive shift from a pre-conventional moral state to a conventional one, or what Jesuit Bernard Lonergan would imagine as a moral conversion moving from self-preoccupation to "self-transcendence" and involvement with social concerns.[13]

The mediation of the Good Spirit prompting conversion comes first from falling in love with Edie, the sister of the man he lured to his death. Casting Eva Marie Saint opposite Brando was an inspired choice. Brando's Terry has brute force and physicality, where Saint's Edie is all innocence and femininity. In fact, this was Saint's first feature film and her inexperience on the set mirrored perfectly the overwhelming energy, eccentricity, and worldliness of her costar. At one point, this contrast is made obvious when Terry picks up Edie's glove in the park and effortlessly puts it on his hands, as if it were a fighting glove. The dainty world of the schoolgirl meets the ex-fighter. As if to further underline their contrast, Terry comes looking for Edie to clarify his alleged innocence in her brother's murder by breaking down the door and overpowering her, even as she shields herself with just a white slip on. Though in love with him, she is furious because of Terry's complicity in her brother's murder. "I don't want you to do anything. Let your conscience tell you what to do," she says. Challenged by the confrontation, Terry screams back, "That—word again! Why do you keep saying conscience, conscience. . . ." Edie answers: "I never mentioned the word before." There is only a passionate kiss and no other physical contact, signifying their trust

---

[13] See, for example, Kohlberg's work on cognitive moral development in Lawrence Kohlberg, *Essays on Moral Development, Vol. 1: The Philosophy of Moral Development* (San Francisco: Harper and Row, 1981). Bernard Lonergan describes conversion as the human subject moving from a "withdrawal of self-enclosure" to "self-transcendence" in a sequence of intellectual, moral, and religious conversion. See Bernard Lonergan, *Method in Theology*, 2nd ed. (Toronto: University of Toronto Press, 1990), esp. chap. 10. From a Lonerganian perspective, Terry's moral conversion opens up a social conscience that was unavailable to him before his conversion.

and love for one another. But in the process, Terry has moved closer to moral conversion by falling in love and understanding its selfless demands. Notable in this exchange between Edie and Terry is the vital freedom that awaits those who engage the first rule: It is the *conscience* that bites, not the insults, condemnation, or coercion of another human being. Edie and, later, Fr. Barry mediate the presence of the Good Spirit, allowing the conscience to bite, to be discovered, stirred up, and speak the truth. In a certain sense, Terry is "seduced" by goodness and genuine love, having spent most of his life as prey to sensuality, childhood behavior, and self-absorbed, sensual desires. When he flees from Friendly's mob attempting to run him and Edie over with a truck in the alley, Terry smashes the glass in a store door in order to find an escape and save them both. I read this action as the redeemed prizefighter using his fists not to throw a boxing match but to rescue and save the one he loves. Terry's conscience is found by the truth of being loved and loving; he has purchased "self-transcendence," the key to moral conversion. As he tells Fr. Barry, Edie "is the first nice thing that ever happened to me." Human love is at the service of conversion and moral knowledge.

But it is not only love that bites and gnaws Terry's conscience in his growing moral awareness and understanding. Fr. Barry was based on a tough, real-life Jesuit priest who witnessed the power abuses and corruption on the docks firsthand. Fr. Barry is relentless in raising the consciousness of the dock workers and Terry himself. He asks: "Who killed Joey Doyle?" Activating those who have gathered in church to testify to the truth, Fr. Barry says, "Boys, get smart. I know you're gettin' pushed around but one thing we got in this country is ways of fightin' back. Gettin' the facts to the public. Testifyin' for what you know is right against what you know is wrong. What's ratting to them is telling the truth for you. Can't you see that?" Things heat up after one of the potential union witnesses, Kayo Nolan, is murdered on the dock with falling cargo hoisted on a crane by one of Friendly's men. As the instrument moving the longshoremen away from the evil of social sin, Fr. Barry becomes more involved in the consciousness raising of the evil of corruption on the docks. Kazan brilliantly stages the climax in the action after Nolan's "accident" by having the priest deliver a long monologue down in the hull of the ship where he continues: "Boys, this is my church. If you don't think Christ is here on the waterfront, you got another guess coming. And who do you think he'd line up with? . . . Every morning when the hiring boss blows his whistle, Jesus stands alongside you in the shape-up. He sees why some of you get picked and some of you get passed over. He sees the family men worrying about getting their rent and getting food in the house for the wife and kids. He sees them selling their souls to the mob for a day's pay." Moments later, the camera shifts to Terry's point of view as he continues to listen to Fr. Barry: "You want to know what's wrong with our waterfront? It's love of a lousy buck. It's making love of a buck—the cushy job—more important than the love of man. It's forgetting that every fellow down here is your brother in Christ. But remember, fellows, Christ is always with you—Christ is in the shape-up, he's in the hatch—he's in the union hall—he's kneeling here beside Nolan . . ." Then, as if rising from the inferno, Fr. Barry is hoisted up with the pallet on top of the deck.

As Fr. Barry names the enemy's tactics—"love of a lousy buck"—there is a lot that might be said about this particular moment in the film, a rightly celebrated moment of religious confrontation with social sin and its denial. In my estimation, an account of the "poetics of space"[14] in the scene of Fr. Barry in the hull of the ship and his "crucifixion speech" begins to gesture at the psychoanalytical dynamics of the collective unconscious of the longshoremen and their eventual liberation. In this reading, the depths of the ship become symbolic of the social evil that has been repressed and awaits freedom. Fr. Barry's sermon associates the suffering of Christ with those on the docks who share in that same reality and raises the buried unconscious to a *conscious awareness* of the evil visible in plain sight. His function, then, is to mid-

[14] See Gaston Bachelard, *The Poetics of Space*, 2nd ed. (New York: Beacon Press, 1992).

wife the Good Spirit by revealing the "sting" of the conscience in those who close their eyes to corruption and murder. As the crane hoists him up to the top of the ship, Fr. Barry's ascent on the pallet with the dead man suggests the victory of the word of liberation, a resurrection, where the dead are brought to life out of the grasp of sin and the grave. More than human consciousness has been raised up.

The priest's speech marks a turning point for Terry himself. He tells Fr. Barry, "I've got something that's chokin' me. I've gotta get it out." Fr. Barry soon responds, echoing Edie's confrontation: "Listen, I'm not asking you to do anything, Terry. It's your own conscience that's got to do the asking." Then Terry: "Conscience . . . I didn't even know I had one until I met you and Edie . . . This conscience stuff can drive you nuts." The scene here underlines perfectly the "stinging" of the conscience with *remorse*. As Terry told Fr. Barry about his continual slippage into moral evil, "It started as a favor—for my brother—you know they'd ask me things and it's hard to say no—a favor—Who am I kiddin'? They call it a favor, but it's do it or else. And this time the favor turned out to be helping them knock off Joey. I just thought they'd lean on him a little but—last night with Edie I wanted to tell her only it—stuck in my throat. I guess I was scared of drivin' her away—and I love her, Father. She's the first thing I ever loved." There are concrete signs of Terry's receiving the Good Spirit because he is about to make a clear break with his sinful past. As Terry ponders the implications of testifying against Friendly and cooperating with Glover and the investigation, Jimmy tempts Terry to hide from the investigator, saying, "You was our first Supreme Commander, Terry. Keep out of sight and I'll tell him you're out." To which Terry replies: "But I ain't out. I'm in. Who's lying to who?" As a kind of last chance to win him over, Charley tempts Terry with a job at a new pier, but Terry tells his older brother he has not made up his mind.

Terry will indeed make up his mind and take action when he finds Charley murdered and hanging on a hook in a dark alley. When he testifies to the Waterfront Crimes Commission, it is the first time we see Terry dressed as an adult, with a jacket and tie. Terry also must bear the responsibility for testifying to his conscience and moving away from sin and a protracted adolescence. This action comes with its share of reparation. His pigeons are slaughtered (he has been identified as a stool pigeon), and Jimmy wants nothing more to do with him. When he confronts Johnny Friendly at the pier, he is brutally assaulted. Bearing the wounds (and punishment) of his past, Terry manages to lead the union longshoremen on the dock into solidarity, all of them now defying Friendly. Together they march into work, with Terry as a leader, a witness to the victory over the spirit of social sin and corruption. Finally, I think it is significant that *On the Waterfront* resists what might be considered as the conventional plot ending for Hollywood. Terry and Edie may or may not see each other again. The closing shots are of Fr. Barry and Edie looking on proudly from a distance as a brutalized and wounded man makes his way to work, a mature, solitary adult man taking ownership of his conscience and leading other union workers into freedom. Terry walks alone to live out his newly discovered interior freedom—a space that has been unearthed in a movement away from the real enemy toward embracing the Good Spirit.

The Second Rule:
Desolation and Grace in *Diary of a Country Priest*

Ignatius's second rule of discernment could not be any more different from the first. Where the first rule finds the enemy content in the midst of those who are cooperating with evil and its attentive seductions, those who face the second rule have moved into a place of valiant resistance, having passed the promptings of the evil one and striving to do God's will as best they can: "In the case of persons who are earnestly purging away their sins, and who are progressing from good to better in the service of God our Lord, the procedure used is the opposite of that described in the first rule. For in this case it is characteristic of the evil spirit to cause gnawing anxiety, to sadden, and to set up obstacles. In this way he unsettles these persons by false reasons aimed at preventing their progress."[15] Therefore the moral status of the person Ignatius describes is not in doubt, or in need of an Augustinian conversion; rather, according to the second rule, the enemy will set up *obstacles* in an attempt to keep the person from progress toward holiness. Ignatius writes in a letter on spiritual direction that the enemy "tries to darken and confuse that good conscience by suggesting sin where there is none, changing perfection into defect, his only purpose being to harass and make one uneasy and miserable. When, as frequently happens, he cannot induce one to sin, or even hope to do so, he at least tries to vex him."[16]

If we are not looking for a dramatic conversion, then we should not be surprised to find a rather slow narrative engagement in an Aristotelian *anagnorisis* to move us forward in a conventional plot. Instead, we face the *internal drama* of often bitter anguish and wrestling with the demons that gnaw their way into a person's heart, biting and stinging, counterbalanced by divine consolations. Ignatius observes: "With persons of this type it is characteristic of the Good Spirit to stir up courage and strength, consolations, tears, inspirations and tranquility. He makes things easier and eliminates all obstacles, so that the person may move forward in doing good."[17] Many of the psalms offer a sense of the movement of the Spirit that the second rule gestures toward. Listen, for instance, to the dialogue between desolation and consolation, despair and hope, in Psalm 119: "My life is always at risk, / but I do not forget your law. / The wicked have set snares for me, / but from your precepts I do not stray" (vv. 109-10). The "snares" here are what Ignatius names as the "obstacles" laid before the just individual by the enemy.

The contrary dynamics of the first and second rules can be discerned in Jesus's celebrated parable of the Prodigal Son. After

[15] Ganss, *Spiritual Exercises*, 121.
[16] Ignatius of Loyola to Sister Teresa Rejadell, June 18, 1536, quoted in Gallagher, *Setting Captives Free*, 23.
[17] Ganss, *Spiritual Exercises*, 121.

rejecting his father and spending his inheritance on a life of dissipation, the younger son returns sorrowful and repentant, his conscience stung by the Good Spirit. The elder son, by contrast, exemplifies the second rule. Bitten by the enemy with sadness, resentment, and envy, he is a tragic figure striving to be righteous and obedient. He awaits the consolation of the Spirit in the Father's words: "Everything I have is yours." But will he attend his brother's banquet? How and in what way the obstacles are overcome becomes the drama of the working of the Good Spirit in the second rule.

If the first and second rules are as different as night and day, *On the Waterfront* could not be any more alien from the culture, director, and overall cinematic dynamics of Robert Bresson's *Diary of a Country Priest*. Although Kazan's film deals with an unusually mature religious topic for Hollywood, the script, direction, and formal structure of the movie are standard studio production material for the 1950s. Additionally, *On the Waterfront* raises issues of American cultural politics in its time, especially those concerning justice and organized crime. By contrast, *Diary of a Country Priest*, adapted from a novel by a devout French Roman Catholic Georges Bernanos, is still classified as one of the highwater marks of European art cinema. The film only gestures at the climate of France in the 1930s, where the novel is set. In a sense, the story of the dying young priest and his recalcitrant parishioners could have taken place at any time in France, and the novel has often been compared to the life and times of St. Jean Vianney. Although Bresson shares with Kazan an interest in naturalism, their approach to such realistic details is entirely different. Kazan paints on a broad palette of gritty, everyday life and shot on location to underline the underside of American urban life; Bresson's attention captures the signature of a minuscule moment in time, local, ambient sound, and almost claustrophobic settings realized in a kind of pre-industrial era, the bucolic and feudal landscape of rural France at Ambricourt. Kazan's Hollywood cast had already gained notoriety in American film and theatrical culture, while Bresson worked with some trained actors who could not really be considered movie stars, to say nothing of exhibiting a new style of acting like the method. The role of the curé of Ambricourt, for instance, was eventually given to the somewhat obscure Belgian actor Claude Laylu, working on the stage and with whom the director worked meticulously for at least a year to get him ready for the role.

Bresson's notorious attention to studied stylistics that adhere to intense, microscopic observations are evident in all of his most famous features.[18] With his close attention to everyday life, it is small wonder why Bresson was interested in writing a film on the life of Ignatius of Loyola, that astute observer of the spirit's labor. But the plan for the film was abandoned in favor of the adaptation of *Diary of a Country Priest* a few years later. Yet the life of a small village and the internal life of the priest who is assigned as its pastor provides an ideal confrontation with the second rule and its testing ground for overcoming the "obstacles" of the enemy. Films such as *A Man Escaped* (1956) and *Pickpocket* (1959) clearly exploit narratives flush with the drama of small gestures and movements. Film historians and art critics alike have weighed in on the characteristics of his narrative style. Among these signature directorial thumbprints include what Susan Sontag would call Bresson's mastering of "the reflective mode." She writes: "In reflective art, the *form* of the work of art is present in an emphatic way. The effect of the spectator's being aware of the form is to elongate or to retard the emotions. For, to the extent that we are conscious of form in a work of art, we become somewhat detached; our emotions do not respond in the same way as they do in real life."[19] The opening shots of *Diary of a Country Priest* call our attention to this reflective character, since these moments are silent silhouettes of introduction to the principal characters, with looks of sadness, suspicion, and distrust, inviting the spectator not so

[18] See, Tony Pipolo, *Robert Bresson: A Passion for Film* (New York: Oxford University Press, 2010).
[19] Susan Sontag, "Spiritual Style in the Films of Robert Bresson," in *Against Interpretation and Other Essays* (New York: Farrar, Straus and Giroux, 1990), 179.

much into a plot, but into what Sontag calls "intelligence."[20] In his *Notes on the Cinematographer*, Bresson says that "a sigh, a silence, a word, a sentence, a din, a hand, the whole of your model, his face, in repose, in movement, in profile, full face, an immense view, a restricted space . . . Each thing exactly in its place: your only resources."[21]

Much of the action in the film occurs inside the interior world of the characters. Indeed, the curé faces a number of assaults from all sides—social, psychological, physical—but mostly the priest wrestles with a herculean battle in the spiritual life. His health compromised (probably, we learn later, from fetal alcohol poisoning and stomach cancer), he has little strength to do much. But he does possess healing gifts that help others in spiritual discernment, one of which—a confrontation with a countess—becomes emblematic for the entire film. The young, inexperienced priest is worn away by spiritual obstacles and more than the occasional dark night of dry prayer, even as he prophetically confronts the spiritual illnesses of his parishioners and becomes a witness of healing and reconciliation. Finally seeking a diagnosis, he dies in the company of a resigned priest and the woman who became the cleric's mistress some years before. The closing words of the film— "What does it matter? All is grace"—discloses both the acceptance and redemption that has been purchased from one who endured suffering and taunts from what Ignatius might have called the evil spirit causing "gnawing anxiety, to sadden" the person from making progress in the spiritual life. As we watch the work of the evil spirit unfold in *Diary of a Country Priest*, however, we also notice the Good Spirit's efforts "to stir up courage and strength, consolations, tears, inspirations and tranquility."[22] That is the essential drama of the *Diary of a Country Priest*: the subtle and intri-

[20] Ibid.

[21] Robert Bresson, *Notes on the Cinematographer*, ed. Per Bregne and Guy Bennett, trans. Jonathan Griffin (Los Angeles: Sun and Moon Press, 1997), 36. See also *Bresson on Bresson: Interviews 1943–1983*, ed. Mylène Bresson, trans. Anna Moschowvakis (New York: NYRB, 2013), 59–80.

[22] Ganss, *Spiritual Exercises*, 121.

cate face-off between the enemy and the Good Spirit in the context of the second rule. Bresson's reflective style captures this movement of the Spirit in action, inviting the spectator to ponder the discernment process of awareness, understanding, and action.

We might note the careful elision between the diary entry written by the priest at the film's beginning and his spoken words—and the subsequent action depicting them both. These cinematic characteristics introduce the spectator to the provincial world of Ambricourt and its world of introspection, a decidedly parochial hostility to strangers, and class divisions. The diary entries throughout the film disclose the high degree of awareness and the unfolding of understanding evolving in the priest's discernment, beginning with his detecting the obstacles he faces in his new parish. These (literal) obstacles are telegraphed when we see the priest in the opening sequence catch sight of the Count (Jean Riveyre) and the governess Louise (Nicole Maurey) behind the gates enclosing a vast estate. The shot of the sign identifying the small town of Ambricourt followed by the transition to the gates recalls the famous opening sequence of *Citizen Kane*, in which the camera pans the gate of the Kane estate like an intruder with a sign that reads "No Trespassing." His passage literally and symbolically blocked, the clergyman already faces a stonewalling by the royalist class, an attitude with a long pedigree of French anti-clericalism and class separation (the priest's tattered cassock and appearance show his own affiliation with the lower classes). In short order, we are introduced to further obstacles that will form a considerable weight on the priest's spiritual and psychological condition. His health is significantly problematized by an undiagnosed stomach ailment that keeps him from consuming anything but stale bread and red wine. He has problems with elderly parishioners like Monsieur Fabragars, as well as younger schoolchildren who make fun of him (one of whom will become something of a nemesis until close to the end of the film). Moreover, the priest cannot seem to find consolation in his mentor priest of Torcy (André Guibert) or Doctor Delbende (Antoine Balpêtré), both of whom drag him further into despair. The curé of Torcy tells him that his function is "to keep order all day long" in the parish and desire "not to be loved," while the doctor tells him to face up to life because they both share an identity as a race that "holds on." Many of the characters in the film barely have a life of their own, serving instead as reflectors of the priest's spiritual state, as all of them face some degree of spiritual torment. The legendary French critic André Bazin observes: "There is no development of character. Their inner conflicts, the various phases of their struggle as they wrestle with the Angel of the Lord, are never outwardly revealed. What we see is rather a concentration of suffering, the recurrent spasms of childbirth or of a snake sloughing off its skin. We can truly say that Bresson strips his characters bare."[23] Bazin might have used a striking scene in which Chantal (Nicole Ladmiral), a resistant penitent, appears as a kind of ghostly remnant of a seance in the shadows of the confessional in her encounter with the priest. Such transparency of characters—the most notable being the curé of Ambricourt himself—allows for the spectator to see the inner workings of the discernment of spirits, since we sense an ethereal presence "never outwardly revealed."

These early moments of the characters' appearances in the *Diary of a Country Priest* set the tone in which the soul's burden from the enemy awaits liberation by the Good Spirit. The characters to whom we are introduced in the early portion of the film only make the priest's life more and more burdensome—even as he becomes ever more aware of these obstacles. Not least of these pastoral difficulties are his parishioners' sins. We learn that the count has been carrying on an adulterous relationship with Chantal's governess, Louise, and that his wife, the countess (Marie-Monique Arkell), has herself ceased to care about his infidelity because she has been grief-stricken for years over the death of her young child

[23] Andre Bazin, "*Le Journal d'un curé de campagne* and the Stylistics of Robert Bresson," in *What Is Cinema? Vol. I*, ed. and trans. Hugh Gray (Berkeley: University of California Press, 1967), 134. Bazin's essay remains arguably the most significant in addressing the issue of "spiritual direction" in the film and especially when it comes to a consideration of adapting Georges Bernanos's novel. See also Paul Schrader, *Transcendental Style in Film: Ozu, Bresson, Dreyer* (Berkeley: University of California Press, 1972).

and submerged in her own desolation. The count's relationship with his mistress obsesses Chantal, who not only detests her governess and falls into toxic states of anger at her father, mother, and Louise but also entertains thoughts of suicide. The priest confronts the young girl's hostility and eventually takes a suicide note addressed to her father away from her. Consequently, he must endure her taunts as well as her eavesdropping on his pastoral visits to her mother, the countess. Highlighting the girl's manipulative behavior is the unspoken sexual tension that exists between Chantal, now at the edge of transitioning from an adolescent to a young woman, and the rather naive priest. He receives an unsigned letter that we later learn is from the girl's governess (Louise is the sole parishioner at daily Mass) advising him to get out. Even the priest's mentor figures leave him without any support. The curé of Torcy (a representation of a certain kind of clergy with pragmatic tools at one's fingertips and very much the opposite of the idealistic cleric) thinks of the younger priest as a dreamy child, impractical and a typical victim of fetal alcohol poisoning. Doctor Delbende, who appears to share some sympathy with the priest, faces spiritual obstacles of his own and commits suicide by shooting himself in the woods. Delbende is an example of where the evil spirit has indeed conquered with tactics of biting despair and dread, machinations that are resisted by the priest throughout the film.

The spectator is gradually drawn into the dynamics of the second rule via the priest's diary entries, which form an interior monologue incorporating us into his world of existential loneliness and darkness. We find ourselves inhabiting the priest's most private moments at 3:00 a.m. when he cannot sleep and goes to pray in the church for hours on end. This is the claustrophobic world of Bresson—ascetic, spare, and hauntingly lit by Léonce-Henri Burel, with which the second rule finds a suitable dialogue partner. Burel photographs the priest as if he were a death mask, with his black cassock obliterating any form. At one point, the rain keeps him confined to his tiny bedroom where he says he cannot pray, even though he needs to pray as he "needs oxygen." He has little hope of breaking through any of his confining obstacles, recognizing before him a "black wall" and concluding that "God has left me; of this I am sure."

Has God really abandoned the priest? Surely one of the most agonizing realities of the second rule is the feeling of abandonment present in the devout human subject inside the experience of the "dark night." Yet that is about to change. The moment of liberation comes slowly as the obstacles are removed, and in a way appropriate for a priest who offers spiritual direction and pastoral counsel. The light of the Good Spirit slowly emerges as the young cleric senses grace unfolding in another, a mirror image of himself. I am now specifically referring to what might be called the *tour de force* of the film, its spiritual center, in which the Good Spirit provides consolation and peace to the countess in the midst of despair The celebrated "medallion scene" in which the priest confronts the countess in her spiritual suffocation and dryness is the sequence that André Bazin praises in no uncertain terms: "It is unlikely that there exists anywhere in the whole of French cinema, perhaps all of French literature, many moments of a more intense beauty than in the medallion scene between the curé and the countess. Its beauty does not derive from the acting nor from the psychological and dramatic values of the dialogue, nor indeed from the intrinsic meaning. The true dialogue that punctuates the struggle between the inspired priest and the soul in despair is, of its very nature, ineffable. The decisive clashes of their spiritual fencing match escape us. Their words announce, or prepare the way for, the fiery touch of grace."[24] Bazin himself makes the parallel between the countess's encounter with the consolation of the Good Spirit and the eventual peace the priest finds in the thrall of his own death. He is perhaps referring also to the very last moments of the film in which the Good Spirit completely eclipses the enemy as the dying priest accounts for his experience of grace, even as he breathes his last.

[24] Bazin, " *Le Journal d'un curé de campagne*," 137.

The "fencing match" between the priest and the countess is remarkable in a number of ways, most notably perhaps in the way that the young priest must face his own desolation and the fear of death in the one to whom he is giving spiritual counsel; he must ask the countess to confront the emptiness of abandonment she has known with the loss of her young son many years earlier. Like Bresson's camera, the countess lives in a myopic world, not far from the claustrophobic one the priest himself inhabits. To permit us some glimpse of the painful realities of such confinement, Bresson allows for the painful, grating noise of a gardener scraping and raking outside the window to slowly penetrate the scene. We see the countess only in her small quarters in the vast estate, and Bresson stages much of the action around the fireplace and the mantel with its numerous photographs of the child (she also wears one in a medallion around her neck, with the boy's portrait). Her flat affect is rather typical among those who are in a state of a long and severe depression. But the priest gets her to talk about her feelings, especially her anger as she says to him: God "has broken me already. He took away my son. What more can I fear from him?" Then her priest-director tells her that this is only "for a time," but that it may be for eternity if she continues to separate herself from God's love. Her only hope is to resign herself and yield to God "unconditionally."

The subtext in this confrontation between the priest and the countess is that she has made an idol of her son and has been living out of the biting anger of the enemy for untold years. Clearly, the countess herself is in the midst of the second rule because she has fallen for what Ignatius says often happens to those who are attempting to move toward God: "He unsettles these persons by false reasons aimed at preventing their progress."[25] The countess falsely reasons that she can continue with her depressed disposition, alienating herself from God, as long as she clings to her son. She imagines they will be united in eternity. But the priest tells her that this union will not be possible if she continues her hostility

---

[25] Ganss, *Spiritual Exercises*, 121.

toward the divine will. The priest breaks that lie, removing a significant obstacle for her by his pastoral intervention and by urging
the countess to say, "Thy Kingdom Come!" The surrender to God's
will causes the countess to admit that "I might have died with
that in my heart." As a sign of the abandonment to Divine Providence, she throws the medallion into the fire. In some sense, the
urge to destroy the image reflects Bresson's final stripping the
character to its very essence; all that remains is what the priest
tells the countess as the ground zero for human experience: "You
are face to face" with God. Representations are an illusion. She
falls on her knees in relief and for a blessing. After the priest returns to his rectory and retires for the evening, a messenger tells
him the countess has expired. He later receives a posthumous letter
from the countess, affirming her resignation, her happiness, and
gratitude to him. We have to wait until the end of the film to see
the priest's final moment of liberation, when he overcomes obstacles
all his own and surrenders, like Christ, to the will of the Father.

Not surprisingly, there is no plot climax following the countess's
interior revelation, just our recognition (or the spectator's *anagnorisis*) that her spiritual obstacles have been removed and that
she may die in peace. Her death causes more in the town to be
suspicious of the priest's counseling methods, which some, including her husband, believe might have caused her early demise. But
what of the priest himself? His removal of obstacles and encounter
with divine grace comes not with a miracle cure for his failing
health, or a recognition of his gifts, but by moving closer and closer
to an identification with Christ's passion. Bazin notes: "The pattern of the film's unfolding is not that of a tragedy in the usual
sense, rather in the sense of the medieval Passion Play, or better
still, of the Way of the Cross, each sequence being a station along
that road. We are given the key to this by the dialogue in the hut
between the two curés, when the one from Ambricourt reveals he
is spiritually attracted to the Mount of Olives. 'It is not enough
that our Lord should have granted me the grace of letting me
know today, through the words of my old teacher, that nothing,
throughout all eternity, can remove me from the place chosen by

me from all eternity, that I was the prisoner of His Sacred Passion.' "[26] With this acceptance of his union with Christ's passion and death, the priest echoes the countess's movement in her own surrender to the will of God. This is the climax of the threefold process of discernment: the action is complete union and surrender to God. The curé of Ambricourt has remained faithful to the end. A Hollywood ending would have probably staged some kind of miracle or recovery for the suffering servant of God.

Ignatius's second rule of discernment is at the service of a movement toward divine life and perfect freedom. As he notes at the beginning of the *Spiritual Exercises*: "Human beings are created to praise, reverence, and serve God our Lord, and by means of doing this save their own souls."[27] In order to facilitate our progress toward this end, the Good Spirit removes the obstacles that thwart us. As the curé becomes subsumed into the Way of the Cross, his obstacles fall away, and he—much like Christ himself—gains the freedom not to defend or justify himself to his accusers. We see another life continuing to take possession of him: Christ's own. When the count confronts the priest about frightening the countess by spiritual melodrama, which may have led to her death, the priest resists showing the countess's letter, which would have proven the opposite was the case. No heroics, just "Thy will be done." He falls on his own "Way of the Cross" in the mud of the forest, and a redeemed Séraphita (Martine Lemaire) wipes his face, like Veronica. Oliver (Jean Danet), who is something of an outsider in the family and serving in the Foreign Legion, gives the priest a ride in his motorcycle on the dreary road, like Simon the Cyrene helping to carry Jesus's cross. The priest's destiny is the end for which he was created: identification with Christ's passion. His final surrender—"all is grace"—suggests the completed work of the second rule: "We ought to desire and choose only that which is more conducive to the end for which we are created."[28]

---

[26] Bazin, *"Le Journal d'un curé de campagne,"* 135.
[27] Ganss, *Spiritual Exercises*, 23.
[28] Ibid.

Conclusion

The first and second of Ignatius's Rules for the Discernment of Spirits are notable for their practical application in the daily lives of men and women. Film culture provides us with a broad array of case studies to explore the concrete expressions of the Spirit's movement inside the human subject, mediated by everyday encounters within the community. The spiritual directors in *On the Waterfront* and *Diary of a Country Priest* are not only Fr. Barry and the curé of Ambricourt; these two priests are simply the principal instruments provoking *anagnorisis* in the lives of Terry Malloy and the countess. In other words, it is the whole context of the New York docks in the 1950s and the rural provinces of France that provide the arena for discernment. Contemporary spiritual directors might remember there are multiple conversation partners in the spiritual direction process—provocations large and small—that move the human heart to conversion and closer to God's will. Finally, spiritual directors should attend "with the ear of the heart," as St. Benedict puts it, in order to engage discernment themselves. Fr. Barry, who himself becomes more aware of the dynamics of God's social justice in the course of the film, allows Terry the freedom to let his own conscience speak the truth; and it was the curé of Abricourt's *second* visit to the countess and listening to her grief that provided her with the mirror of God's consolation just before she died. The priest learned from that very encounter in spiritual direction the difficult, steadfast path of grace so characteristic of the second rule. The lesson underneath Ignatian spiritual direction is to meet the directee wherever he or she may be and to mediate the labor of the Spirit for the sake of the kingdom that even now is making itself known.

CHAPTER NINE

Everything That Rises Must Converge: Spiritual Direction and Literature

Fr. Denis Robinson, OSB

The expression "Everything that rises must converge" has two important connotations in modern Catholic thought. Originally, it refers to the insight of the Jesuit anthropologist-philosopher Pierre Teilhard de Chardin (1881–1955). In his landmark work *The Phenomenon of Man*, Chardin deals with the fundamental unity of all things, of the endeavors of the human person. This ideal he identifies as the "Omega Point," the place where all reality meets. Concerning the Omega Point, Chardin observes: "Remain true to yourself, but move ever upward toward greater consciousness and greater love! At the summit you will find yourselves united with all those who, from every direction, have made the same ascent. For everything that rises must converge."[1]

This sweeping insight forms the core of thought for a fiction writer and essayist far removed from the milieu of Teilhard de Chardin's world, that of the Catholic author from the American South, Flannery O'Connor (1925–1964). O'Connor's stories of "hillbilly" spirituality can seem disconnected from the theological-philosophical-scientific insights of Teilhard de Chardin. The persons

---

[1] Pierre Teilhard de Chardin, *The Phenomenon of Man* (New York: Harper Perennial, 2008), 64.

of O'Connor's rural Georgia do not appear to share the intellectual and spiritual concerns of a post-nuclear Europe. Yet there are connections, at least in O'Connor's mind, connections that also help modern audiences—so accustomed to the segmentation and specialization of areas of thought—see the essential unity of all things, all thought, all expressions of the human intellect. O'Connor, like Chardin, was searching for the Omega Point, which she identifies very readily with Catholicism and Christian spirituality.

In this chapter, I propose to look at the question of the spiritual quest and spiritual direction, particularly as it relates to sources. What are the means by which spiritual ideals and patterns for a spiritual life are expressed? Is it the case that only specialists in the field of spiritual guidance can help chart the course for spiritual formation in individuals and communities? These questions raise important considerations for today's spiritual seeker: How are we to gain access to the mind of God and, perhaps more importantly, how prevalent is the spiritual world in our modern, secular society?

In the first part of this chapter, I examine the dance between literature and spiritual direction, understood in a very broad context of discipleship. In the second part of the chapter, I examine the writings of three contemporary Catholic fiction writers: O'Connor, Muriel Spark, and Fr. Robert Hugh Benson. From this brief analysis, I hope to demonstrate that literature has the power to move both mind and heart to be on the lookout for the presence of the divine in daily life.

Literature and Spiritual Direction

A preliminary investigation of the relationship between literature and spiritual direction takes us back to the beginnings of all things Western, the Greeks. In our contemporary context, we tend to view the two great Homeric epics, those touchstones of Western literature, as remarkable works of fiction. They are, in contemporary parlance, "myths" understood as something "made up." The reality at the core of the *Iliad* and the *Odyssey* could not be more different. These works are literary and, indeed, entertaining, but they are also primarily spiritual and theological documents.

In the *Iliad*, the struggle of the Greeks and the Trojans is but a stage for the internal struggles of the individual kings and warriors whose lives and souls are played out on the narrow beach of Troy. The struggles of Achilles and Agamemnon, of Hector and Priam with the gods are microcosms of the human struggle, the authentic nature of spiritual engagement. For Homer, the primary virtue for these warriors is piety, in Greek, εὐσέβεια, a virtue by which they are always true to who they are, their place in the world, and the gods who guide human destiny. Indeed, Greek "literature" could mostly be construed as an extended meditation on the virtue of piety. In the *Odyssey*, the warrior hero Odysseus must maintain piety toward his homeland and his family. He is tested by the gods, but his desire to remain true to his wife and son eventually leads him home. When the ancient bard recited the great epics of literature, they certainly entertained, but they also conveyed essential truths about the human condition, morality, and the relationship we mortals have with the gods.

The same ideal is expressed in dramatic literature in the Greek world. As audiences gathered in the *theatron* of ancient Athens, they were reminded, through the foibles of the dramas of Sophocles or Euripides, or the characters of Jason or Medea, of what was important and essential in life—messages forgotten by those who suffered tragic ends in their dramas. The most important thing in life was maintaining faith with the divine. The same patterns of using literature to convey essential truths about living rightly applied in the Roman world. Virgil teaches the importance of the Roman virtues of patriotism and uprightness (*pietas*), through the exploits of Aeneas, his family, and his companions. The moral and theological lessons of ancient literature were also performative, not material to be read and consumed, but realities to be imbibed in the public arena. They were indeed public virtues and their consumption was for all. The gods were for all. The ancient Greeks and Romans understood this very complexly. They did not rely upon an unthinking assertion of the reality of the divine. They

allowed simultaneously for the existence of the traditional pan-
theon and the expression of the divine "impulses" in more subtle
and, indeed, natural ways. They allowed for the piety of the person on the streets to collate with the esoteric thought of groups
like the neo-Platonists with no real tension.

In the early Christian environment of Europe, this changed
somewhat. Some in the early Church distrusted the ambiguity
found in ancient Greek and Roman literature. They wanted their
teachings to be clearer ways of conveying the essential message
of the Church. Literature in the patristic world took a back seat to
the preferred genres of apologetics and homiletics. Early Christians told the truth primarily in these ways, although there are in
addition the often fantastical works of hagiography, the lives of
the saints, that sometimes invoke an older Greek and Roman ideal.
The lives of the early martyrs and saints relate stories about heroes.
They also tell the truth about how Christians are to conduct their
lives, the virtues they need to imbibe in order to achieve salvation
in heaven. For example, in book two of St. Gregory the Great's
Dialogues, the church doctor tells the vastly entertaining story of
the father of Western monasticism, St. Benedict. In Gregory's story
of Benedict's life, he encounters the follies of his younger charges
by engaging in a bit of fantastical miracle making, retrieving an
ax head from the bottom of a lake. The story of Benedict's last
encounter with his sister, St. Scholastica, while theologically relevant, also explores the dynamics of sibling rivalry in an entertaining way. The adventures and exploits of the saint certainly convey
an important spiritual message, but their reading in various contexts in the early Christian world must also have had the effect of
engaging the hearers at levels other than spiritual and cerebral;
they were quite simply fun.

Because of the widespread challenge of literacy, the written
exploits of the saints eventually found a more popular mode in the
mystery plays of the high Middle Ages. These spiritual comedies
and dramas, usually performed in front of churches and in con-
junction with major church feasts (and therefore holidays), were
both enlightening and entertaining. An important moral story

could be told while engaging the imaginations of many viewers who could never fathom the tomes of theology and spirituality being produced, even if they had access to them, which they did not. These plays and other physical expressions (such as the visual arts and stained-glass windows) were the catechetical methods of the medieval Church. This is the way men and women had access to the profound truths of Scripture and theology. It was also remarkably effective.

All of this began to change with the advent of a single revolutionary figure, Dante Alighieri (1265–1321). Dante made two momentous contributions to Western religious thought: he revived the ideal of storytelling as an essential way of conveying essential truth and did it in a more serious way than perhaps the medieval world experienced in the morality plays; and, second, he wrote in the vernacular, the language of the people. In the *Divine Comedy*, Dante invokes the serious attitudes of the ancient world toward literature as an essential vehicle for truth-telling. His connection with the thought of Homer and Virgil is conveyed in the narrative, Virgil being an essential guide for Dante in the first two-thirds of the work.

The importance of Dante's storytelling can be illustrated in a couple of incidents from the first part of his work, *Inferno*. In Canto V, Dante meets the recently departed lovers Paulo and Francesca. In Dante's salvific economy their adulterous love affair is punished by their being bound together and tossed through all eternity. Francesca comments to Dante on their fate:

> Love, which in gentlest hearts will soonest bloom
> seized my lover with passion for that sweet body
> from which I was torn unshriven to my doom.
> Love, which permits no loved one not to love,
> took me so strongly with delight in him
> that we are one in Hell, as we were above.[2]

---

[2] Dante Alighieri, *Divine Comedy: Inferno*, trans. John Ciardi (San Francisco: Berkeley, 2003), 100–106.

Her theological acumen is augmented by her poetic instinct. The image Dante creates of the lovers does not exonerate moral guilt, but it makes the circumstances of their relationship more compelling by its poetic beauty. Later in the *Inferno*, in the unforgettable Canto XXIII, Dante recounts the story of his near contemporary Ugolino, who was imprisoned for fraud with his sons. In the end, Ugolino is faced with the necessity of eating his own children in order to survive. In the recounting of the story, Dante finds a powerful emotional core in the sorrow of the wretched Ugolino. This is the point where literature can assist the reader in finding nuance that more prosaic forms of theology or history cannot always uncover.

Dante's time is also an important point of convergence for a number of developments. As the Middle Ages gave way to the Renaissance, the primary literary development was not about writing at all; it was about technology. When Johannes Gensfleisch zur Laden zum Gutenberg (1400–1468) invented the moveable-type printing press, he must have imagined the revolution that such an innovation would provoke. Now printed works could be produced en masse. New literacy also provided for new forms of literature. New audiences provoked new ideas.

For the first time in history, written works took the lead in provoking ideas among ordinary people. Vernacular versions of Scripture began to appear. New spiritual writings developed as groups like the Brethren of the Common Life gained traction, influencing the spiritual direction of the man and woman in the street, men and women who desired to take in new ideas not only in preaching, but in writing as well. In the new world of printing, literature also began to change. In Spain, Miguel de Cervantes Saavedra (1547–1616) raised the old troubadour tales to new heights in *Don Quixote*. In England, dramatists such as Christopher Marlowe and William Shakespeare brought drama out of the restrictive conventions of the mystery plays and into the Renaissance light of the playhouses, places in which profound ideas mingled with popular entertainment. A good example of this can be found in Shakespeare's late play *The Winter's Tale*. In the play, Shakespeare uses a contemporary love story to illustrate the conflict inherent in his own time, the warfare between Catholicism and Anglicanism for the soul of England. In the final scene of the play, the heroine and queen of Leontes, Hermione, who was believed dead, the victim of a slander perpetuated by her own husband, the king, is found in the form of a statue hiding in the attic of the palace. The narrative focuses on the folly of kings (read perhaps Henry VIII) and the perfection of ideals, sometimes kept in hiding (as many Catholics had to do during Shakespeare's time). In the end the queen stands in for the pure virgin, Mary, and remains hidden until a suitable time for her "rehabilitation." Throughout his works Shakespeare uses images of popular religious culture to appeal for the return of the "old faith."

This close synthesis between spiritual ideas and literature began to break down with the advent of the Enlightenment. While some reformers questioned the morality of "popular" forms of literature, such as works performed at the playhouses, the late Reformation, in general, saw the specialization of literary works. Spiritual works were spiritually attuned. Theological works spoke to theologians. The vast spiritual revolution of the late sixteenth and early seventeenth centuries paved the way for a specialized realm of spiritual direction. The popularity of works like St. Francis de Sales's *Introduction to the Devout Life* not only instructed average Christians that they *were* to think about their relationships with God; it also taught them *how* to think about that relationship. New patterns of thought and new vocabularies were thereby ushered in by the dissemination of spiritual guidance for everyone. The ideal of spiritual direction began to be viewed literally as a distinct genre, and other forms of literature, including fiction, came to be seen as fulfilling other goals, but not necessarily spiritual ones.

While the increasing number and variety of spiritual works for the masses began to appear, literature, likewise, started to take new forms. The rise of the novel in almost every cultural and geographical center of the West became a new way of conveying truths about the human story, truths sometimes linked to the eternal verities of religion, but more often to new, Enlightenment-era convictions rooted in the ideal of "secularity." Fiction, especially the novel, offered a means of indoctrinating audiences with new values. It has that power. Novels like *The History of Tom Jones, a Foundling* by Henry Fielding (1743) evoke a world in which hypocritical religious ideals are best forgotten. Indeed, a great deal of literature from the Georgian and Regency periods subtly (or not so subtly) challenges organized religion as a way of organizing life and the social order. Sometimes religion is gently lampooned, an example being Samuel Richardson's *Pamela: Or, Virtue Rewarded* (1740). Sometimes it is outwardly criticized, as in the Gothic thriller by Matthew Gregory Lewis, *The Monk* (1796).

The evolution of the novel in the nineteenth century brought a subtler interplay of themes concerning religion and faith. The novels of Dickens, Tolstoy, Dostoevsky, Trollope, and many others provide road maps for the spiritual life that, at times, surpass the specialized literature of spirituality in the West. An important example of this ideal is the work of George Eliot (1819–1880). Eliot's novels are still as powerful as when they were written, almost a century and a half ago. One of her novels, *Daniel Deronda*, speaks of the condition of Jews in England in the mid-1800s. The novel is also about identity and how our self-identities are formed. It is also a character study in spiritual greed. It is also a moral treatise on cruelty and its effects. It is, in addition, a very rewarding love story and coming-of-age novel. Eliot makes a novel like *Daniel Deronda* work on many levels. She also uses language in a passionate and masterful way. A great novel has the ability to make one think, fulfill an emotional catharsis, inspire and provoke. In this way, novels and fiction become authentic vehicles for spiritual formation.

Many consider George Eliot's most famous novel, *Middlemarch*, to be one of the greatest novels of all time. It is a long and complex narrative about the spiritual effects of modernization on a small English town. It covers a great deal more ground, however, in reflecting on such issues as the nature of religious faith, marriage, technology, science and its proper usages. It is also a highly philosophical novel, which can easily be read as a study in epistemology—that is, of the ways in which different people approach life and the effects that these different approaches have. It is also a highly ethical novel and an important "conservative" novel in that Eliot is advocating for a simpler England, an England of tradition and an agrarian past. It is also just a good read, with characters that the reader learns to care about deeply and that never appear as types.

The one thing that Eliot knows about is personality, and she conveys different classes of folks with sympathy and real affection. The central character of *Middlemarch* is Dorothea Brooke. Dorothea is one of the author's "Protestant heroines." She is a devoutly religious person, who is intent upon doing good for everyone with whom she comes into contact. Her great desires in life are to be useful and spiritually fulfilled. She seeks to marry for "meaning" and not for status or money, and she does so by finding favor with the ancient Mr. Casaubon, a local clergyman and scholar. What she discovers, in her search for meaning, even above personal happiness, is that her marriage is a sham and a cause of great disillusionment. However, Dorothea is not down for long. When she becomes a widow, she trades some of her old piety for a new sense of love and adventure in marrying the more rebellious artist Will Ladislaw. Her need for values meets her desire for happiness. In many ways, she represents us. Much of the work of discipleship is the ability to discern the depths of the human personality. Novels help us gain insight. No one does this better than George Eliot, the woman with a man's name, a philosopher's mind, and a generous heart. At the end of *Middlemarch*, the very end, there is a powerful passage that speaks of Dorothea's final contributions, but it might readily apply to all who have the will to serve, to make a difference in the world, and to touch profoundly the lives of others:

> Her finely-touched spirit had still its fine issues, though they were not widely visible. Her full nature, like that river of which Cyrus broke the strength, spent itself in channels which had no great name on the earth. But the effect of her being on those around her was incalculably diffusive: for the growing good of the world is partly dependent on unhistoric acts; and

that things are not so ill with you and me as they might have been, is half owing to the number who lived faithfully a hidden life, and rest in unvisited tombs.[3]

O'Connor, Spark, and Benson

I now turn to three examples of modern Catholic novelists who in their works of fiction shed light on important spiritual ideals and whose work offers good examples of the ways in which literature can contribute to spiritual formation. Each of these writers brought distinct cultural and personal perspectives to their shared vocation, but all were similarly intent upon conveying in their fiction important Catholic, spiritual themes. Flannery O'Connor was born in Savannah, Georgia, in 1925. Raised as a Roman Catholic in the predominantly Protestant, fundamentalist South, she infused her short stories and short novels with the essence of "coded texts." Indeed, while Catholic faith and Catholic identity were fiercely ingrained in O'Connor's personality, few of her stories have an outright Catholic theme or feature Catholic characters. Rather, her fiction centers on what she describes as misfits and freaks who end up conveying religious truths more strongly than any overtly Catholic characters possibly could.

A good example of this may be found in her short story "Revelation."[4] Published posthumously in 1965 (O'Connor had died from the effects of lupus the year before at the age of thirty-nine), the story centers on Ruby Turpin, an opinionated, middle-aged woman sitting in a doctor's waiting room somewhere in central Georgia. As she espouses her opinions about everything around her, it is evident that this "good Christian woman" is, in fact, a hypocrite. In the course of her lecturing to the other inhabitants of the waiting room, another patient, a sullen girl named Mary Grace, literally throws the book at Mrs. Turpin. The book is called *Human Development* and its projection is accompanied by the girl's

---

[3] George Eliot, *Middlemarch* (New York: Everyman's Library, 1930), 889.

[4] Flannery O'Connor, *Collected Works* (New York: Library of America, 1988), 633–54.

wish: "Go back to hell where you came from, you old wart hog."[5]
Having been assaulted by "Grace" and "Human Development,"
Mrs. Turpin returns to her farm, the girl's curses resounding in
her mind. Later in the day, as she is attending to the pigs on her
farm, she has a vision:

> Mrs. Turpin remained there with her gaze bent to them as if
> she were absorbing some abysmal life-giving knowledge. At
> last she lifted her head. There was only a purple streak in the
> sky, cutting through a field of crimson and leading, like an
> extension of the highway, into the descending dusk. She
> raised her hands from the side of the pen in a gesture hieratic
> and profound. A visionary light settled in her eyes. She saw
> the streak as a vast swinging bridge extending upward from
> the earth through a field of living fire. Upon it a vast horde
> of souls were tumbling toward heaven. . . . And bringing
> up the end of the procession was a tribe of people whom she
> recognized at once as those who, like herself and Claud, had
> always had a little of everything and the given wit to use it
> right. She leaned forward to observe them closer.
>
> They were marching behind the others with great dignity,
> accountable as they had always been for good order and com-
> mon sense and respectable behavior. They, alone were on key.
> Yet she could see by their shocked and altered faces even their
> virtues were being burned away.[6]

O'Connor's vision evokes the images of her great predecessor
Dante. Those climbing the mountain of Mrs. Turpin's backwoods
purgatory are just like her, they are her. They are also O'Connor.
They are also the readers. O'Connor sets up scenes in her writing
that stir the imagination, sometimes shocking, sometimes very
amusing, but they are always related to explaining an important
theological point. Her eschatological teaching takes on the decided
air of a modern, Southern American sensibility. This is precisely
how fiction and literary forms can convey authentic doctrine and

---

[5] Ibid., 646.
[6] Ibid., 653–54.

authentic truth about faith in ways that more patently didactic material cannot. Flannery O'Connor certainly entertains, but she also teaches, and those who are fortunate enough to meet her at that crossroads may discover themselves inspired.

Another important story of O'Connor's also gives the title to her first short story collection, *A Good Man Is Hard to Find* (1955). In the short story, a typical family from Atlanta finds themselves at the mercy of a notorious serial killer named "the Misfit." The story centers on the conversation near the end between the murderer and the grandmother of the family, a woman who would never be mistaken for anything but a lady. The old woman's (again) hypocritical opinions about everything in the world are available for all who are willing to listen, though few are. She is particular about the way she dresses. She treats others according to accepted rules (most of which are of her own making). She offers her ideas to the air quite literally, until finally she is silenced by a trinitarian gun blast to the chest. The killer, taking the time to clean his glasses, offers the definitive word: "She would have been a good woman, if it had been somebody there to shoot her every minute of her life."[7] Interestingly, it may be argued that the Misfit is the Christlike figure in the story. O'Connor is caught up in a meditation on how grace is communicated, its violence, and its unusual qualities in the modern world. This is O'Connor's world of discipleship: Grace is everywhere. It is experienced in church, certainly, but also in the woods and fields. It is found in the things we find important and meaningful, but it is also found in the things we find problematic, even repulsive. O'Connor's world is filled with grace; all is tipping toward the Omega Point; everything that rises converges and does so precisely in God. She does not recognize, like her great inspiration John Henry Newman, the idea of the secular; everything is God.

O'Connor was a Catholic author writing about Catholic themes like grace, salvation, revelation, the cost of discipleship, the centrality of Christ, and many others, but she approached them in

[7] Ibid., 153.

ways that stimulate reflection and remain with the reader long after the short story is completed. In her provocative story "The River," the theme of child suicide is interwoven with a reflection on the sacramental nature of baptism. In "The Enduring Chill," a headstrong youth is forced into a long meditation on mortality by his own egotistical recklessness. In "Temples of the Holy Ghost," a pair of Catholic schoolgirls inspires, by negative example, a young child to stronger faith. All of O'Connor's stories touch of paradox, the unexpected encounter with God and the hidden but decisive nature of God's hand. From her cultural place, O'Connor is commenting on the spiritual health (or sickness) of the world around her. Literature becomes a vehicle of spiritual direction for the discerning reader.

It is no coincidence that her final collection is titled *Everything That Rises Must Converge*, which also is the title of the lead story. In that story, the two protagonists (or antagonists) are a young son, Julian, a typewriter salesman, and his elderly mother. The two never see eye to eye; indeed, the son's identity seems constructed around rejecting everything his mother believes and finds meaningful in the world. In the midst of their endless arguing, they find a moment of convergence when the mother, trying to do good in talking down to an African American "double" on the bus, is struck by the woman. The son insists his mother deserves what she got, and they are completely at odds until the incident causes the woman to suffer a stroke, drawing the two antagonists together in a way they could have scarcely imagined. In the end, the mother and son converge in death. The death of the mother demonstrates something essential to the son, their point of connection. All are connected, the mother and the son, the two women who encounter one another on the bus. All are rising, and everything that rises must converge. That is the spiritual direction of Flannery O'Connor. It is a direction of hope and the fulfillment of human promise and desire, but it is not easy.

Muriel Spark (1918–2006) could hardly have been a more different figure from Flannery O'Connor. Born in Edinburgh, Scotland, to a Jewish father and Presbyterian mother, she was raised as a

Presbyterian and lived a quite complex life, married to a manic-depressive husband, trying to raise a son by herself, and working in intelligence during World War II. In 1953, she was baptized as an Anglican, but a year later became a Roman Catholic, a decision that set the course of all her future endeavors. Her career as a novelist began with her conversion. She later remarked about the relationship between her new faith and her writing: "I was just a little worried, tentative. Would it be right, would it not be right? Can I write a novel about that—would it be foolish, wouldn't it be? And somehow with my religion—whether one has anything to do with the other, I don't know—but it does seem so."[8] She spent much of her later life in Italy, dying in Florence at the age of eighty-eight.

Perhaps Spark's most famous work is the short novel *The Prime of Miss Jean Brodie*, a tragic story of a middle-aged woman who teaches in an exclusive, all-girls school in Edinburgh in the years leading up to World War II. The story follows Miss Brodie and her elite set of chosen apostles, "her girls," through the school years and into the vicissitudes of adulthood. Miss Brodie inspires her girls with images of Cimabue, the heroism of the *fascisti*, music, poetry, and everything that is fine. While she remarks that "it is obvious . . . that these girls are not of cultured homes and heritage,"[9] she intends to help them become "the crème de la crème" even if they do not wish to do so. The novel eventually settles on a clash of wills between Miss Brodie and one of her girls, Sandy Stranger. Sandy believes that Miss Brodie's self-delusions have eventually convinced her that she is the "God of Calvin."[10] She believes herself to be getting even with Miss Brodie and betraying her in that, after leaving school, Sandy has an affair with a much older married former teacher whom Miss Brodie has placed in her path. In the novel, Miss Brodie uses Sandy as her "surrogate," tempting the young woman to have an affair with a much older man whom Miss Brodie actually desires. At first, Sandy seems to

---

[8] From an interview between Muriel Spark and John Tulsa on Radio 4.

[9] Muriel Spark, *The Prime of Miss Jean Brodie* (New York: Harper Classics, 1999), 51.

[10] Ibid., 129.

be fulfilling Miss Brodie's will, but ultimately there is a betrayal in that, when the affair ends, Sandy becomes a Roman Catholic, like her married lover, and then a nun. As Sister Helena of the Transfiguration, she observes of her betrayal of Miss Brodie that, "it is only possible to betray where loyalty is due."[11] In other words, there is a degree to which Sandy feels loyalty to Miss Brodie, or perhaps to the Calvinist/Scottish ideal the teacher represents. Perhaps she needs to understand the loyalty she has to both. The betrayal of Miss Brodie, as much by her conversion as by her affair, becomes a betrayal of a whole world. The conversion also comes from a place of depth, a depth that none of the other characters show. It is almost as if Spark is asking us to look deeply into ourselves, and when we do we may find that many of the loyalties we think we hold, or should hold, are not the fulfillments of the soul we need.

Spark's tangled interactions between Calvinism (Miss Brodie) and Catholicism (Sandy Stranger) undoubtedly speak to the spiritual journey of the author herself. *The Prime of Miss Jean Brodie* is a kind of spiritual autobiography. Certainly, Spark is a very different author from O'Connor, not only in her background, but also in the hiddenness, the covertness in which she (Spark) finds Catholic truth interwoven in life. Both writers, however, engage Catholicism as something quite alien to their received cultural places and, therefore, revolutionary, certainly for their protagonists, but also for their readers and ultimately themselves. Both writers, in this sense, see Catholicism as a radical choice to heal a world radically marked by sin and error. Both provide spiritual guidance for readers who sense that such a radical journey is not only worthwhile, but necessary.

A final Catholic author to consider as a spiritual director is Robert Hugh Benson (1871–1914). Benson had a rather unusual beginning for a Catholic author and priest in that he was the son of Edward White Benson, an archbishop of Canterbury. Ordained as an Anglican priest, Benson converted to the Catholic faith in 1903 after the death of his father. He was ordained a Catholic priest

[11] Ibid., 136.

one year later. Benson produced a great deal of literature in the course of his short life, much of it fiction and all of it somewhat unapologetically apologetic. He wrote several novels of historical fiction, focusing on the effects of the Reformation on Catholics (e.g., *The Queen's Tragedy*, 1907). In these works, some of which are set in Lambeth Palace, the former home of his father, he examines how religious division brings upon struggle and tragedy in families. It must have been a thought very close to his heart. In other works, Benson offers religious critique of the trends toward supernaturalism in his time. In 1909, he published *The Necromancers*, a novel that explores the question of spiritualism and its effects on a middle-class family. For Benson, the search for the spiritual is not a matter of looking for the occult, but looking closer at the reality of God present in the world as we know it. His output also included works of science fiction, a relatively new type of literature in his time.

It is in this last genre that Benson has made what is arguably his most lasting impact with *The Lord of the World*. Published in 1907, the novel is a complex dystopian narrative set in twenty-first-century London. The interestingly prescient narrative predicts the advent of the Antichrist in the form of a socialist regime that dominates culture and persecutes the church. The story concerns the engagement of a single family as they struggle to maintain faith, juxtaposed to the fate of the larger Catholic Church. Again, Benson's theme of the family and the effects of ideas on families is tantamount. The Brand family patriarch, Oliver, is a Labour MP, intent upon realizing the new socialist philosophy in a completely secular England. He is thwarted in his efforts, first by his mother, a staunch adherer to Catholicism, and later by his wife, Mabel, a young woman who is seeking truth. Mabel's struggle forms the center of the book's plot. Her conversion to faith and her move away from faith lead to what Benson sees as the last stand of secularism. She checks herself into a voluntary euthanasia clinic and takes her own life. The novel, in the persons of the Brand family, chronicles the overweening secularism that in Benson's mind was beginning to take hold in England, indeed in all of Europe in his time. The culmination of the story occurs in Nazareth, where the church has taken refuge in the final days. The despotic Lord of the World—a bureaucrat who has risen to power on a populist platform and who uses his political clout to further his own ends, the Antichrist—personally bombs the city, but the church, gathered in the adoration of the Blessed Sacrament, is caught up in a vision at the end, the return of Christ in which "this world passed and the glory of it."[12] *The Lord of the World* is a novel that has gained new Catholic audiences in recent years and some new notoriety for Robert Hugh Benson. It has done so primarily as a political allegory. Politics devoid of faith, pure secularism, leads to the downfall of human persons, their dehumanization.

Critics are divided about the quality of Benson's writings. Some have critiqued his work as rather crude in its bald apologetic. If *The Lord of the World* offers a crude conclusion, a bald apologetic, it does not negate the truths told by Benson in its pages. The themes of secularization, rank politicization, the increasing persecution of religion, and the trials of a church under fire are all meaningful themes for Catholics today. They are also eternally meaningful. Like O'Connor and Spark, Benson uses the vehicle of fiction to offer some important spiritual insights. He notes, like them, the need for a greater appreciation of the role of faith, of finding timeless rather than timely truths. They are not writing abstractly, or rather they are writing abstractions centered in the here and now, in our culture, our time, our world. All three focus on the way in which faith is not an "accessory" to life. It is the core of life. When Benson's heroine, Mabel, loses her faith, her only recourse is suicide. She cannot go on in a world without faith. O'Connor and Spark see this as well.

Conclusion

Throughout human history, literature has often been employed for lofty ends. The lessons taught by the ancient Greeks and Romans, by the medieval poets, and by modern novelists are offered

---

[12] Robert Hugh Benson, *The Lord of the World* (South Bend, IN: St. Augustine's Press, 2011), 260.

not only for our education and entertainment, but also for our edification. They provide probing insights into human nature and our relationship to God, gesturing in the direction of salvation. In short, they offer new hope that everything that rises must converge.

Benson, Spark, and O'Connor all stand as new apostles in a long tradition of using literature as a means of conveying spiritual ideals. All three accomplish in their writing what is essential in the great tradition of literature: They capture their time (and to a degree their personalities), but they also capture something eternal. O'Connor finds transcendence in the culture in which she lives. She raises her hillbillies to the position of archetypes. She crafts her plots as essential narratives, determined by a great Creator who, though to some anonymous, is nevertheless the Lord of the World. O'Connor is fierce in her defense of this God. There is a theology in her stories that has the potential for teaching lessons that extend beyond the didacticism of more theoretical works. Spark, likewise, works out timeless themes in her own time and place. In *The Prime of Miss Jean Brodie*, the protagonist Sandy was a "stranger" who ultimately finds transcendence, in spite of the best efforts of her culture (Miss Brodie), who in Spark's estimation is long past her prime. Sandy finds fulfillment in Catholicism, as Spark herself did. Spark uses her fertile mind to challenge readers to ask the important questions: What should our "names" be? Where do we belong? Benson also employs his creative energies to assist seekers on the way. In all of his works, the reader senses the urgency of telling the truth about God. When the truth is found it must also be lived. This is a theme that all of these writers share: Faith has consequences. Sometimes it is easier for us to learn that lesson through the vivid examples presented in literature.

In my years as a spiritual director, I have found much usefulness in the great works of spirituality by authors like St. Ignatius, St. Francis de Sales, and the Carmelite mystics. We need to be able to offer those on the spiritual journey the insights of these giants of the Catholic tradition. They understood the spiritual journey because they had engaged it so successfully. They understood the crises faced by people of their own times, those for whom they composed their works, because they cared for them and were involved with them. In no way can the insights of these great authors be displaced, but they can be augmented. Since becoming a spiritual director, I have been aware that spiritual truth can also be conveyed in other forms, particularly in the visual arts and in literature. Inspired works of literature have the capacity to convey profound insights in ways that are particularly compelling. God can be found in the very impetus to write, to create, to make something lasting.

Literature is true and literature lasts because it is made in a place of spiritual insight in the human person. Sometimes this is very purposeful. The three authors considered here, I believe, wanted to share their Catholic faith and the truth of Catholicism in focused, creative ways. In other writers, for example someone like George Eliot, this spiritual impulse may not even be fully known to *them*. Recognizing the presence of an anonymous God in literature and art is a challenge that in some way surpasses the discovery of truth in more explicitly spiritual writings. The discovery of the anonymous God in great books is a challenge that can be undertaken with a good director. Uncovering God in literature can serve as a powerful tool for discerning the hand of the living God in the processes of daily life, and for understanding more fully how to live one's life properly oriented toward God. Literature, at its best, brings all of these things to light, but it does something else, something equally beautiful and spiritual: It delights us. It delights us precisely by *our* discovery in its pages of the depth and beauty we so strongly seek.